IMAGES
of America

FORT DRUM

IMAGES
of America

FORT DRUM

Robert E. and Jeannie I. Brennan

ARCADIA
PUBLISHING

ISBN 978-0-7385-1037-8

Published by Arcadia Publishing
Charleston, South Carolina

Printed in the United States of America

Library of Congress Catalog Card Number: 2002103652

For all general information contact Arcadia Publishing at:
Telephone 843-853-2070
Fax 843-853-0044
E-mail sales@arcadiapublishing.com
For customer service and orders:
Toll-Free 1-888-313-2665

Visit us on the Internet at www.arcadiapublishing.com

Contents

ACKNOWLEDGMENTS

Information used in this publication came from the archival collection of Robert and Jeannie Brennan. Images and text are also drawn from the Pickering-Beach Museum in Sackets Harbor, Jefferson County Historical Society, the Watertown Daily Times, the Fort Drum & 10th Mountain Division Historical Collections (FDMDHC), the National Archives in Washington, D.C., and the private collections of James McNeff and Jerry Charley.

We also wish to acknowledge the kind assistance of the owners and the library staff of the Watertown Daily Times, Watertown City Clerk and Historian Donna Dutton, and James Neville at the Fort Drum & 10th Mountain Division Historical Collections. A special thank-you also goes to our daughter, Constance Brennan Barone, who suggested the publication, encouraged our efforts, and assisted in preparing the captions and introduction.

All proceeds from the sale of this book are donated to the Sackets Harbor Area Cultural Preservation Foundation, for the preservation of the early-19th-century stone hospital at Madison Barracks.

—Robert E. Brennan and Jeannie I. Brennan

INTRODUCTION

The logical publication to follow our previous book, *Images of America: Sackets Harbor*, is *Images of America: Fort Drum*. In the final chapter of *Sackets Harbor*, readers learn about the origins and military importance of Madison Barracks. Picking up from that last chapter, this book links Fort Drum's presence with its historical beginnings at Madison Barracks.

Our own personal histories were intangibly linked to the military presence in Sackets Harbor when our families moved to the harborside community in the early 20th century. Patrick X. Brennan was a civil service employee at Madison Barracks from 1910 to 1945. Stephen Kafka was ship-keeper of the Sub Chaser No. 431 at the Navy Point, Naval Militia station from 1928 to 1937. Since we grew up here, surrounded by the history and presence of the military, our goal is to share an awareness and understanding of the vital link between Sackets Harbor's Madison Barracks and Fort Drum. This collection of photographs tells that story.

During the War of 1812, Sackets Harbor, on Lake Ontario, was the eastern terminus of an important military transportation route that stretched across the Adirondack Mountains, linking strategic military posts on Lake Ontario to Lake Champlain. That route from Sackets Harbor passed through Pine Plains, which later became the site of Fort Drum.

At the height of the War of 1812, between the United States and Great Britain, the village of Sackets Harbor housed over 4,000 troops. Following the war, military security on the northern frontier was bolstered by the construction of Madison Barracks in Sackets Harbor. Thus, the military presence that continues today in northern New York State was established.

Pine Plains, near Watertown, evolved from the military presence at Madison Barracks, 23 miles away. In 1906, Col. Philip Reade, stationed at Madison Barracks, approved the location for summer maneuvers at Pine Plains, which was purchased by the federal government and named Camp Hughes. In 1908, army engineers began constructing the military camp that was to be named Pine Camp.

In the summer of 1935, the "greatest military maneuvers in the peacetime history of the United States" took place at Pine Camp, with "more than 40,000 officers and men." Five divisions of the 1st U.S. Army took part in this mock warfare exercise.

Just prior to World War II, a major expansion took place at Pine Camp when it was designated a training post for the development of armored divisions to contend with Germany's growing blitzkrieg tactics. The camp's acreage expanded from 16,000 to 90,000 acres. During

World War II, three divisions were stationed at Pine Camp: the 4th and 5th Armored Divisions, along with the 45th Infantry Division.

In August 1952, Pine Camp was dedicated as Camp Drum, honoring World War II–era 1st U.S. Army Gen. Hugh A. Drum. The name Fort Drum was given in 1974. The 107,000-acre post today supports a variety of military missions. The famous 10th Mountain Division (light infantry) is stationed at Fort Drum. The Army Reserve and the National Guard still train there, not only in summer months as they did in 1908, but also in the harsh winter months of northern New York.

Today, a strong military presence remains in northern New York State. The economic impact of the enormous Fort Drum complex bolsters the region. Historic Madison Barracks in Sackets Harbor has become a multifaceted community where Fort Drum service personnel reside and students of American history can glimpse reminders of a bygone military past.

From the War of 1812 to the present day, northern New York State has boasted a prominent military presence. We invite you to follow the course of this military history as you turn the pages of *Fort Drum*.

One

MADISON BARRACKS

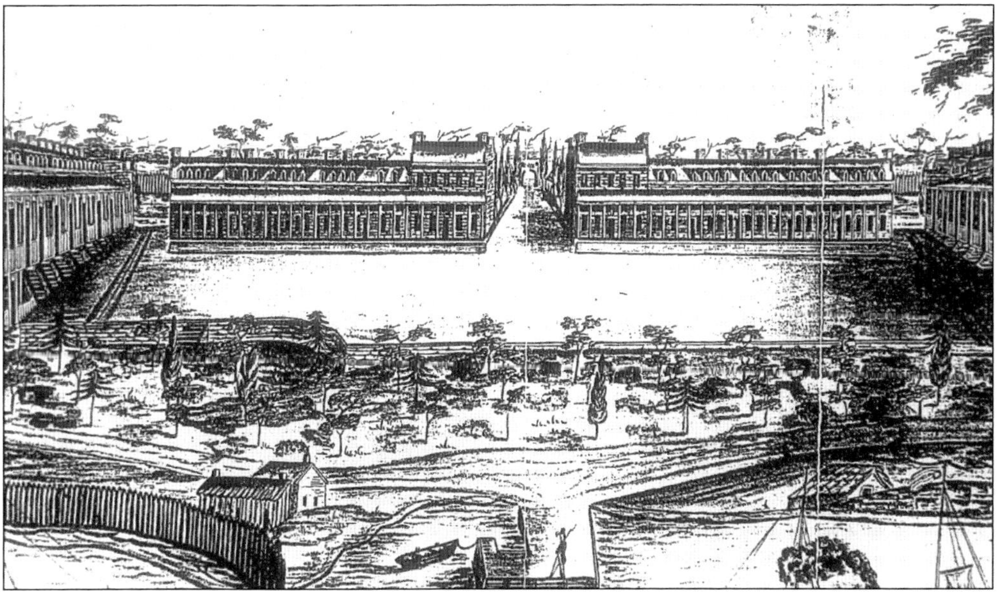

Located in Sackets Harbor, near the border between the United States and Canada, Madison Barracks originally encompassed over 39 acres. This military facility provided a training site for troops until it was decommissioned and abandoned on August 30, 1945. The U-shape layout of buildings, constructed between August 1816 and October 1819, includes a straight row of officers' quarters dubbed the Stone Row, separated by a passageway called the sally port. The two rows of enlisted men's barracks faced each other on the east and west sides of the U. These buildings were designed by William Smith of Watertown. Soldiers of the 2nd U.S. Infantry, under the supervision of Thomas Tupper of the Quartermaster Department, assisted in the construction. Of the three rows, only the Stone Row remains today. (Courtesy National Archives, Washington, D.C.)

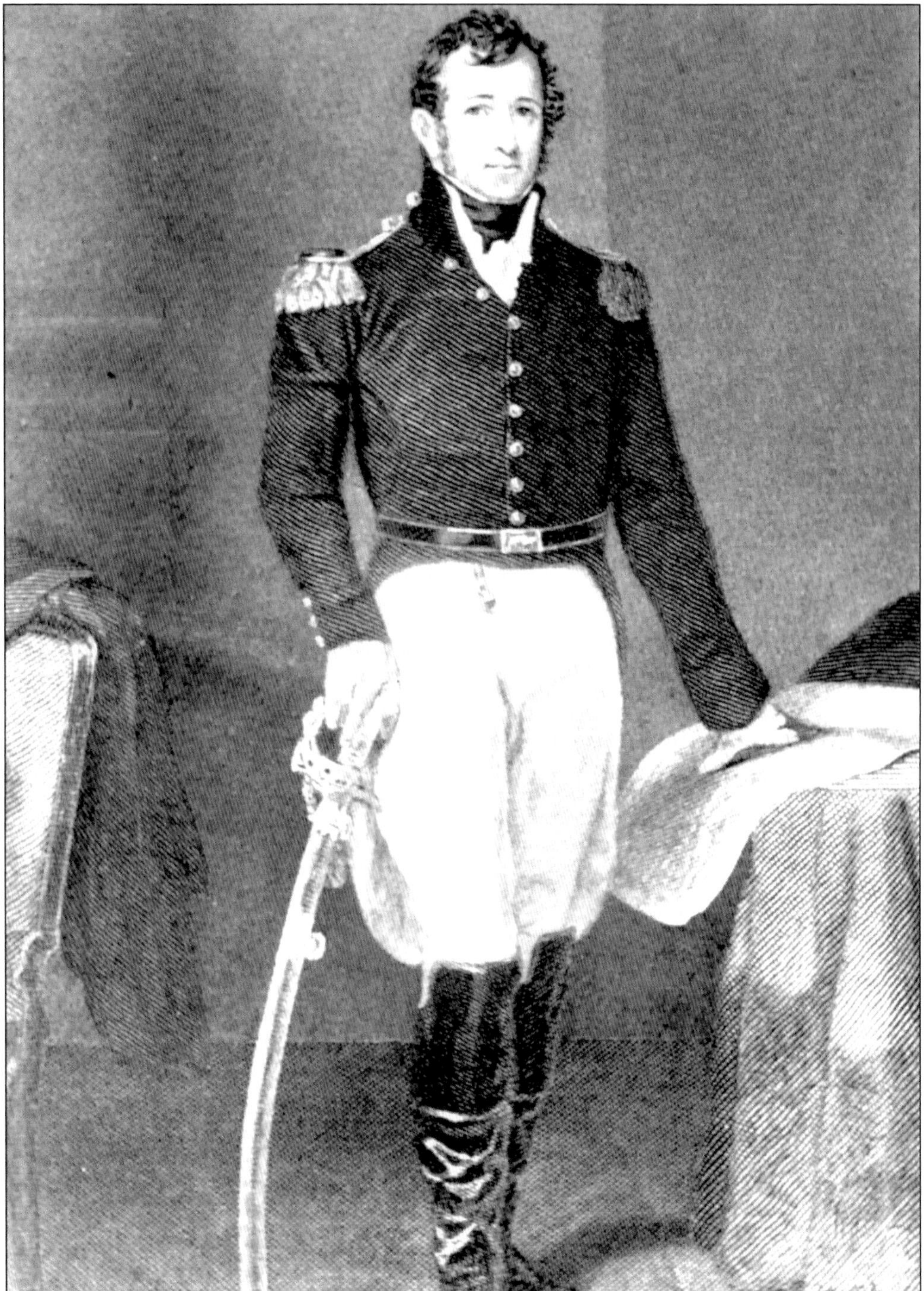

During the summer of 1815, Gen. Jacob Jennings Brown ordered Madison Barracks constructed as a border post at the eastern end of Lake Ontario on Black River Bay at Sackets Harbor. During the War of 1812, Brown served as general of the militia. In 1821, he was appointed general in chief of the armies of the United States.

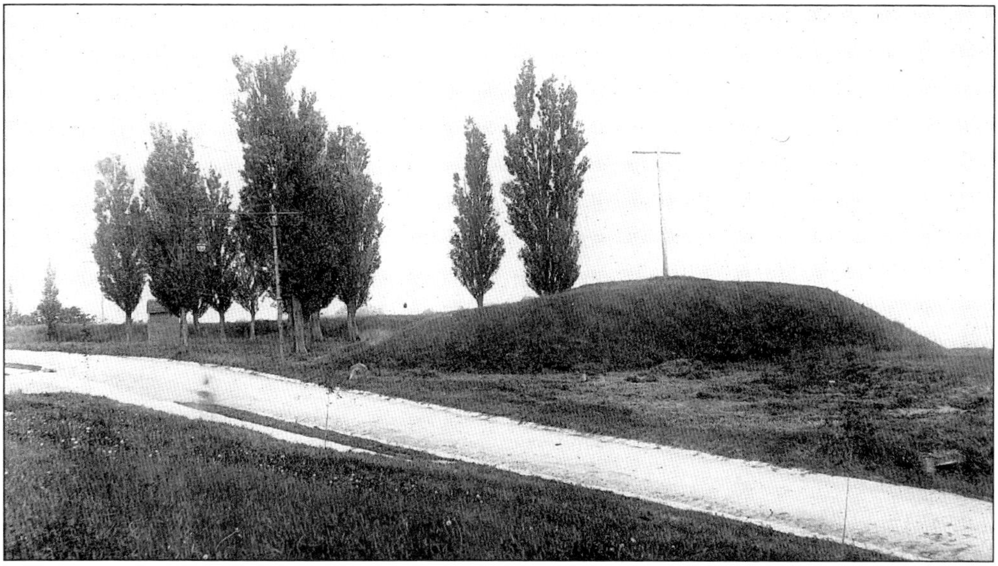

This photograph shows the remains of Fort Pike (originally Fort Volunteer), an earthwork and water battery used to defend Sackets Harbor during the War of 1812. The fort occupied about one third of the Madison Barracks waterfront. A two-story blockhouse was located in the center of the fort. Originally built by veterans of the Revolutionary War, the Silver Grays, the fort was named Fort Pike in honor of Gen. Zebulon Pike. Pike was killed on April 27, 1813, during the War of 1812, while leading American troops at the Battle of Fort York (now Toronto, Ontario).

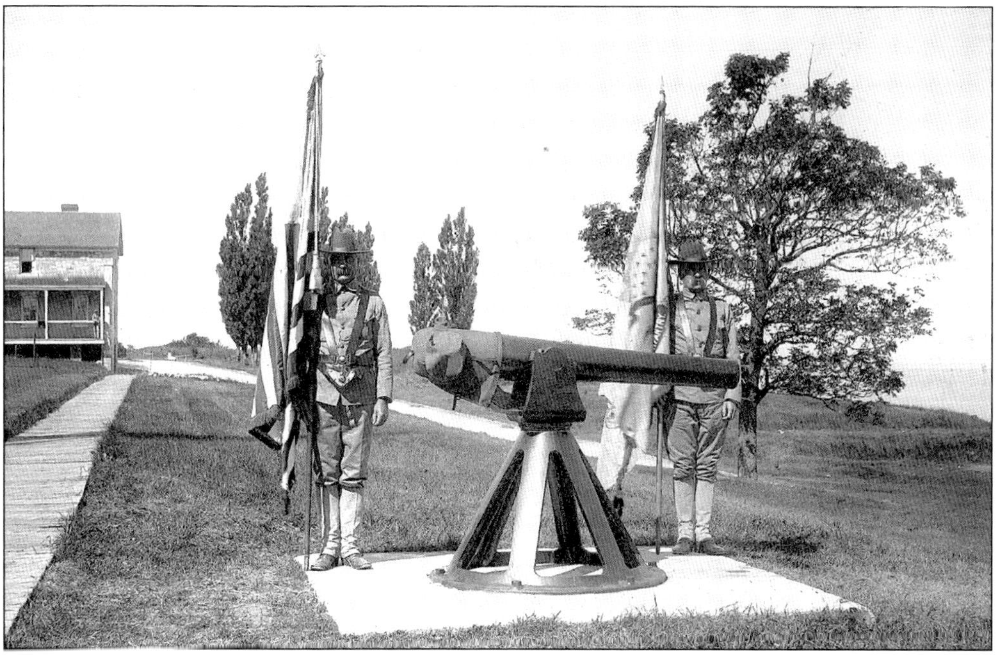

In the early 20th century, a color guard of the U.S. 23rd Infantry stands at attention beside the salute gun. The color guard raised the garrison flag in the morning and presented a gun salute ceremony each evening. A portion of the enlisted men's barracks is seen at the left, and the poplar trees of Fort Pike stand in the background.

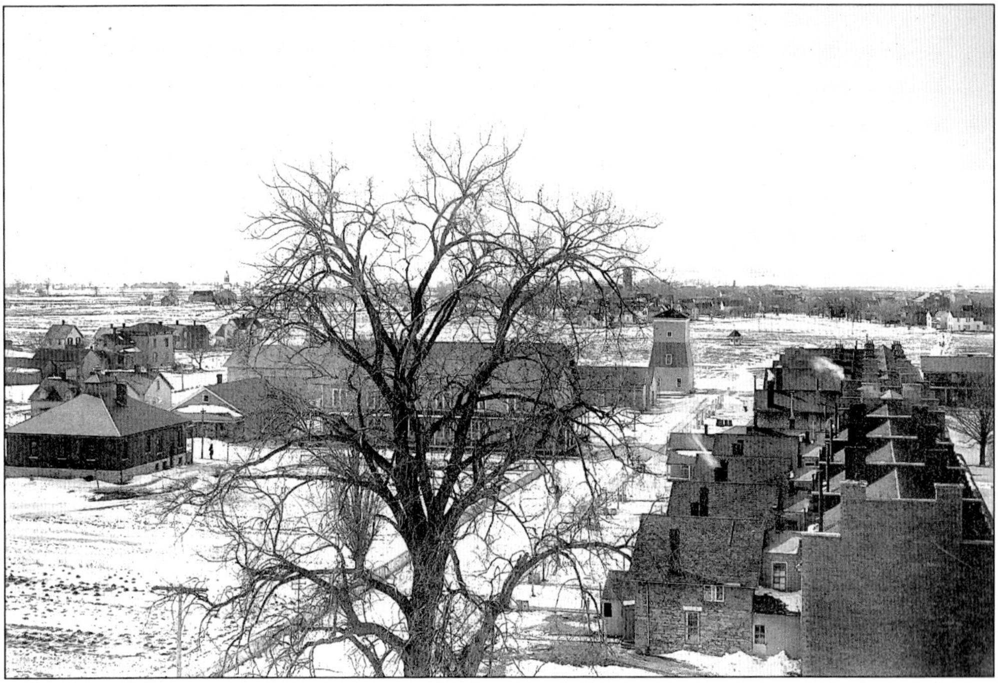

A 1902 photograph of Madison Barracks, taken from the stone water tower, looks northwest toward the village of Sackets Harbor. On the right is the Stone Row officers' quarters. The wooden water tower, Dodge Hall, and ordnance warehouses are in the center. The new brick and old limestone guardhouses are on the left. Beyond the guardhouses are two-family noncommissioned officers' (NCO) quarters and the quartermaster warehouses.

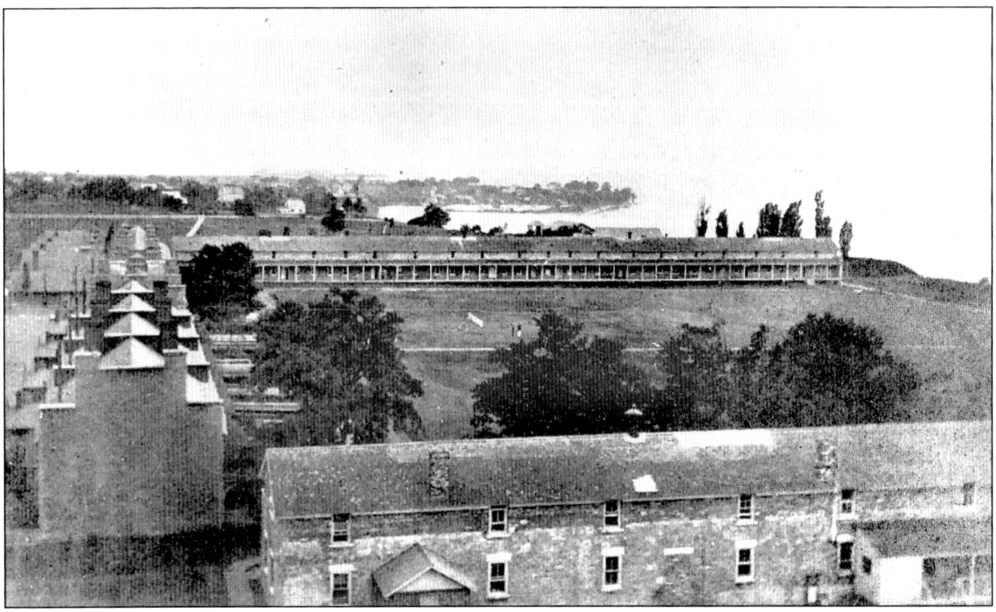

Another early-20th-century photograph taken from the stone water tower looks northwest toward the village of Sackets Harbor. The west wing of the enlisted men's quarters and poplar trees on Fort Pike were landmarks of Madison Barracks.

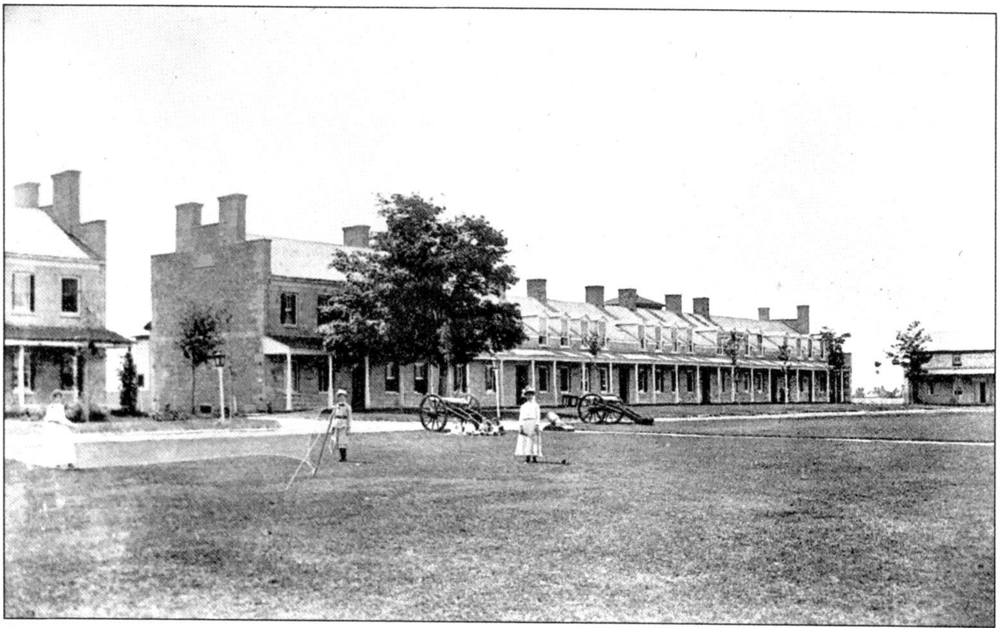

On a summer day, officers' wives enjoy a game of lawn tennis in front of the sally port in the Stone Row. Civil War cannons serve as a reminder that Madison Barracks was a recruiting station for the formation of regiments during the American Civil War.

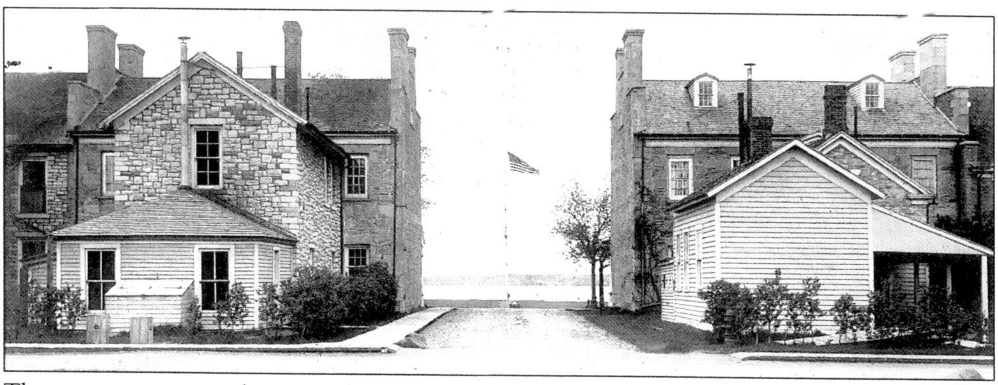

The open passageway between the two sections of Stone Row is called the sally port. Guard mounts passed through this area on their way to the main flagpole twice a day to raise and lower the garrison flag. Quarters on the west side of the sally port were occupied in 1848 by future Pres. Ulysses S. Grant. Living quarters immediately on the right were occupied by the post's first commander, Col. Hugh Brady, in 1816.

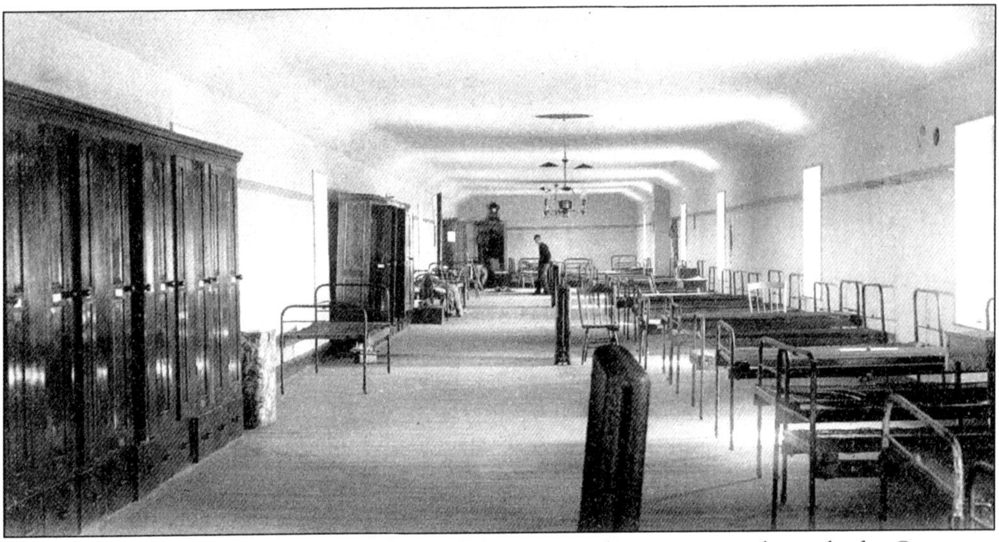

This 1905 view shows the interior of one of the two cut-limestone row barracks for Company L, 9th Infantry. Eighty men were housed in a barracks. A row of hot-water radiators lined the center of the barracks, and iron bedsteads replaced canvas cots. A three-compartment locker provided more space for the soldiers' belongings. The east row of barracks was demolished in 1907 and the west row in 1908.

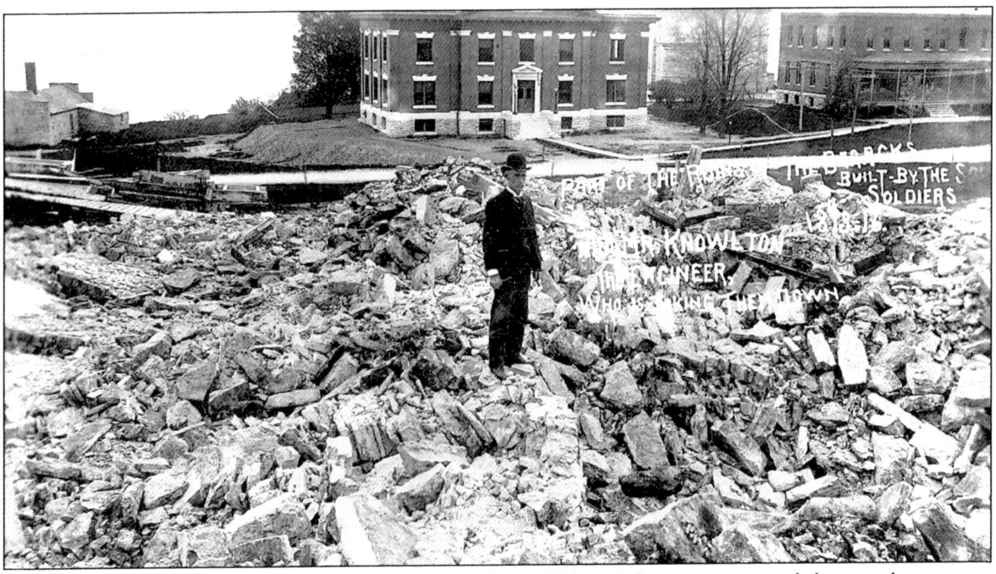

Post engineer Edwin C. Knowlton stands on the rubble of the east wing of the cut-limestone barracks during demolition in 1907. The post exchange, just two years old, is seen in the background.

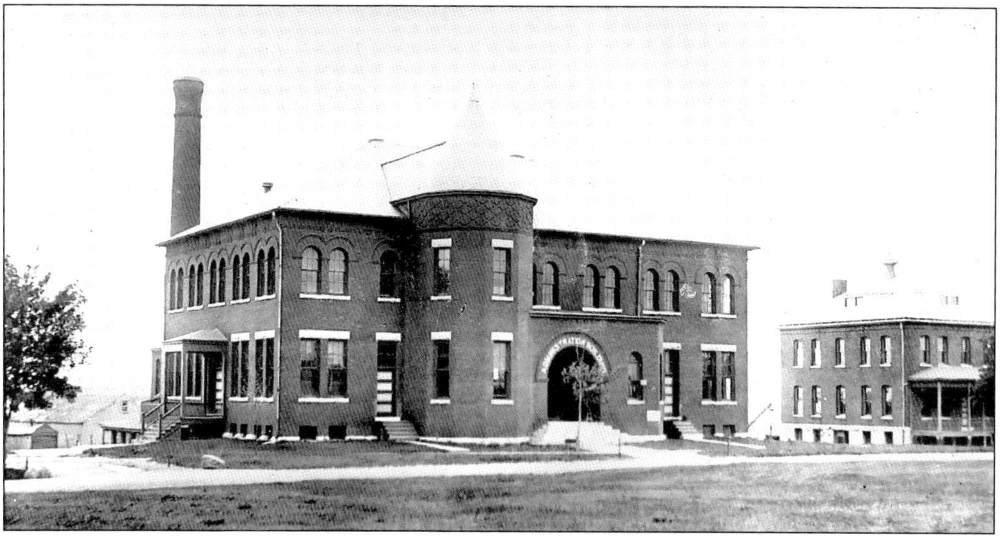

The central mess hall, built in 1892, was located at the west end of the enlisted men's barracks along the shoreline. At one time the mess hall was used as quarters for the post's regimental band. In the late 1920s, the mess hall became the administration building.

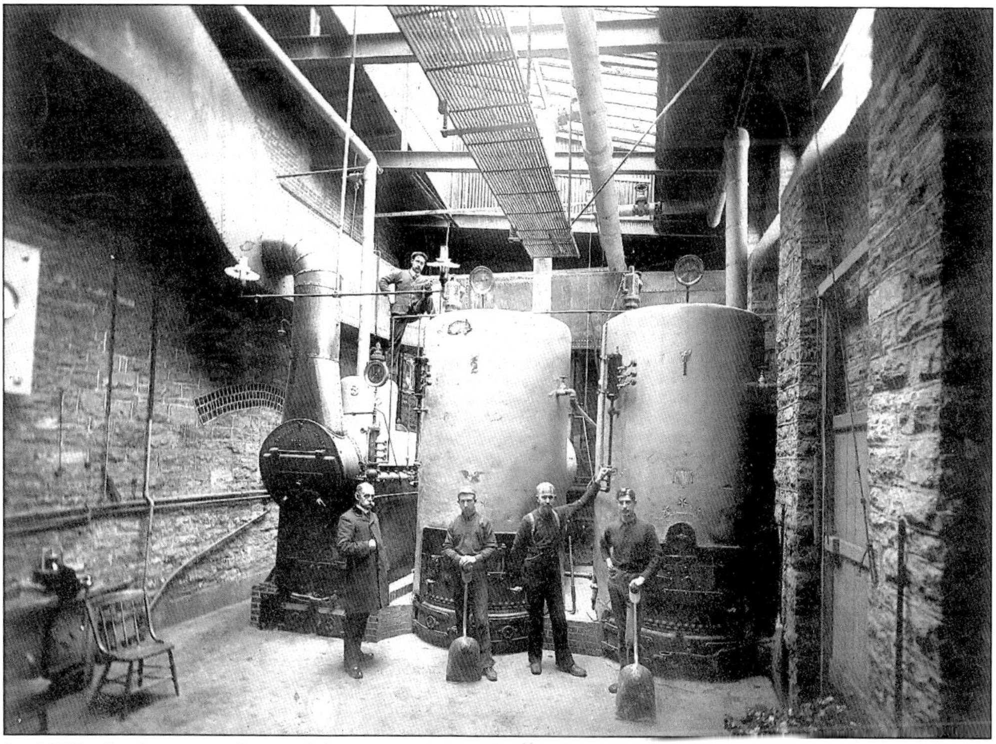

In 1893, the heating plant of the central mess hall contained two coal-fired hot-water boilers. Coal was dumped down a manhole into the storage bin located on the right. At the left is post engineer Edwin C. Knowlton, who was in charge of all post maintenance. Civilian workers were responsible for the maintenance and operation of the boilers.

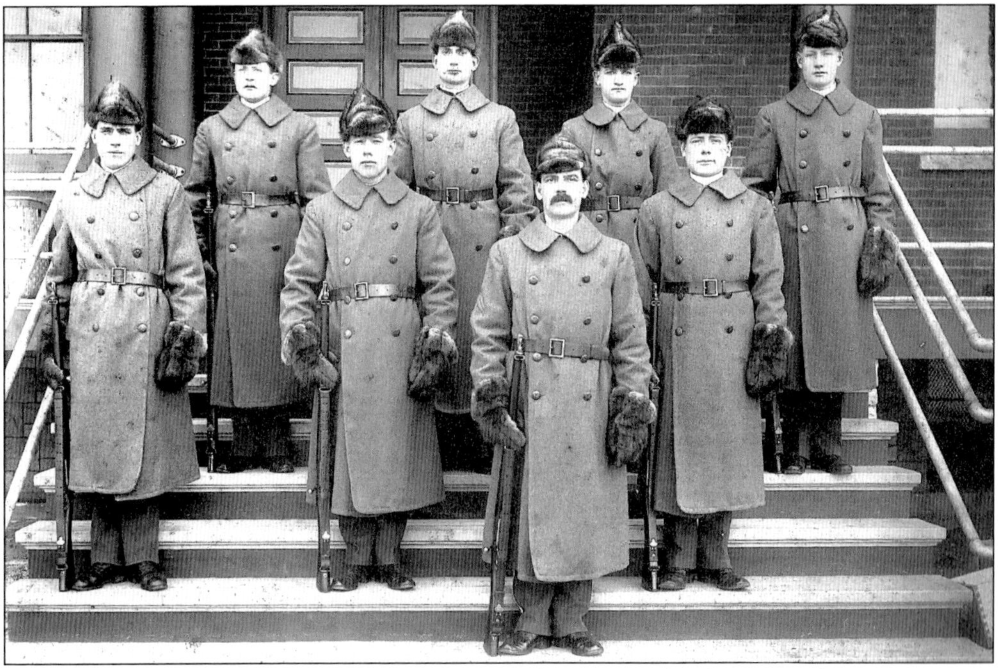

Members of the 9th Infantry, stationed at Madison Barracks from October 9, 1892, to April 23, 1905, stand in front of their barracks. Dressed in fur hats and gloves, they are prepared for guard duty in typical north country winter weather. Second from left in the front row is William Osborne. In 1900, Osborne was in the military contingent sent to China during the Boxer Rebellion.

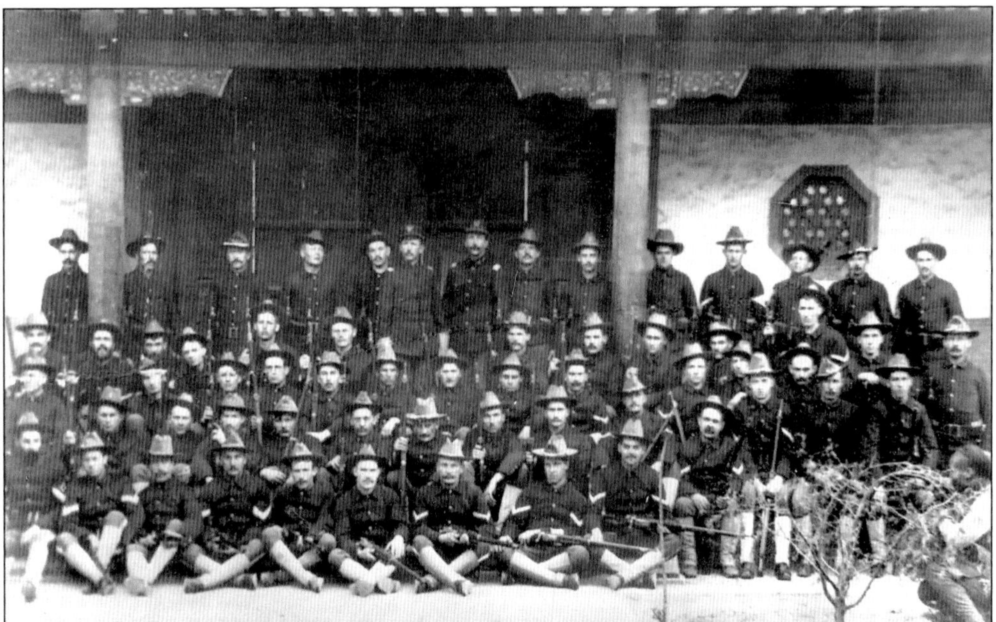

Members of the 9th U.S. Infantry pose outside the gate to the Forbidden City in Peking, China. They are preparing to leave for their home post at Madison Barracks after the Boxer Rebellion. They arrived at Madison Barracks on July 5, 1902.

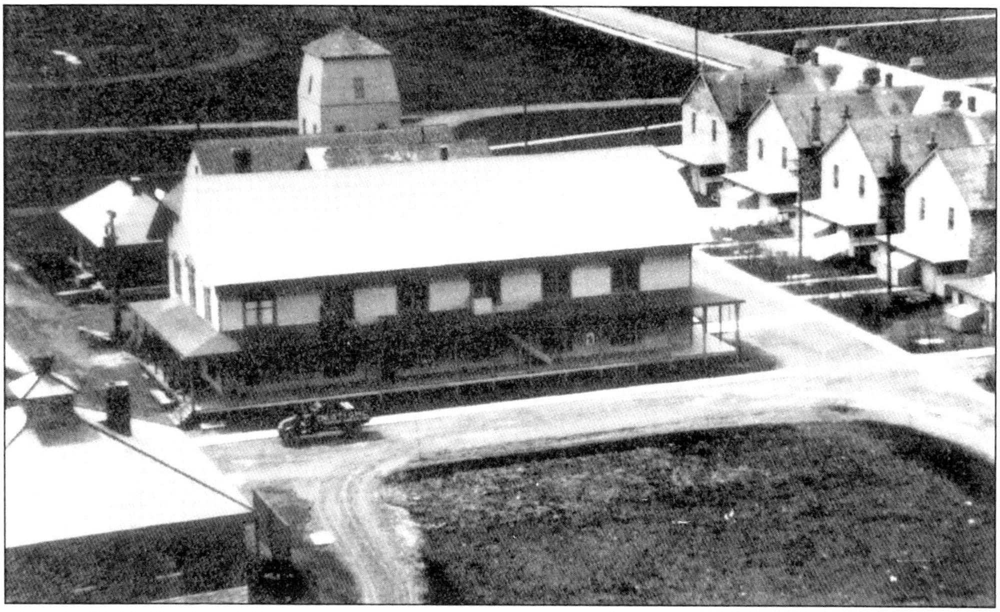

Built in 1888, Dodge Hall was the first administration building with ordnance and quartermaster offices on the first floor. A library, a theater for silent movies, and a dance hall on the second floor provided an entertainment facility for post personnel. The wooden structure was destroyed by fire in April 1932.

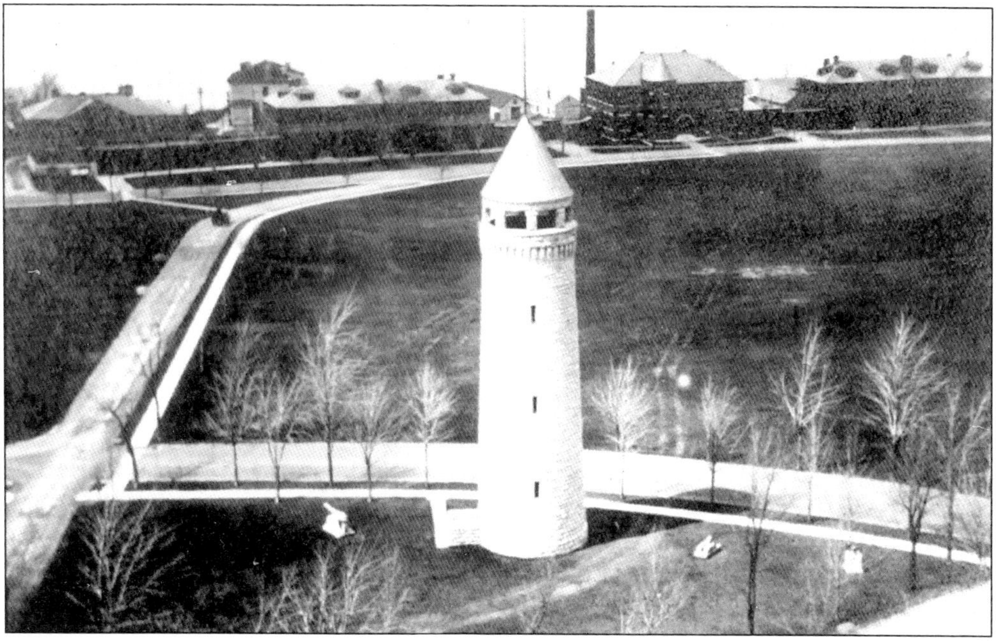

The cut-limestone water tower occupied the first building site to the east of the original barracks during the expansion in 1892. The tower held a 55,000-gallon water tank. Attached to the tower, on a copper plaque, is a list of 238 names of 9th Infantry enlisted men and 9 officers who were casualties of the Cuban War, the Philippine Insurrection, and the Boxer Rebellion in China. The 9th Infantry was stationed at Madison Barracks from 1892 to 1905. The water tower remains a historical landmark in Madison Barracks.

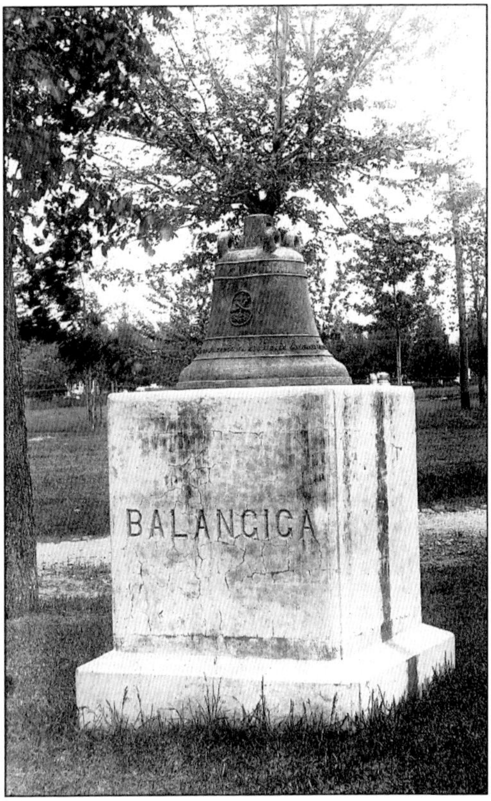

On September 28, 1901, during the Philippine Insurrection, this bell was rung by Filipino prisoners at Balangiga, Samar, to signal an attack on Company C, 9th Infantry. Three-quarters of Company C were massacred. In 1904, the bell was brought to Madison Barracks and placed on a concrete pedestal beside the stone water tower. Today the bell is kept in the 9th Infantry Museum in Korea.

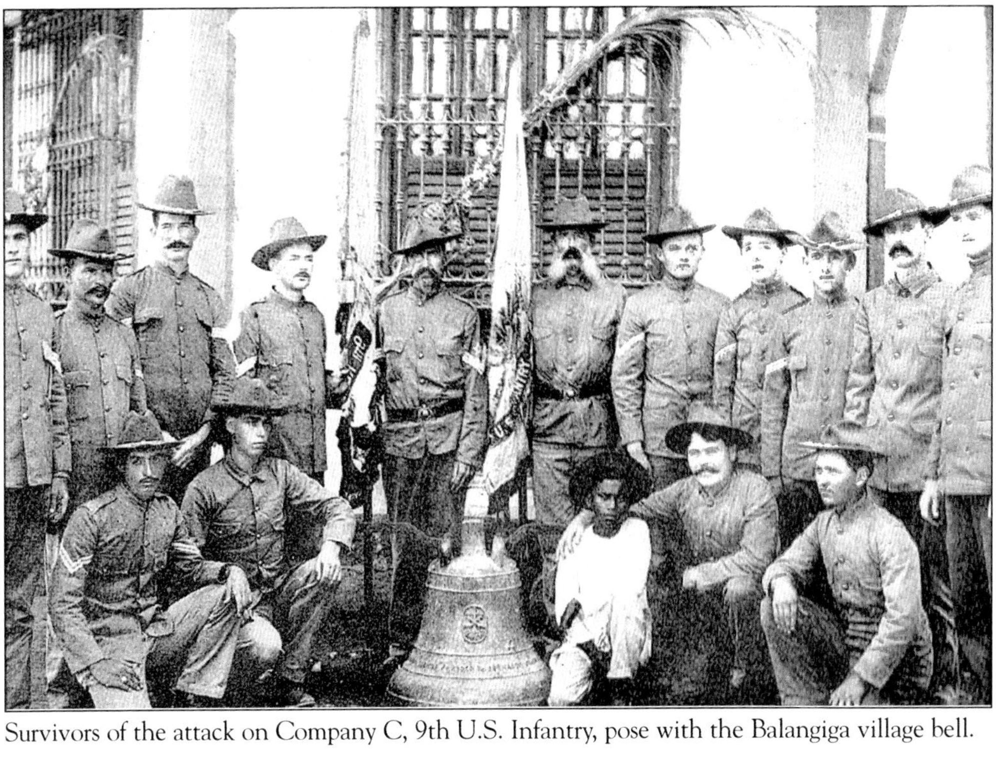

Survivors of the attack on Company C, 9th U.S. Infantry, pose with the Balangiga village bell.

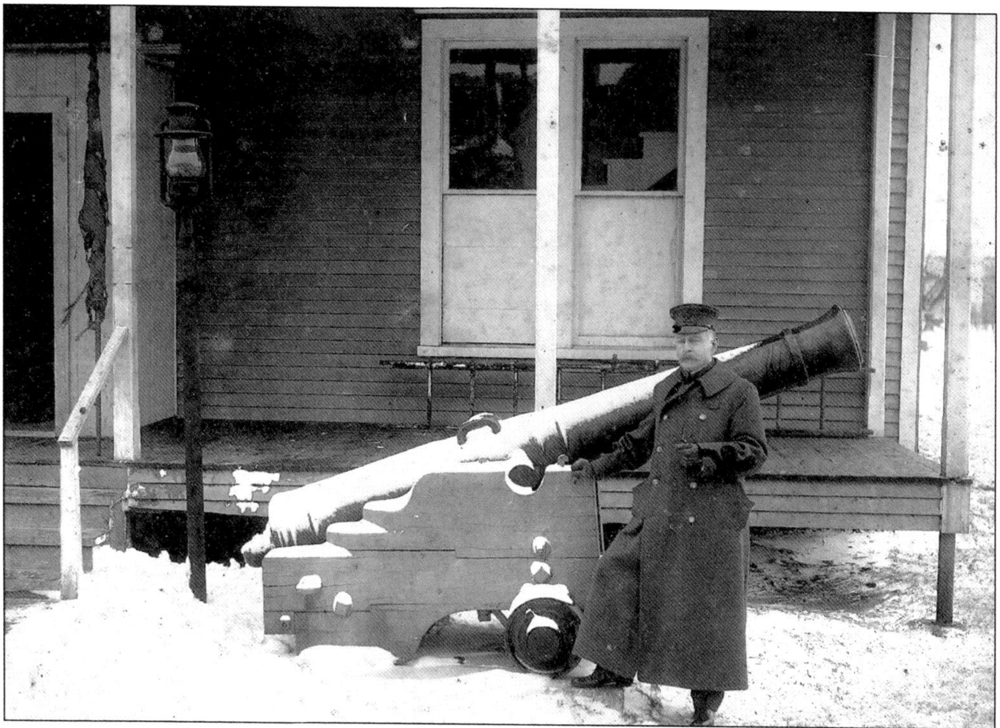

On a winter day, Col. Philip Read poses beside a Spanish cannon by Dodge Hall. The cannon was mounted on a gun carriage made of wood from the dismantled War of 1812 ship *New Orleans*, which stood abandoned on Navy Point in Sackets Harbor for 75 years. (Courtesy of Pickering Beach Museum.)

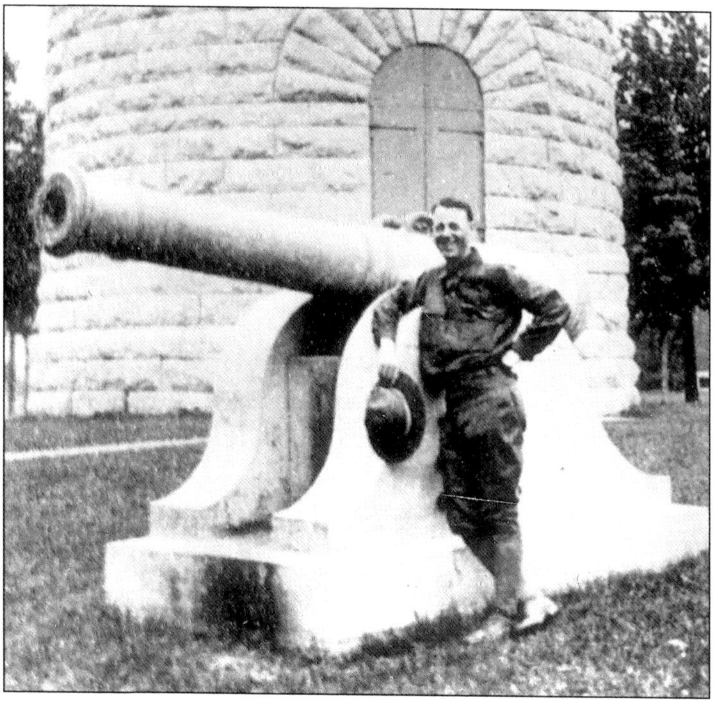

The cannon that stood beside Dodge Hall was brought from the Philippine Islands by the 23rd Infantry after the Philippine Insurrection of 1899–1901. The cannon was later relocated to an area beside the stone water tower, where it still rests today.

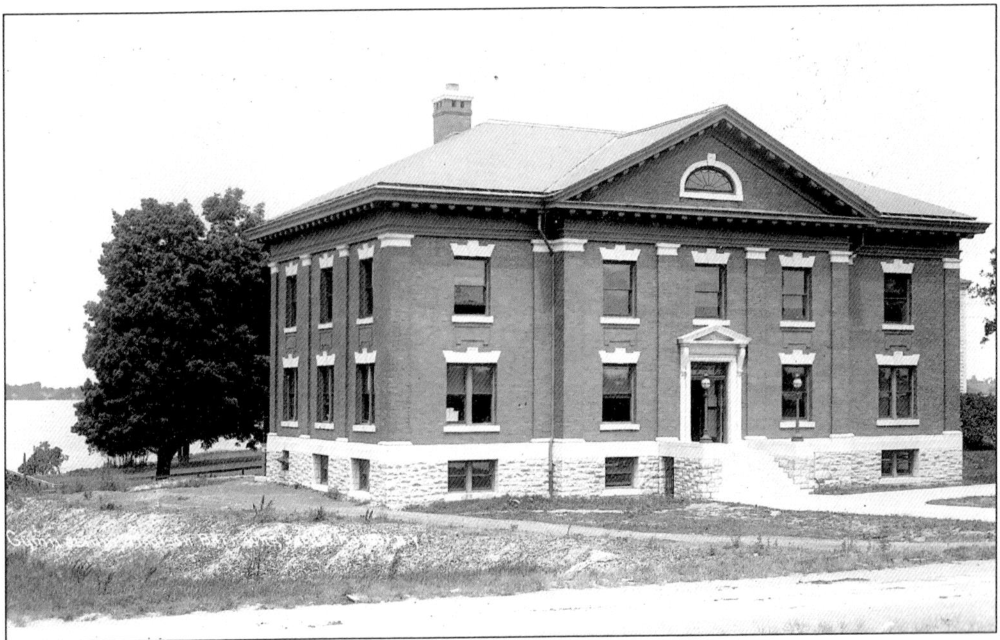

Built in 1905, the Post Exchange housed a variety of services such as a library, a barbershop, a variety store, a restaurant, a gymnasium, a bowling alley, the Red Cross office, and a taproom (bar).

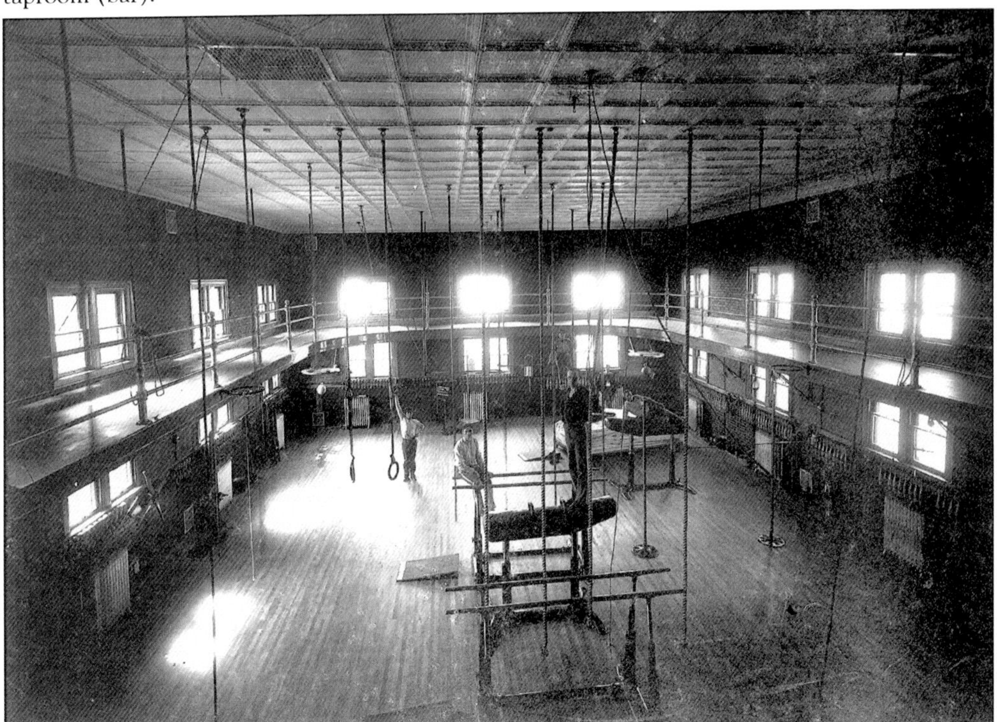

This 1908 view of the gymnasium shows an enlisted men's facility for exercise activities. The equipment was moved aside during popular athletic events like boxing matches. Both civilian and military spectators sat in the balcony.

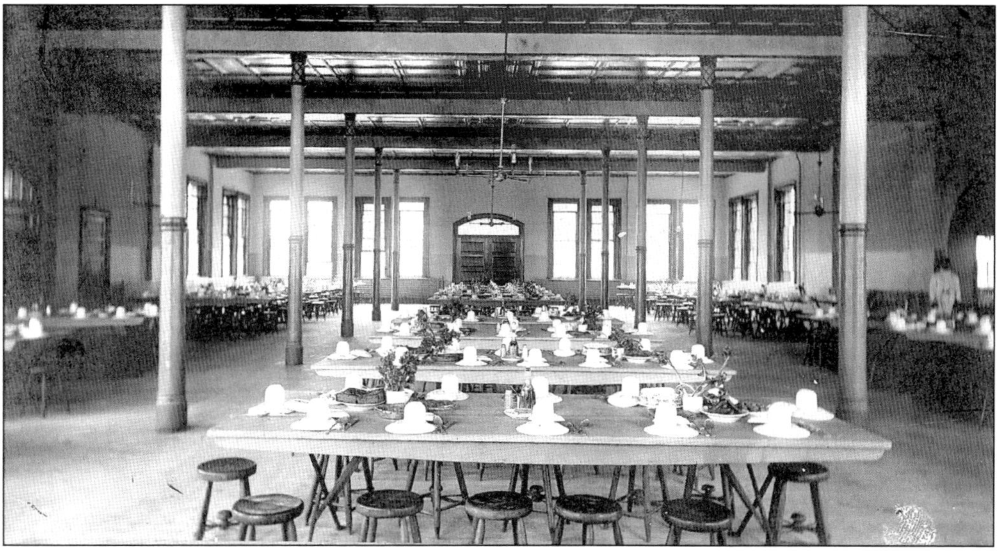

Soldiers of the 9th U.S. Infantry were the first to have breakfast in the new central mess hall dining room, built in 1892. Four hundred troops could be served at one sitting. Food was served family style on white ironstone crockery. At meal's end, the four-legged stools were turned upside down on the tabletops so that the floors could be cleaned.

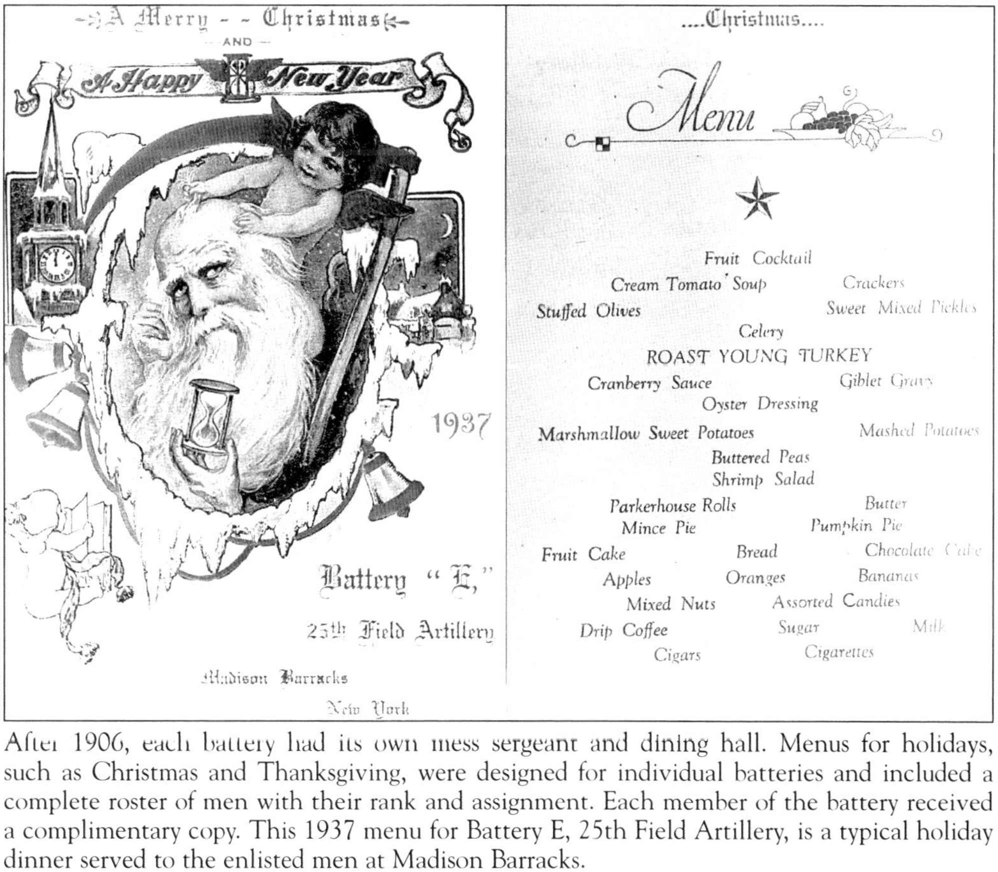

After 1906, each battery had its own mess sergeant and dining hall. Menus for holidays, such as Christmas and Thanksgiving, were designed for individual batteries and included a complete roster of men with their rank and assignment. Each member of the battery received a complimentary copy. This 1937 menu for Battery E, 25th Field Artillery, is a typical holiday dinner served to the enlisted men at Madison Barracks.

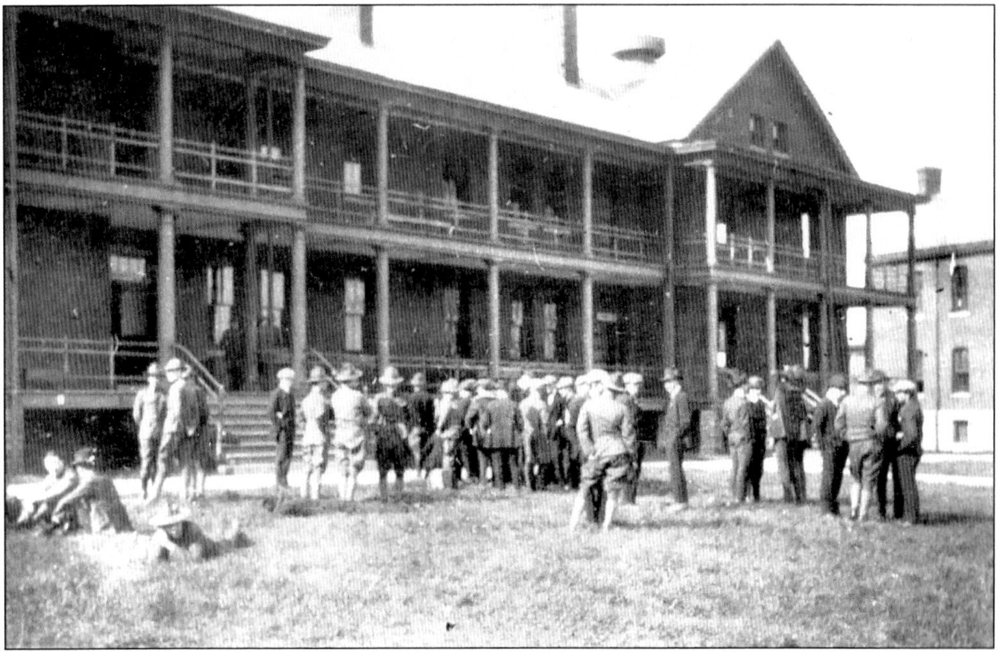

Opening day of officers' training camp at Madison Barracks, May 14, 1917, shows a group of recruits assembled in front of an enlisted men's brick barracks along the shoreline.

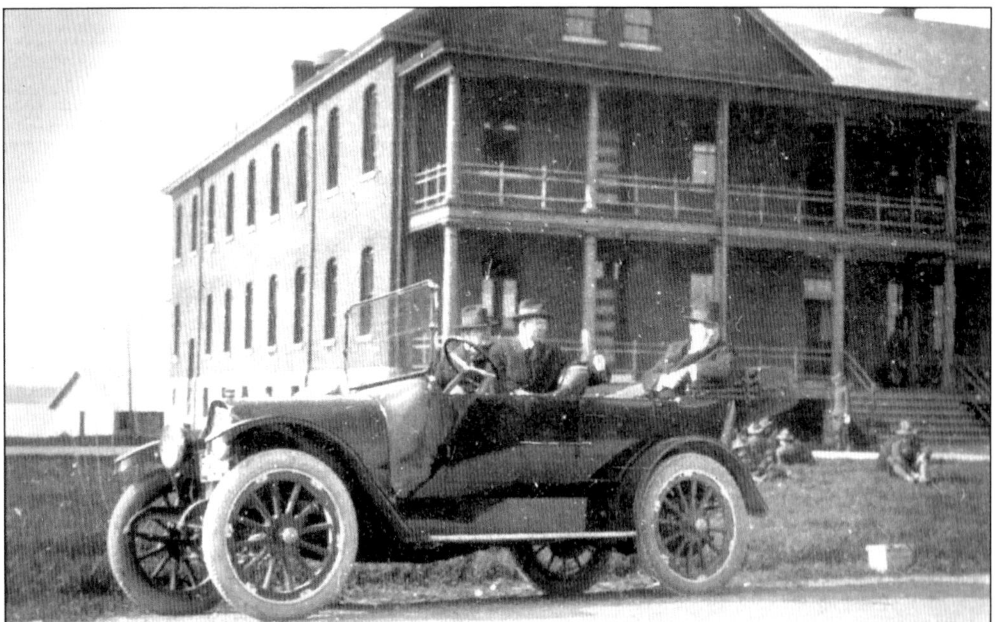

An article in the *Watertown Daily Times* of May 19, 1917, stated that "Another recruit arrived at Madison Barracks in a large automobile with his father. Another student officer arrived with his valet."

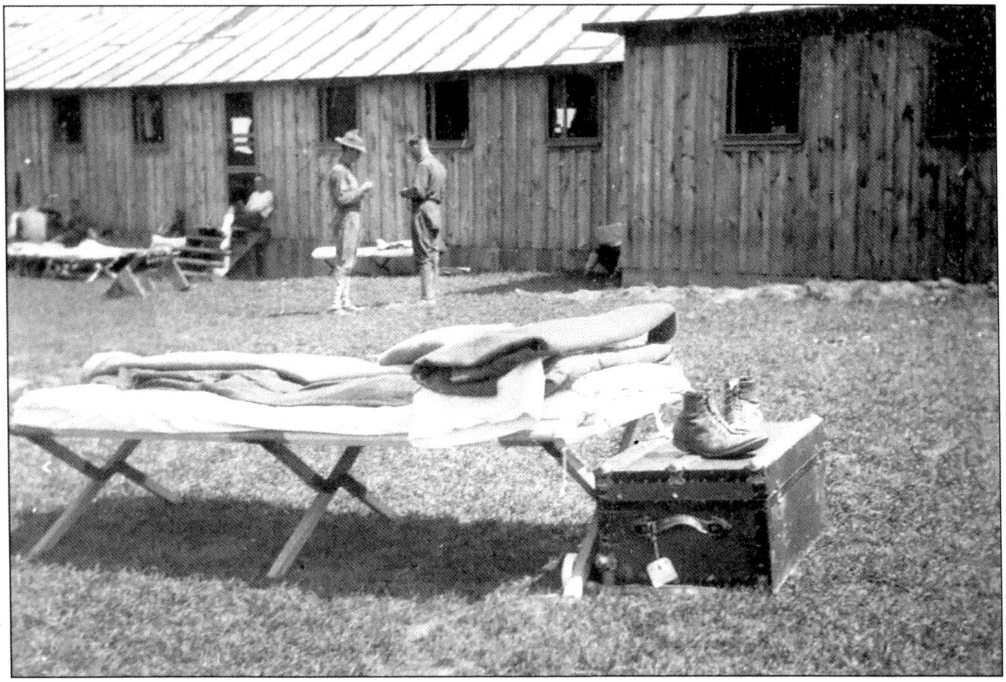

Temporary wooden barracks, located near Mill Creek along the eastern border of Madison Barracks, were used for troop accommodations during World War I. In this photograph the folding canvas cot and a footlocker demonstrate how a soldier's belongings and equipment were placed inside the barracks.

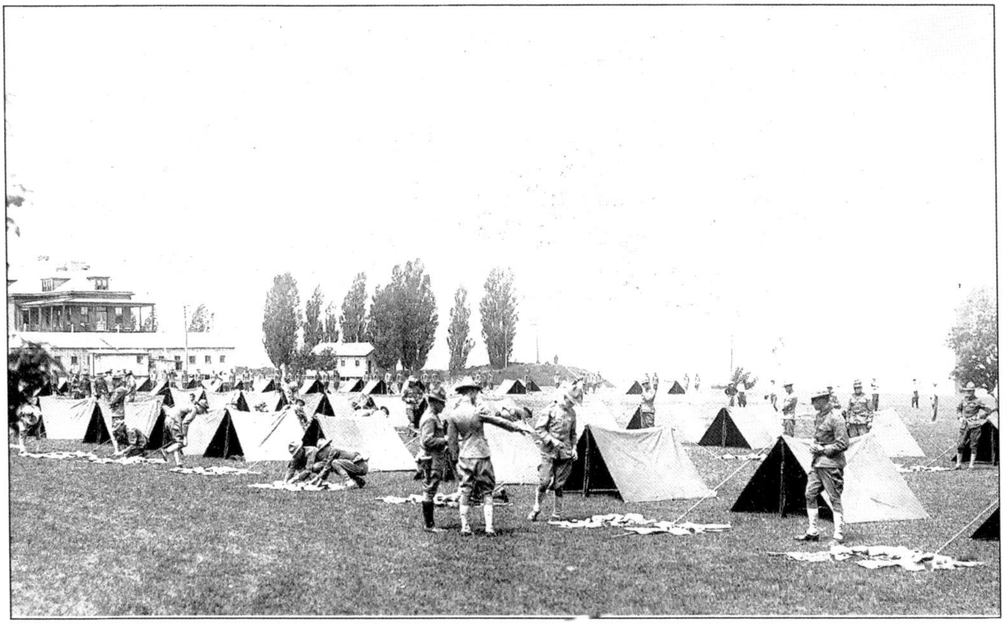

During World War I, those in Officers' Training Camp (OTC) used the parade grounds for training exercises. Men were given instruction on setting up temporary camp facilities in tents. Note the brick hospital and Fort Pike in the background.

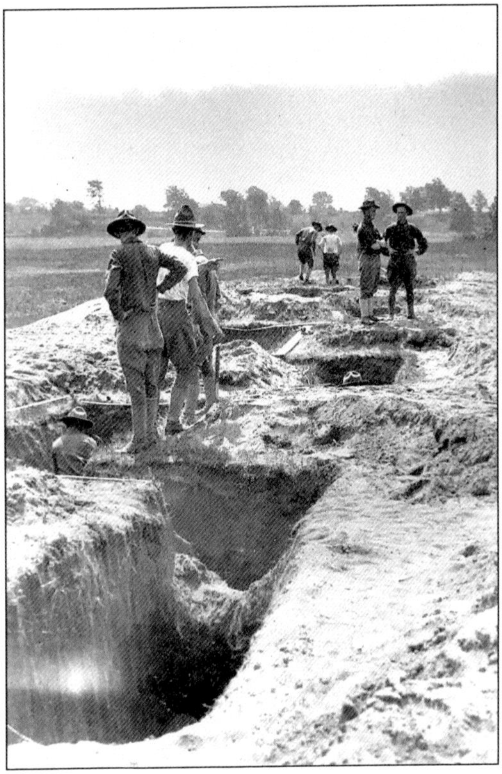

While training for World War I, troops rest after digging the ubiquitous trenches.

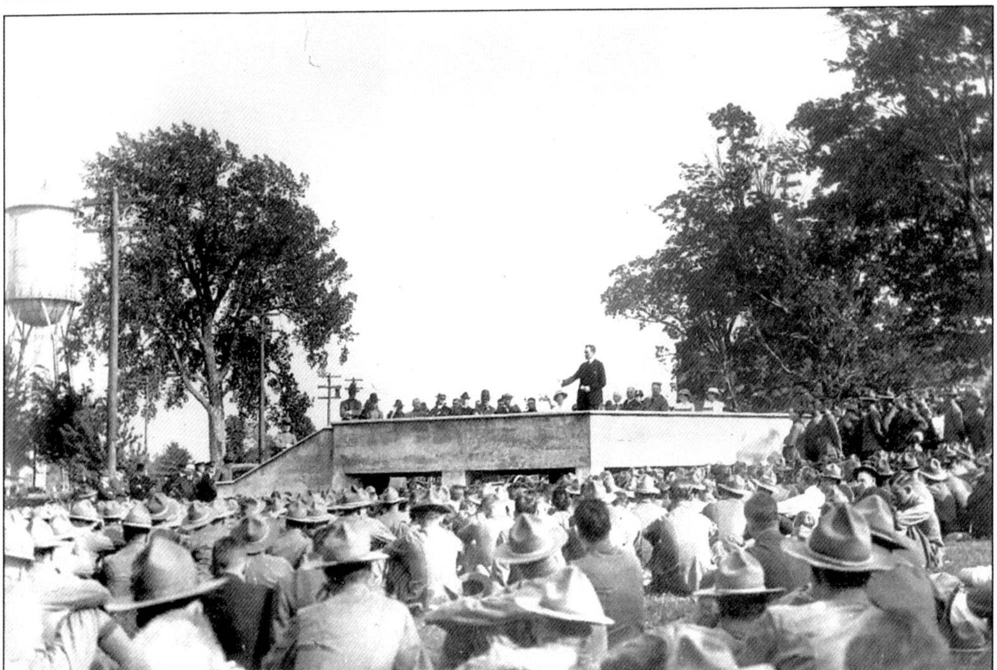

On July 19, 1917, the bandstand at Madison Barracks served as a speaker's platform for New York City Mayor John P. Mitchell. After addressing Rotarians in Watertown, he visited the post of Madison Barracks, where he spoke to the student officers.

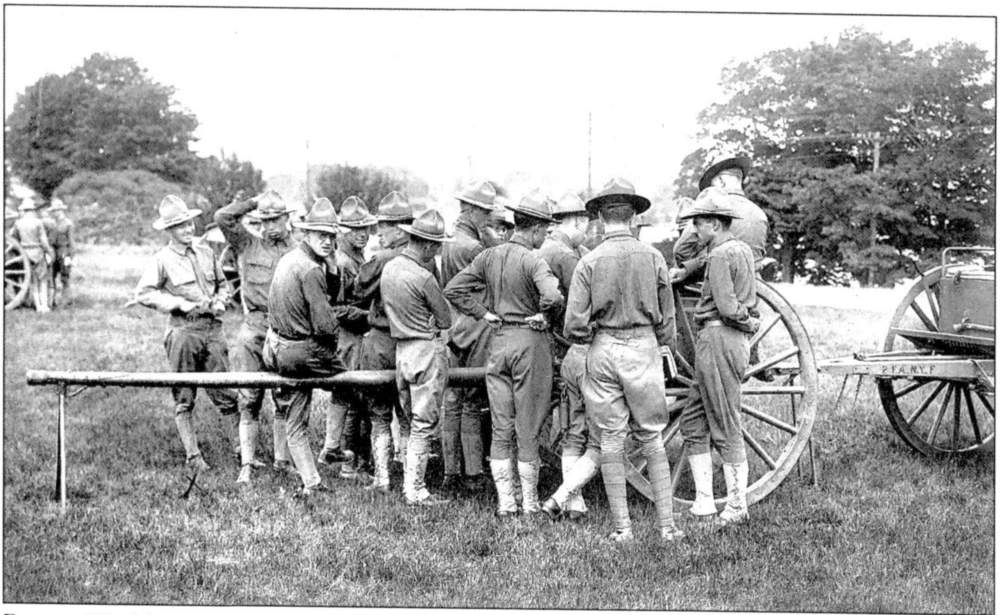

During World War I, the New York National Guard 2nd Field Artillery, Battery F, arrived at Madison Barracks for training with a detachment of 30 men and 12 three-inch pieces (cannons). Eventually the unit reached a complement of 450 men.

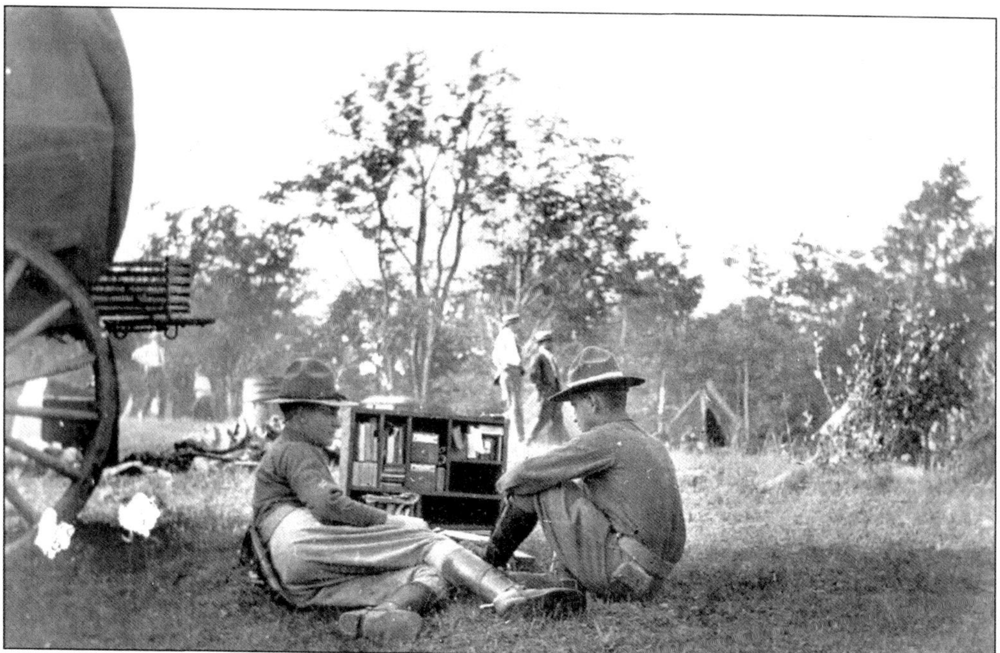

Troops from Madison Barracks stop for a break in Watertown on their way to Pine Plains, near the village of Great Bend, where they will fire artillery pieces. Battery clerks in front of a portable library were responsible for personnel and equipment records.

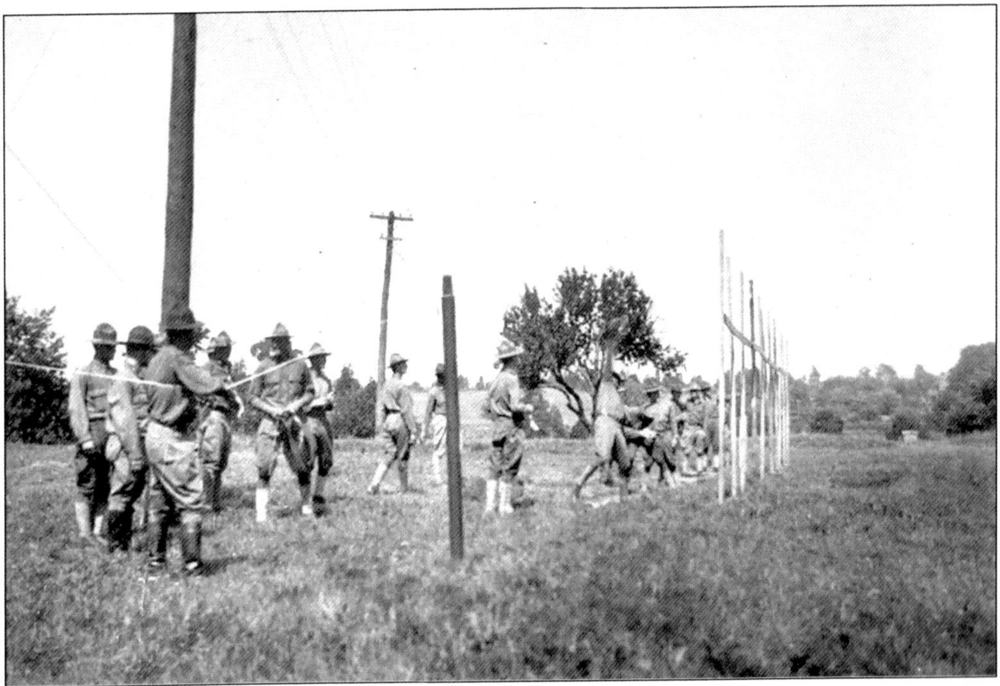

At Madison Barracks, trainees receive instruction in throwing hand grenades over make-believe obstacles such as this row of wooden posts.

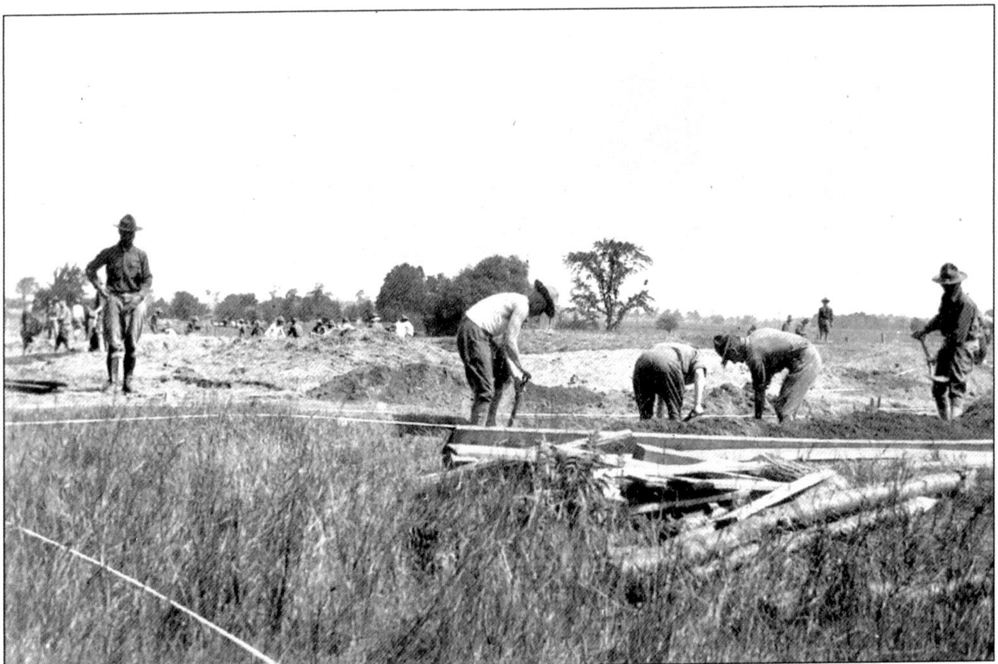

Also during World War I, student officers are shown in the process of constructing model fortifications on leased land east of Madison Barracks outside the village of Sackets Harbor.

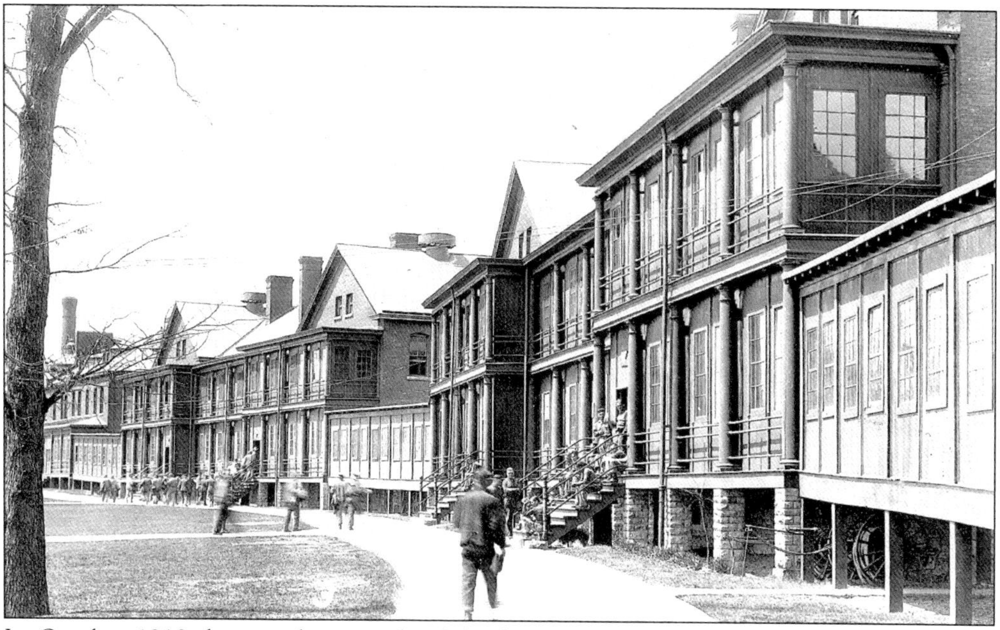

In October 1918, late in the war, the federal government designated Madison Barracks a general convalescent hospital for American Allied Expeditionary Forces returning from overseas. Their housing consisted of a row of seven enlisted men's barracks along the shore, which were connected by covered porches. By March 1919, over 500 patients had recuperated and were discharged. In addition, French war brides of infantry soldiers were brought to Sackets Harbor to join their new husbands.

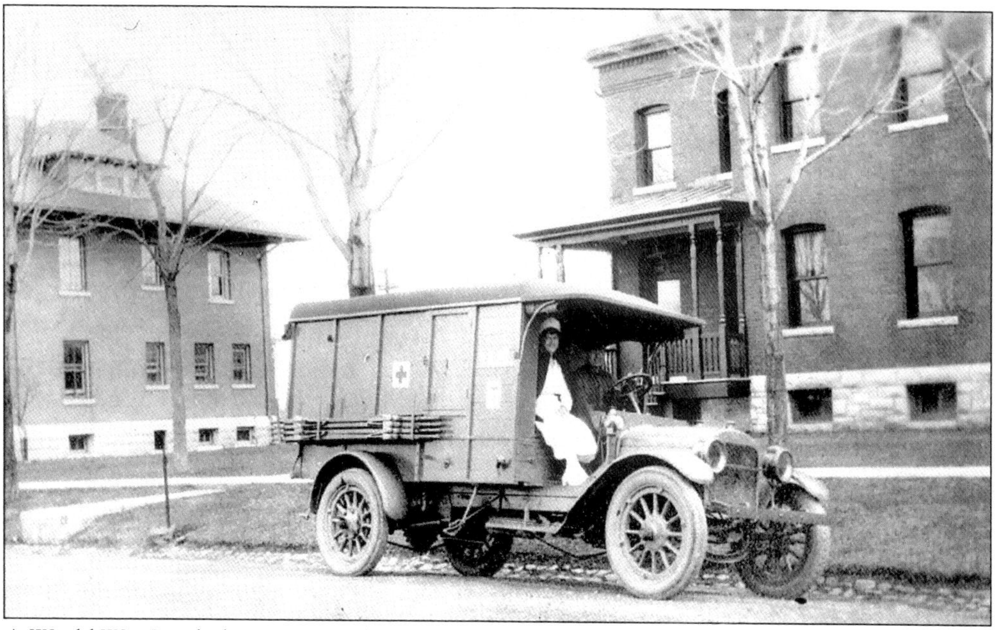

A World War I ambulance assigned to Madison Barracks is parked in front of the post chaplain's quarters on officers' row. The commandant's house is on the left. A detachment of the 142nd Medical Corpsmen had been at the post several months when the post was used as a general hospital after World War I.

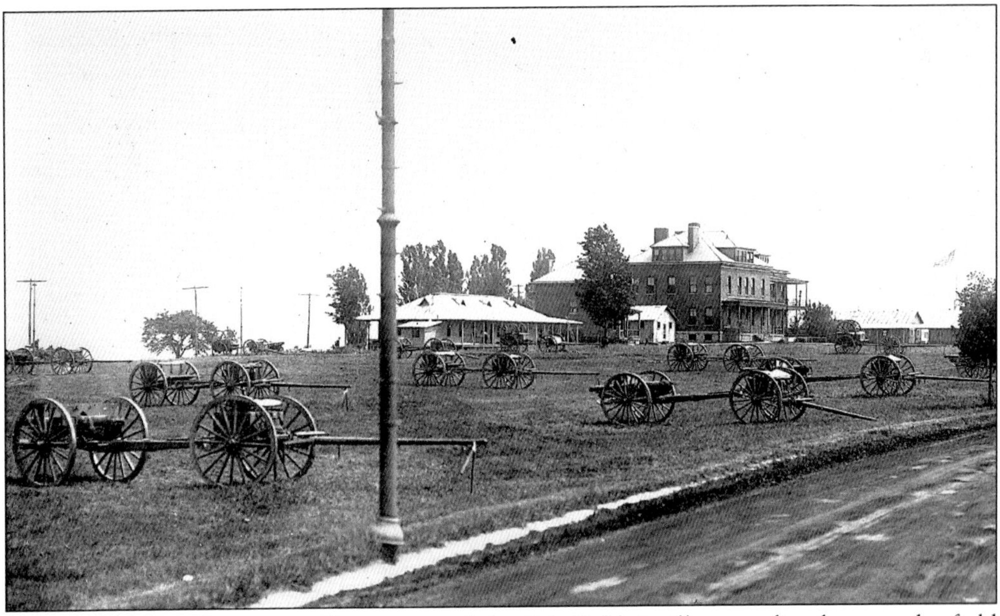

Old French 75-millimeter artillery pieces of the 7th Field Artillery are lined up on the field west of the brick hospital. In the background, the white-roofed building stored tents used during summer training.

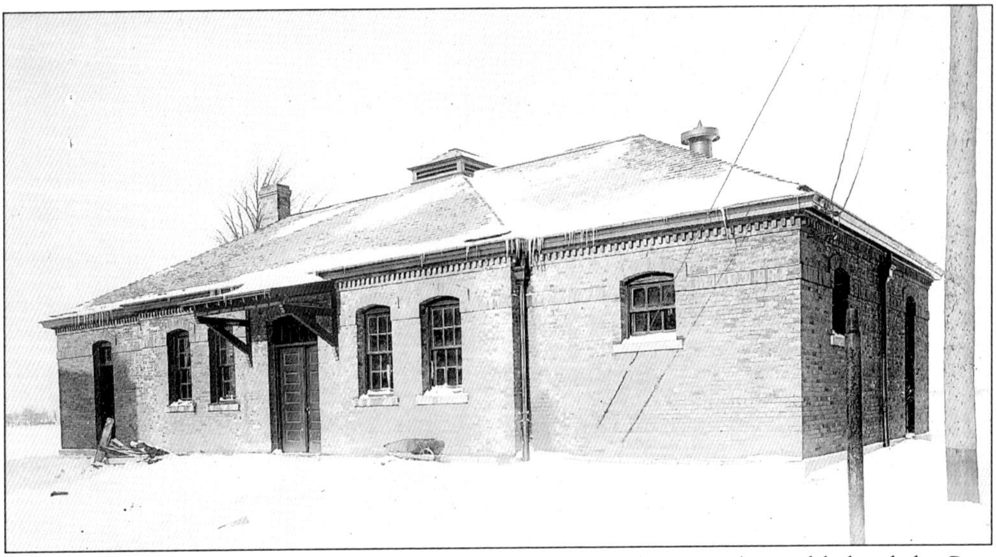

Built in 1910 at a cost of $6,200, the Madison Barracks bakery was located behind the Post Exchange. It was built to replace the original bakery, now restored as part of the Barracks Inn restaurant. An electric mixer and two ovens enabled the bakers to produce 6,000 pounds of bread daily. This bread was supplied to the mess halls and sold in the post commissary.

A soldier of the 3rd U.S. Infantry, stationed at Madison Barracks from 1911 to 1915, poses with his steadfast animal. Mules were used to transport equipment, while officers rode horses.

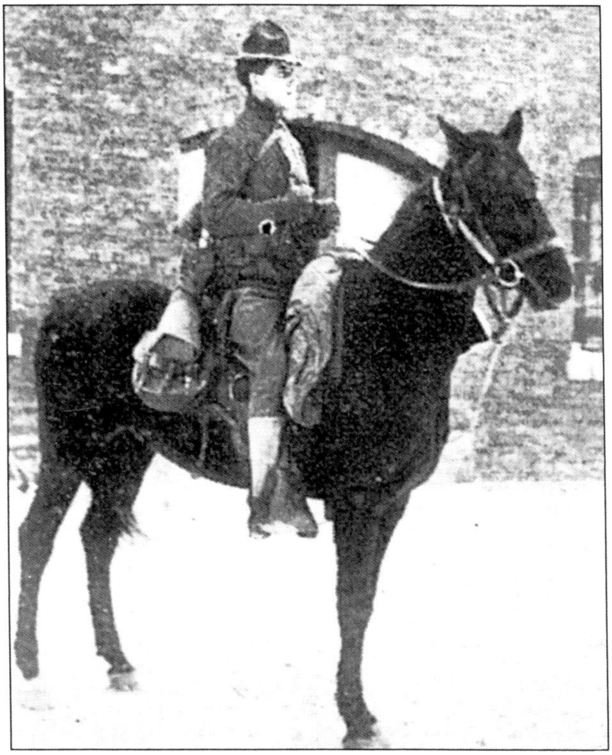

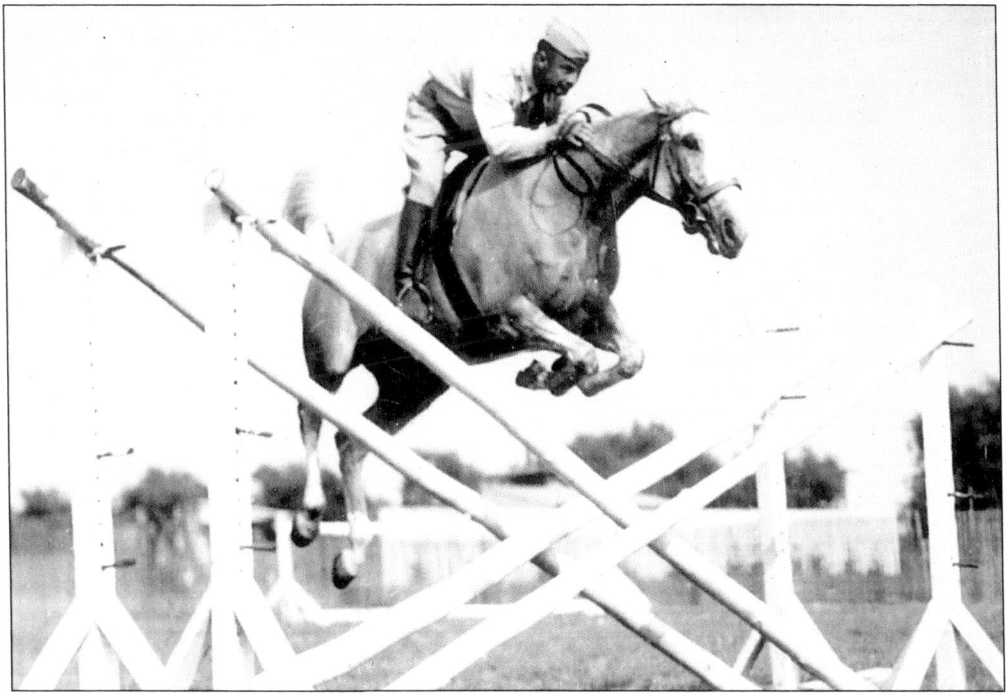

During the summers of the 1920s and 1930s, horse shows at Madison Barracks were popular events on Sunday afternoons. Officers who participated owned their own horses. Members of local riding clubs were invited to participate.

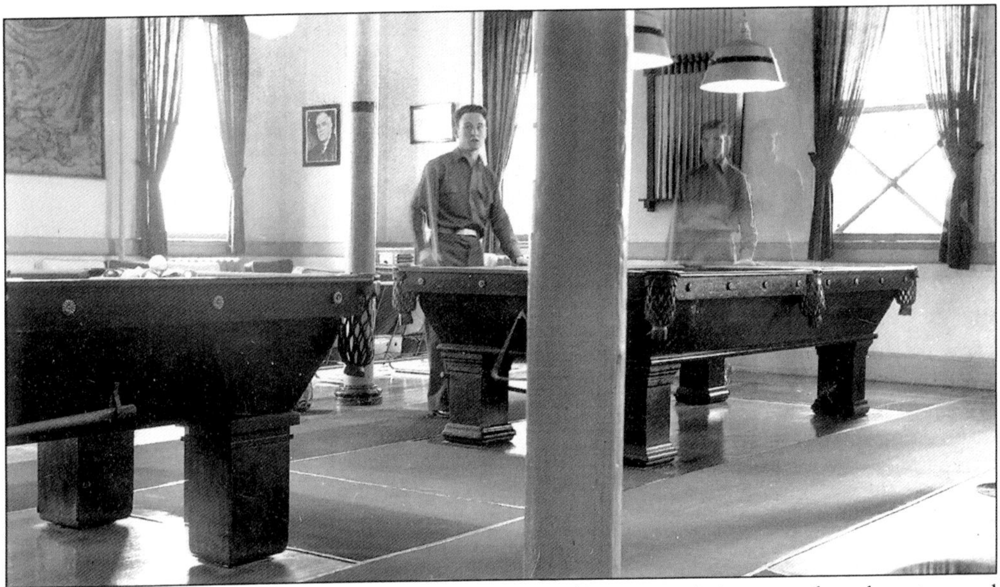

In the 1930s, the dayroom of D Battery, 25th Field Artillery, provided an area for relaxation and entertainment. A portrait of Pres. Franklin D. Roosevelt hangs on the wall.

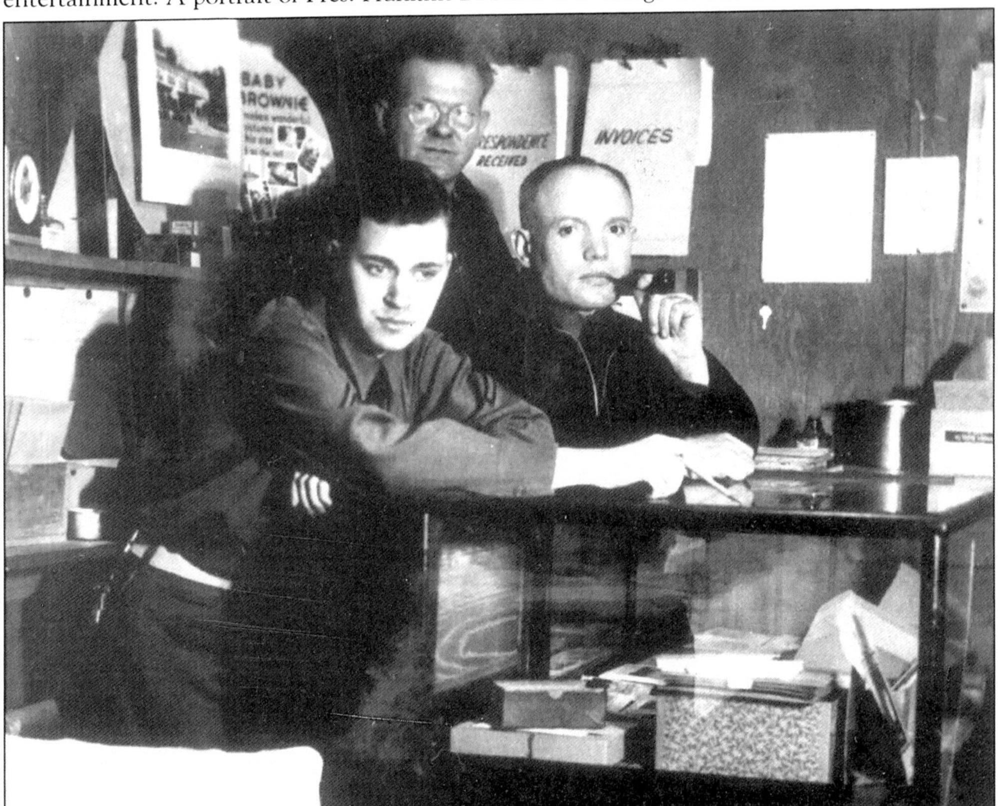

Pfc. Merle Saunders, member of the service battery and band, is seen in the center of this photograph. Saunders sold and developed film in a photography shop located in the barracks dayroom, where soldiers spent off-duty time.

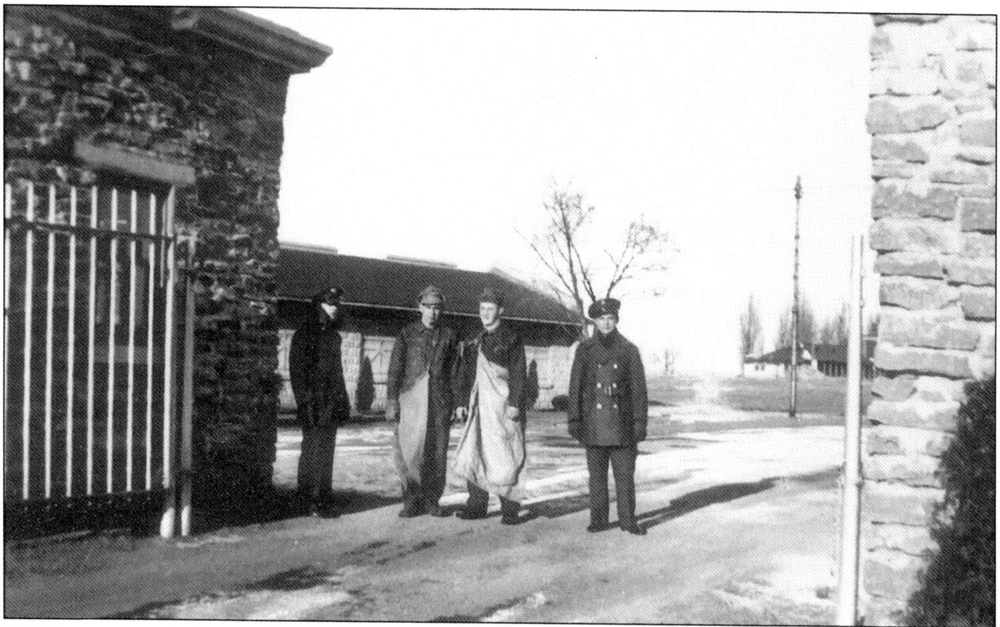

Soldiers accused of an infraction of rules were sentenced to serve time in the guardhouse. They were placed on cleanup detail to police the grounds. Dressed in blue denim outfits, with a large white P on the back of their jacket, they were guarded by military police. This photograph was taken *c.* 1930.

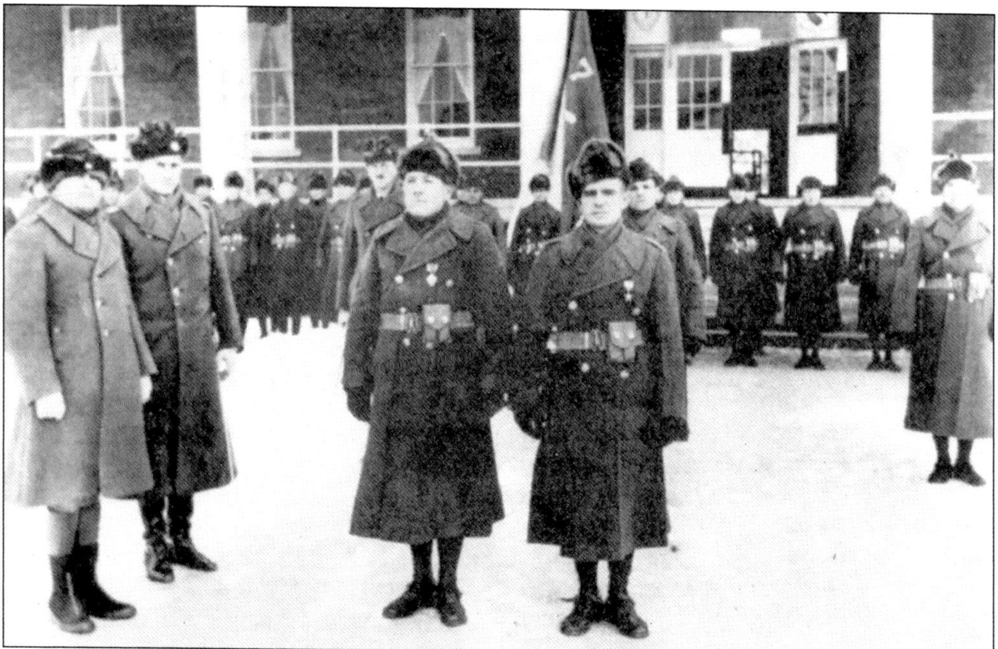

On November 20, 1932, members of the 7th Field Artillery, Battery E, stand at attention in front of building No. 76. The occasion was to honor a recipient of the Silver Star. From left to right, in the front, are Capt. Norbert Manley, Col. William Fergus Kernan, Sgt. Meczyslaw J. Suwicki (recipient of the Silver Star for heroism in World War I), unidentified, and 1st Sgt. Andrew Bostock.

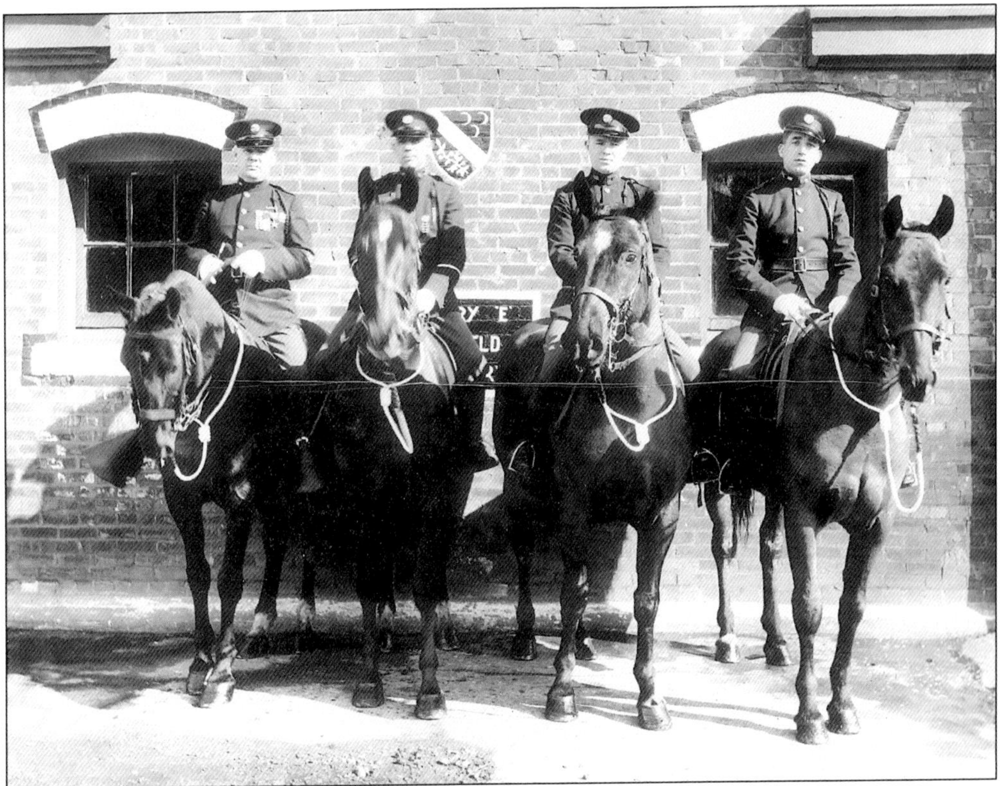

In the 1930s, members of the 7th Field Artillery, Battery E, stop in front of the stables near Mill Creek. They are, from left to right, 1st Sgt. Andrew Bostock, Sgt. Thomas Greene, unidentified, and Sgt. Ralph Golightly.

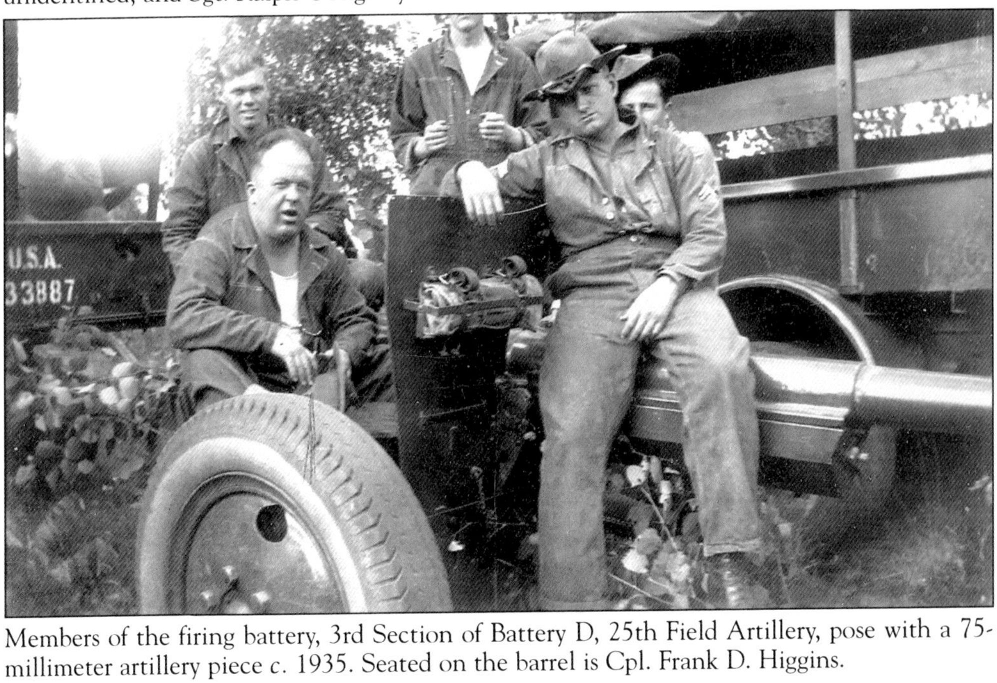

Members of the firing battery, 3rd Section of Battery D, 25th Field Artillery, pose with a 75-millimeter artillery piece c. 1935. Seated on the barrel is Cpl. Frank D. Higgins.

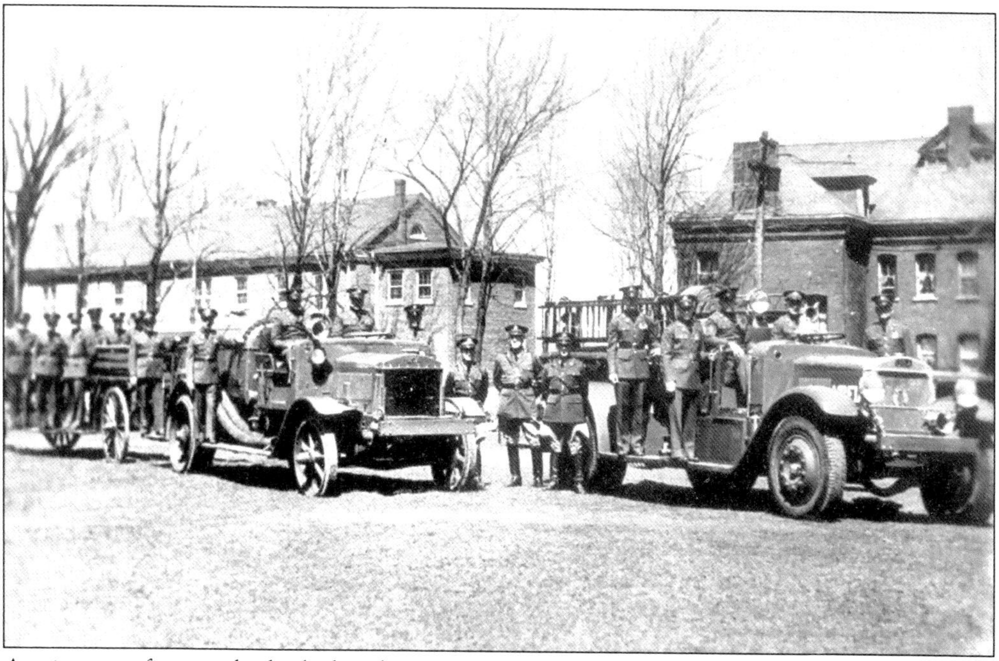

A nine-ton fire truck, built by the Camp Holabird Quartermaster Corps in Baltimore, Maryland, upgraded the fire protection equipment in 1934. The new fire truck was housed in the fire station garage built in 1929. The practice of firing a three-gun alarm to signal a fire was replaced by an electric siren mounted on top of the stone hospital.

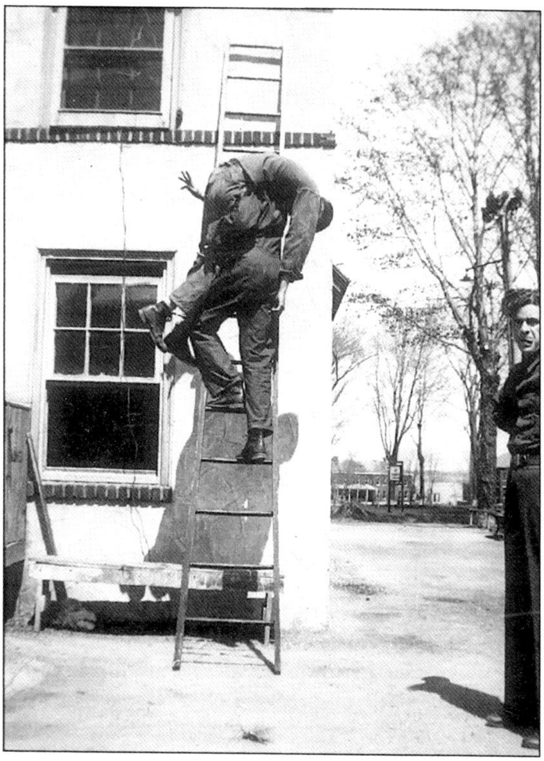

Qualified enlisted men served as firefighters in the post fire department. A practice rescue drill is shown in progress at the fire station.

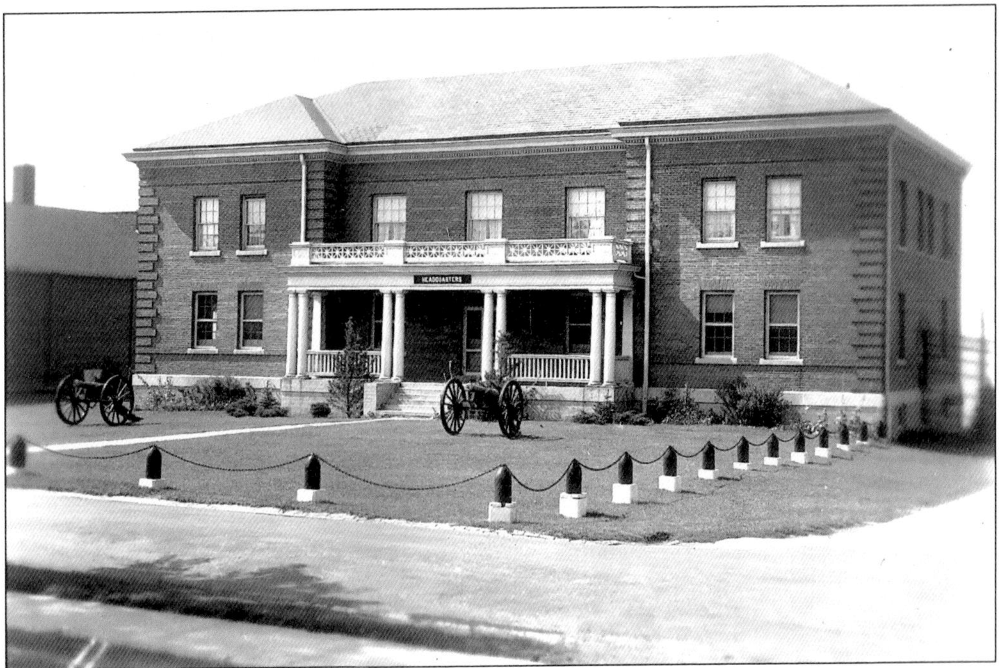

A fence of deactivated artillery shells marks the front lawn of the post headquarters, built in 1926.

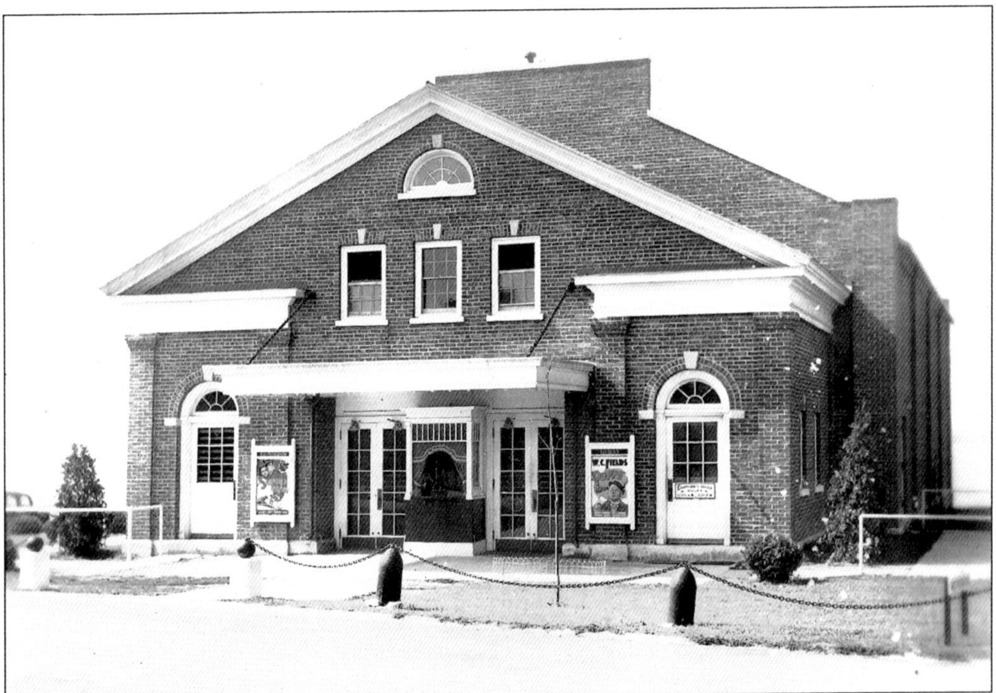

A new theater was constructed in 1932 on the waterfront. Movies with sound were shown every night, and matinees were shown on weekends. Before the new theater, silent movies were shown on the second floor of Dodge Hall administration building.

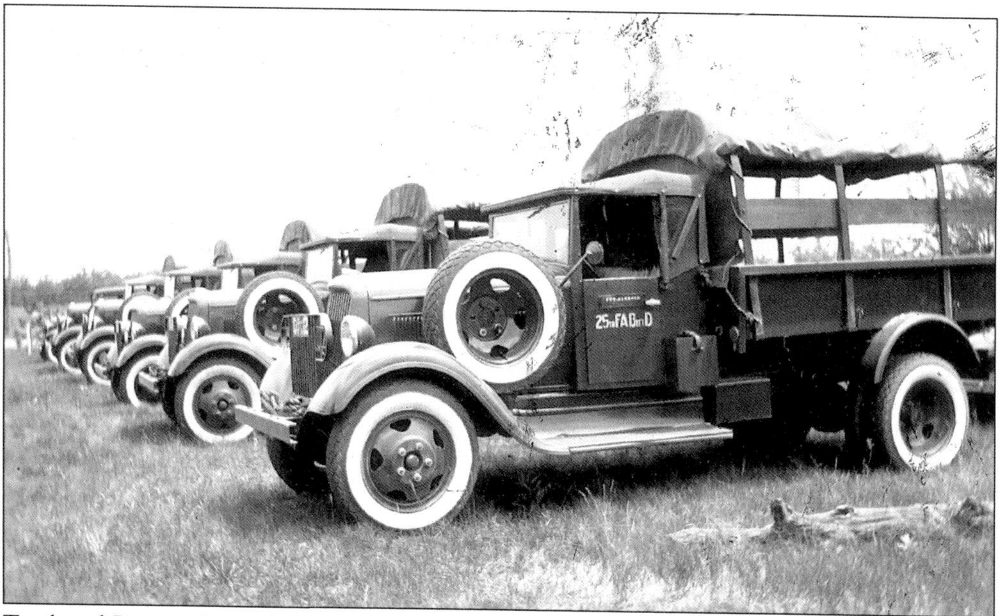

Trucks of Battery D, 25th Field Artillery, are lined up in preparation for a convoy to Pine Camp near Great Bend village. The tires are hand-painted by the soldiers with white tire paint simulating whitewall tires.

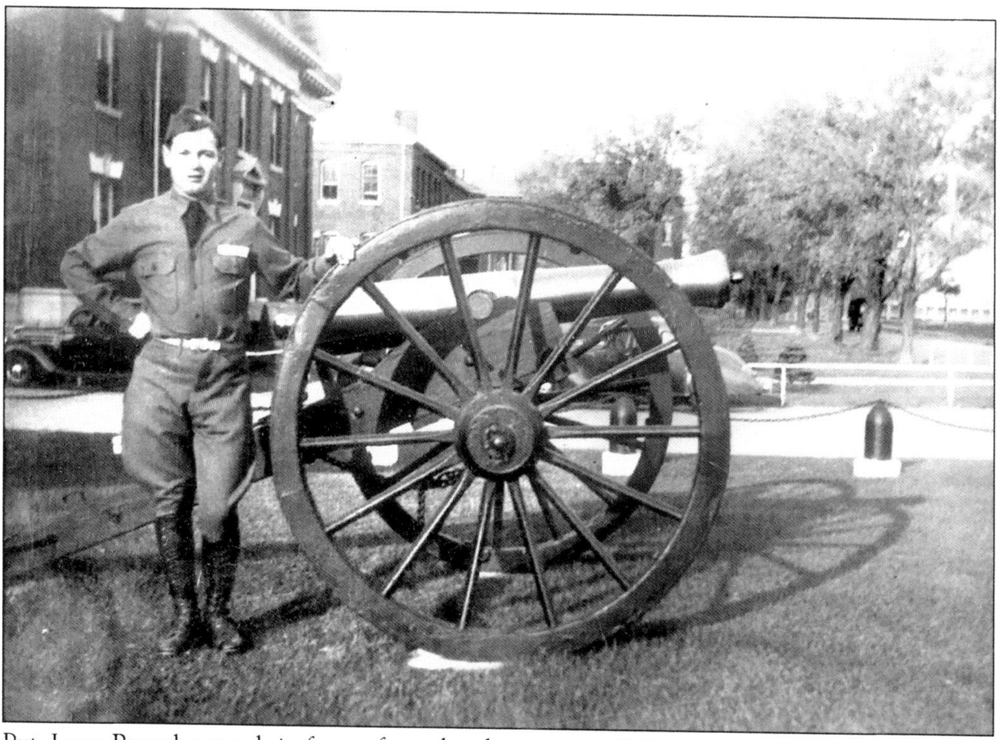

Pvt. Leon Branche stands in front of post headquarters in 1938 beside a Civil War-era cannon. This cannon is now in front of artillery headquarters at Fort Drum.

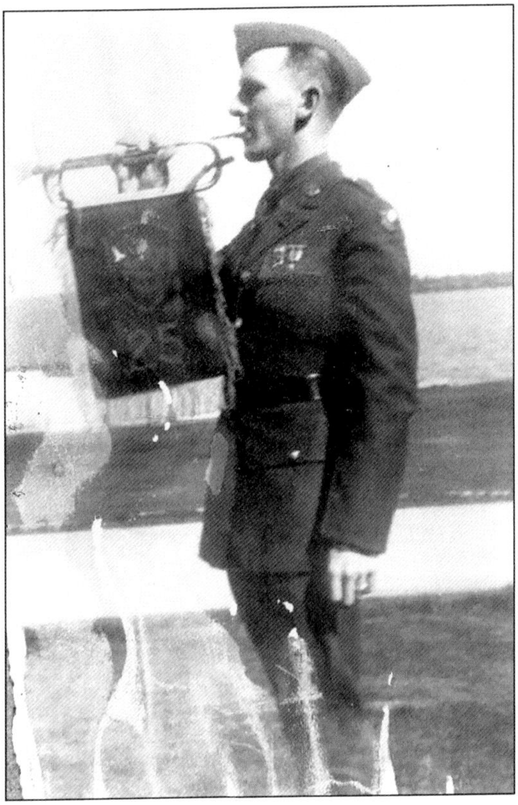

Pfc. Clair V. Ingram of Battery E, 25th Field Artillery, 9th Division, was bugler and chauffeur for the battery commander from 1933 to 1940 at Madison Barracks. He was responsible for all required bugle calls.

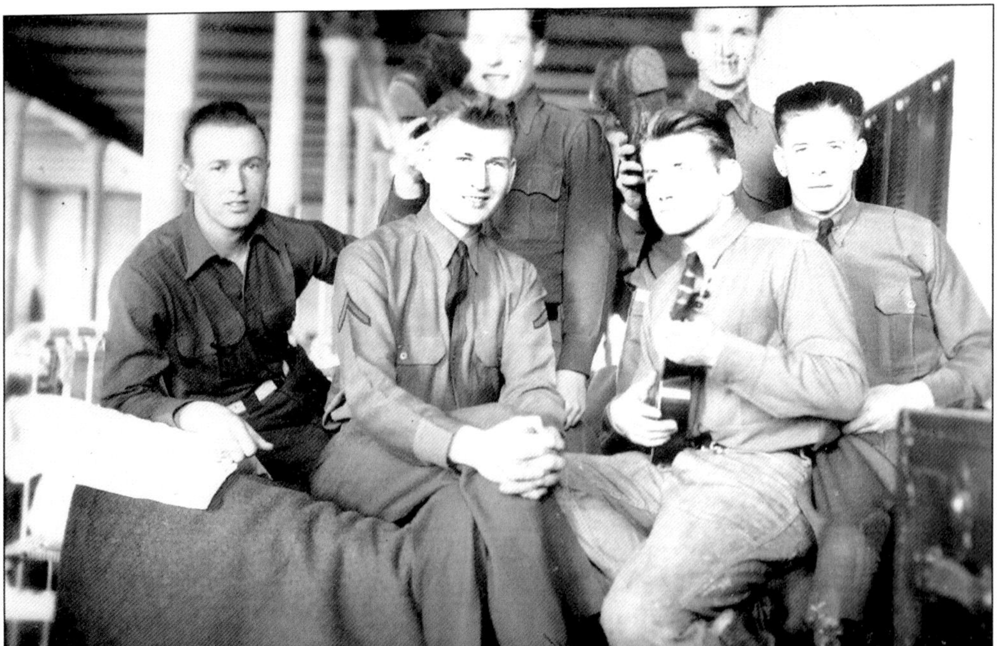

Soldiers of Battery D, 25th Field Artillery, appear ready to silence the ukulele players.

Col. Maxwell Murray arrived at Madison Barracks on August 13, 1936, to assume command of the post. The 5th and 25th U.S. Field Artillery units were in residence. He left on August 15, 1938, was promoted to brigadier general on December 1 of the same year, and was assigned to Hawaii in 1940.

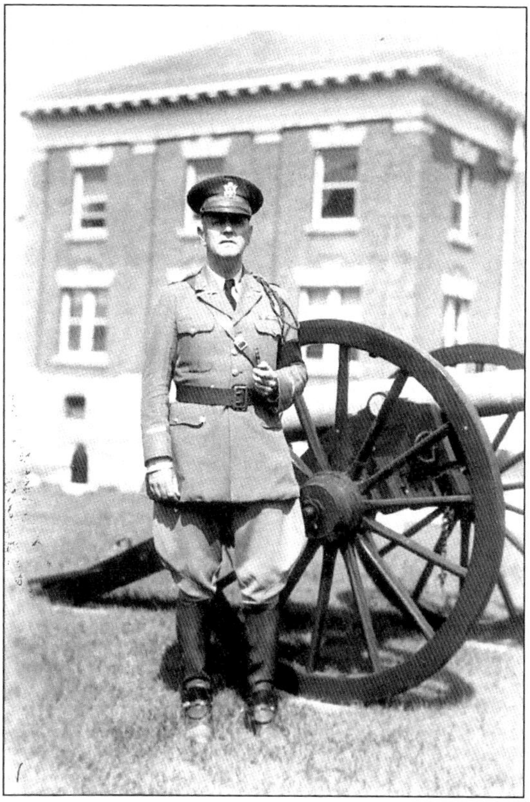

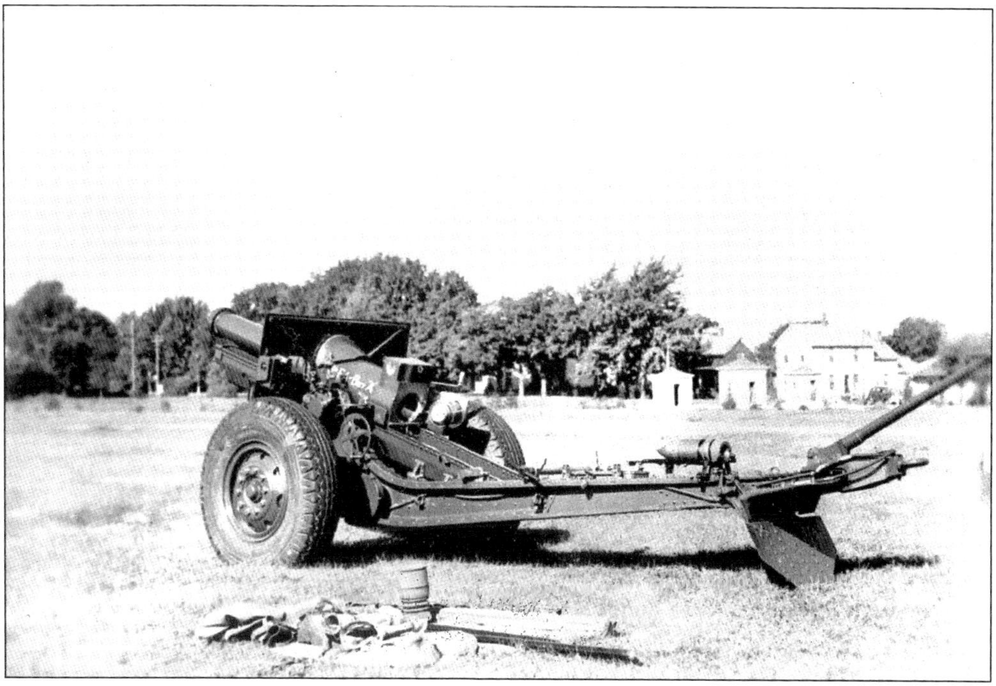

A 155-millimeter piece used by Battery A is prepared for inspection in 1935.

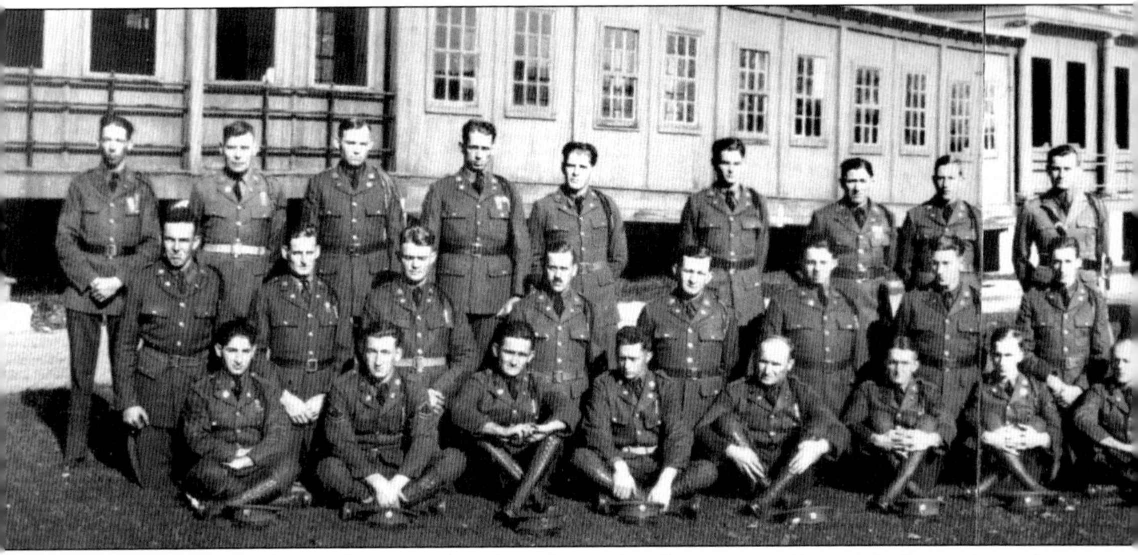

The first mechanized unit, the 5th Field Artillery, arrived at Madison Barracks on October 28, 1931. On November 7, 1931, Battery B poses in front of the enlisted men's

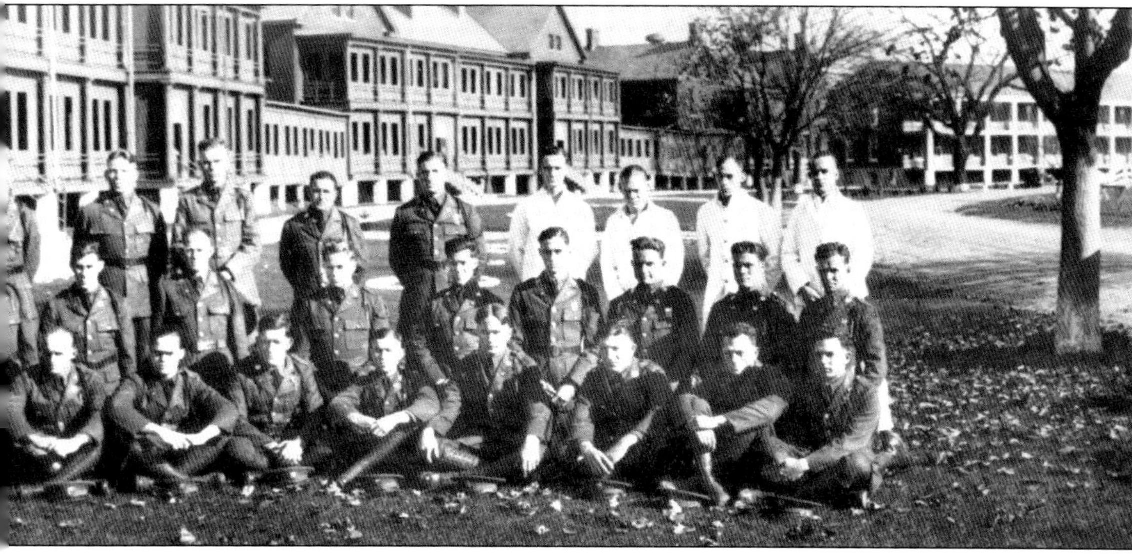

barracks. The covered porches, built in 1917, allowed convalescing soldiers to move easily between buildings.

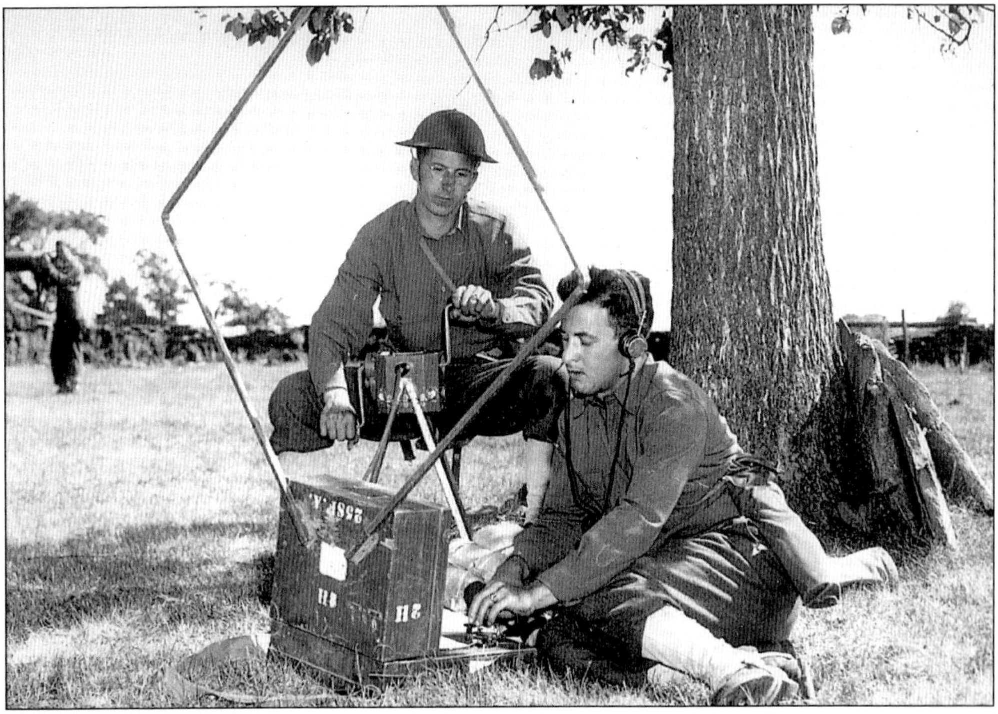

During two-day field maneuvers in July 1941, soldiers set up a field radio at the junction of the Sackets Harbor-Smithville Road and Route 3. Pvt. Clyde Fittelli, wearing earphones, and Cpl. John S. Meckowski communicate with adjacent units on firing missions.

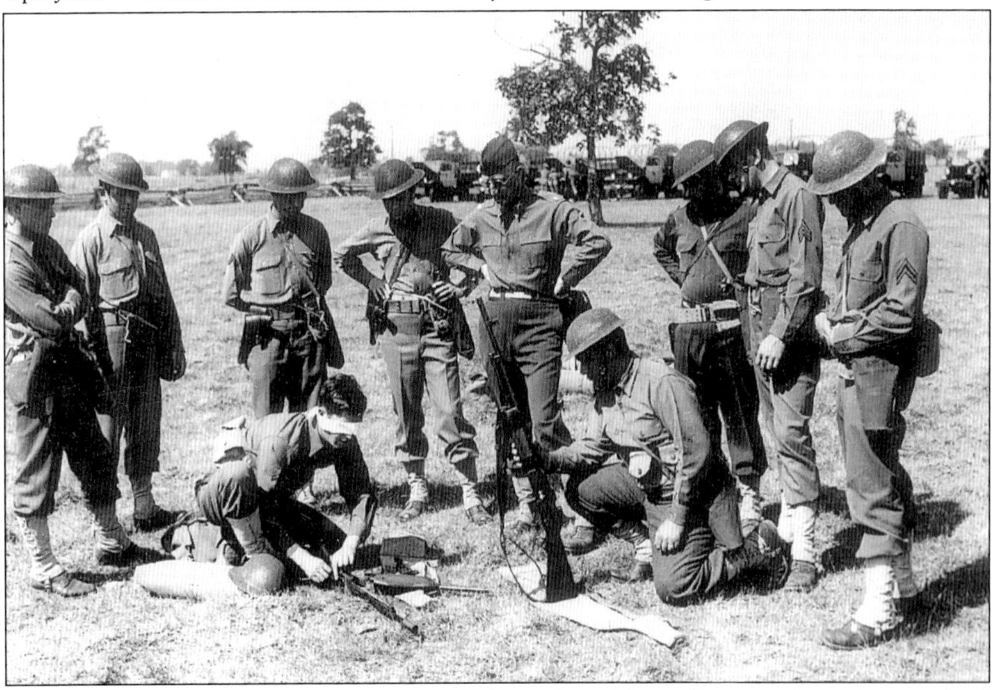

In July 1941, soldiers of the National Guard 258th Field Artillery watch as Pvt. Michael Kennedy, Battery E, assembles a Browning rifle. Kennedy is blindfolded.

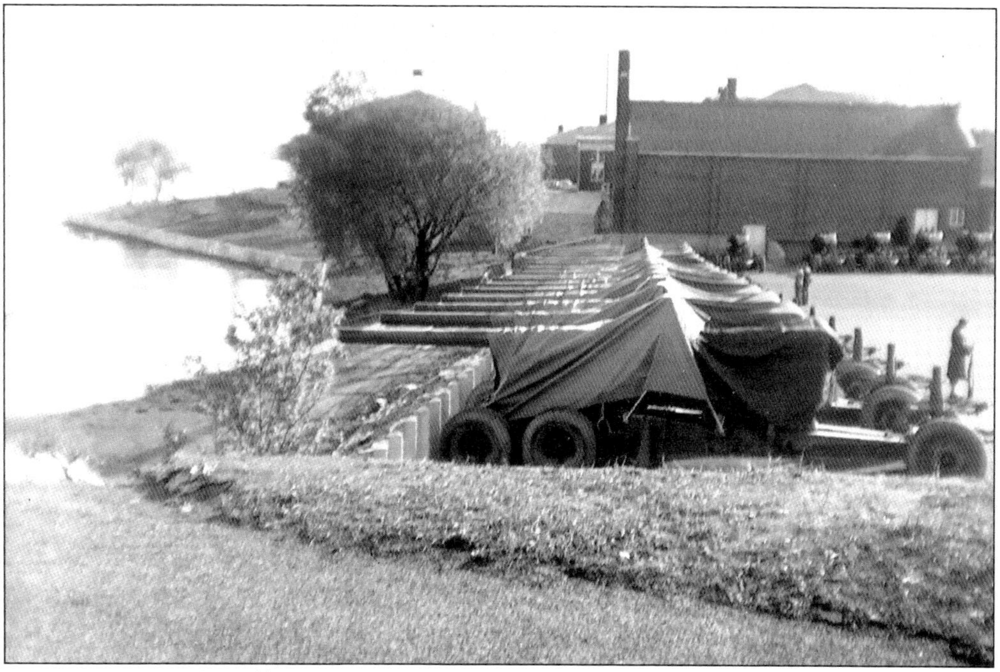

In 1941, "Long" 155-millimeter pieces are lined up in the parking lot of the post theater. The National Guard 258th Field Artillery from the Bronx had replaced the 5th Field Artillery. Note the post theater in the background.

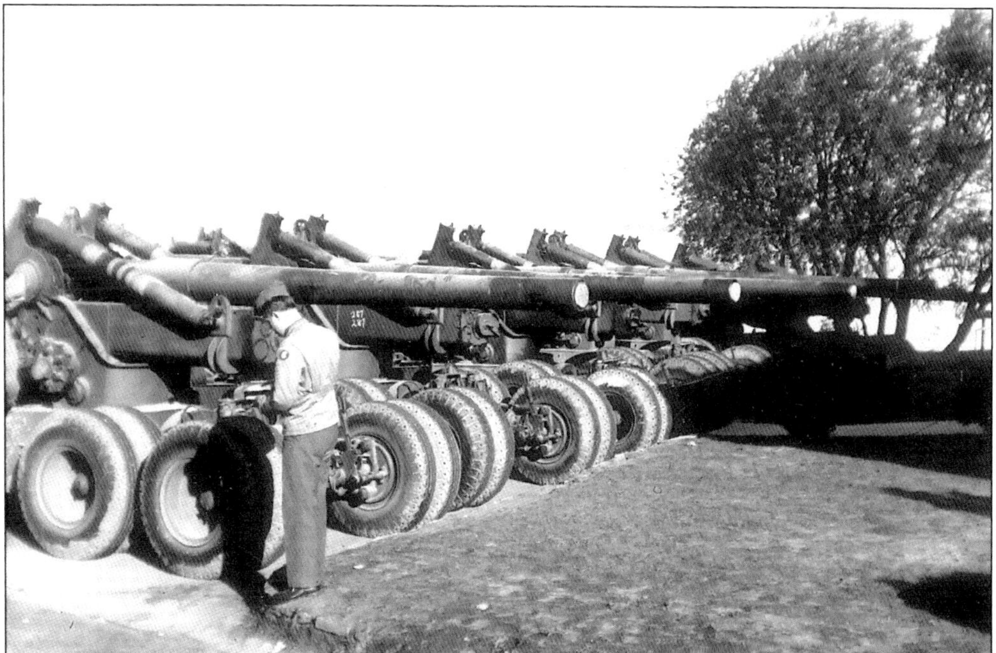

In 1941, the National Guard 258th Field Artillery, stationed at Madison Barracks, moved these 155-millimeter cannons to Pine Camp for firing practice, as these artillery pieces could not be fired at the post in Sackets Harbor. The cannons, with a range of 15,000 yards, were manned by a squad of eight.

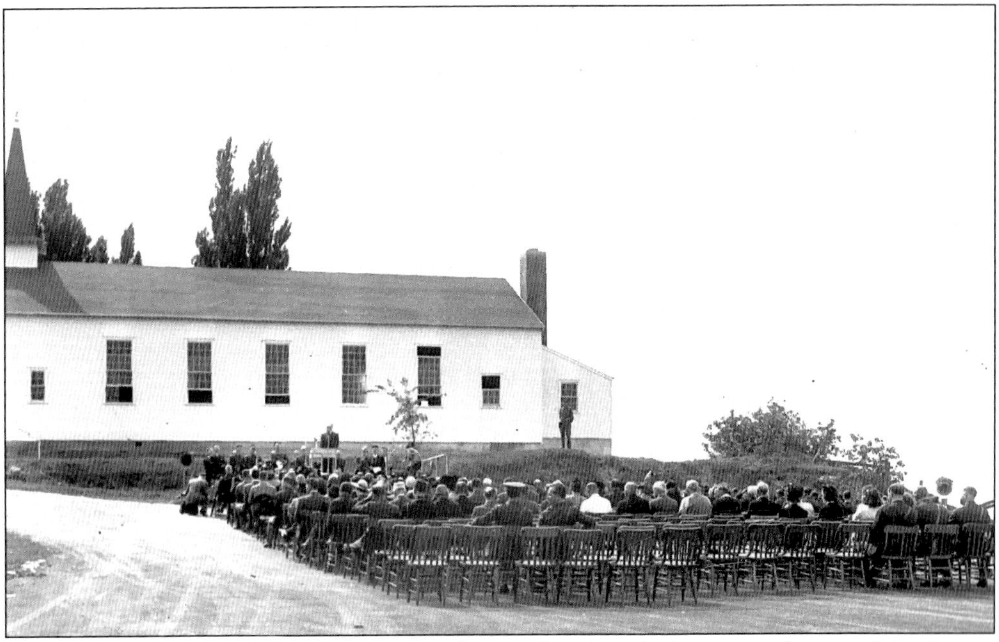

In 1941, the federal government constructed a wooden chapel adjacent to the site of the former Fort Pike. The chapel was dedicated on September 11. Three faiths were represented at the dedication by Protestant chaplain Capt. E.J. Kroencke, Rabbi Hyman Goodkowitz, and Roman Catholic 1st Lt. R.C. Goodenow.

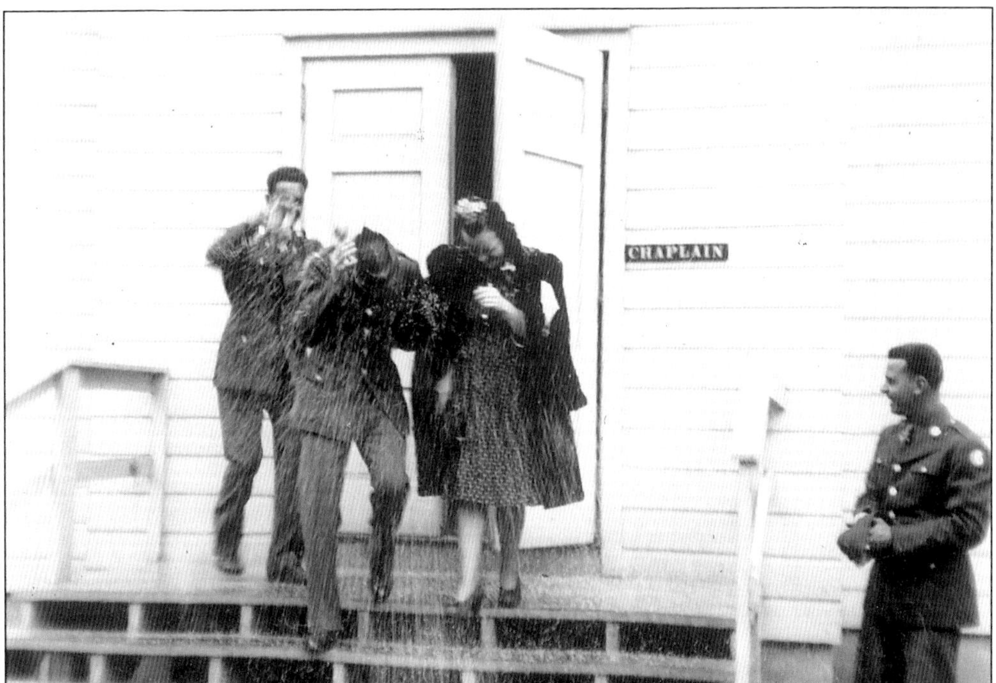

The wedding ceremony of R. Walton Shively and his fiancée was held shortly after the chapel was opened. The structure was sold to the Assembly of God on November 2, 1954, and was moved to Lockport.

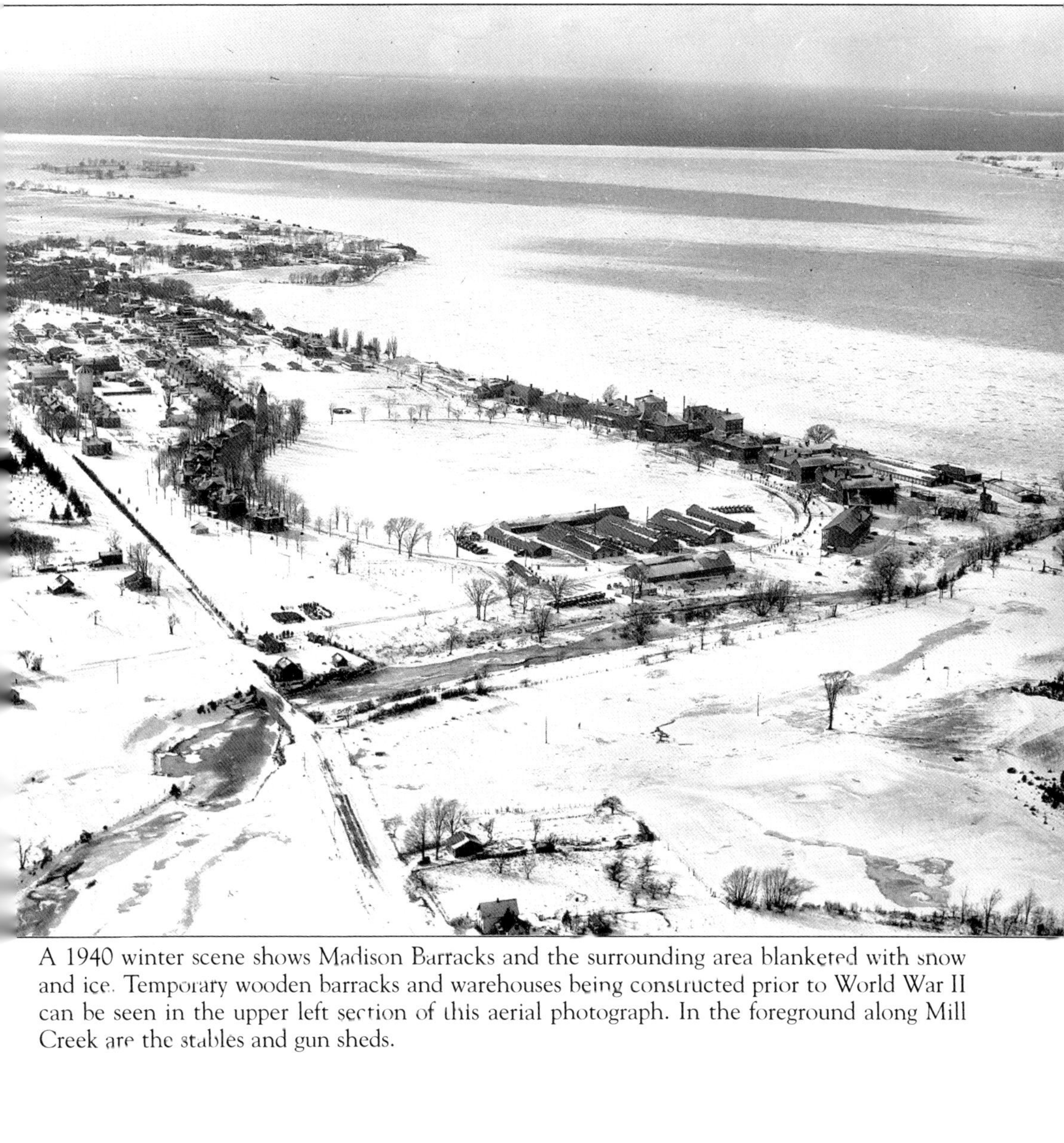

A 1940 winter scene shows Madison Barracks and the surrounding area blanketed with snow and ice. Temporary wooden barracks and warehouses being constructed prior to World War II can be seen in the upper left section of this aerial photograph. In the foreground along Mill Creek are the stables and gun sheds.

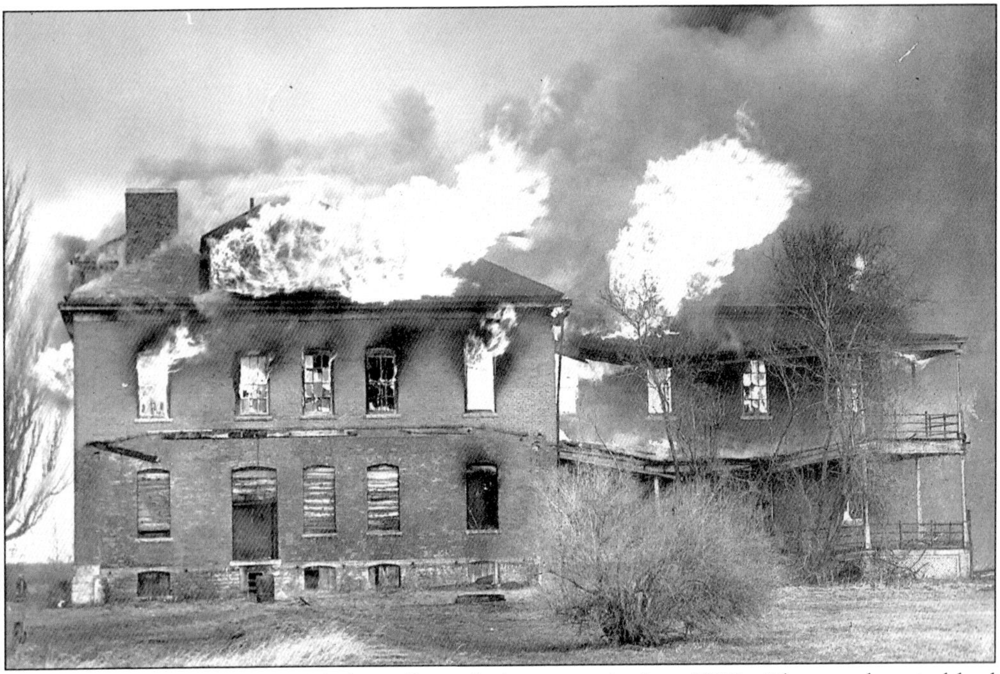

The leveling of structures at Madison Barracks began in the late 1970s. The post hospital had opened on August 4, 1900, next to Fort Pike on the west side of the Barracks. The interior of the hospital contained dental and surgical offices, an examining room, an operating room, two 12-bed wards, a dining room, and a kitchen. The hospital was demolished by means of a controlled fire on December 9, 1979.

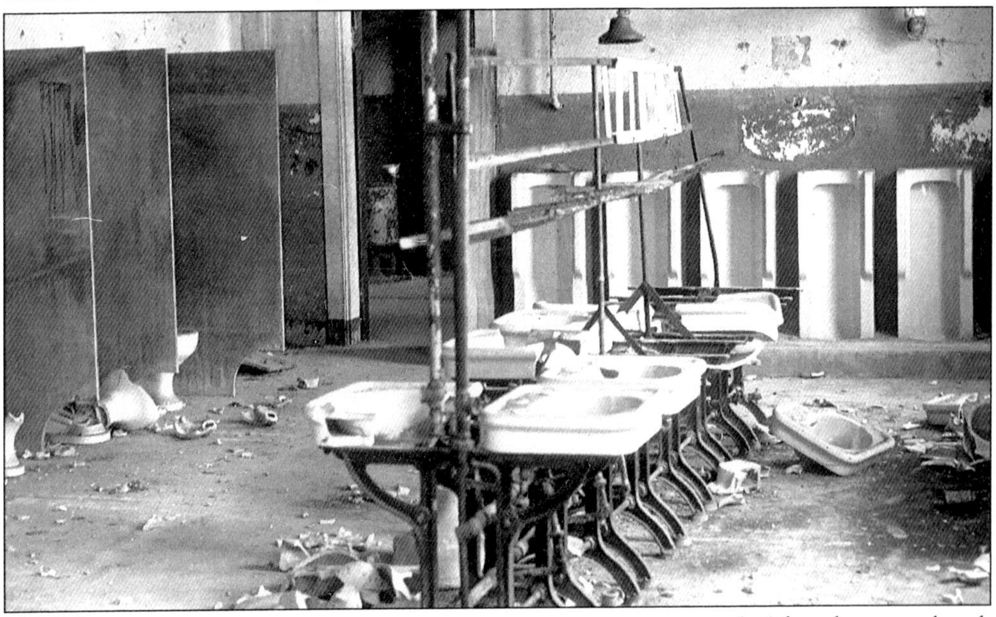

Madison Barracks was abandoned by the federal government in 1945. After the post closed, buildings fell into neglect. This photograph shows the derelict condition of the latrine in the basement of E Battery, 25th Field Artillery's building No. 76, which had been constructed in 1927, the last barracks before the row of stables.

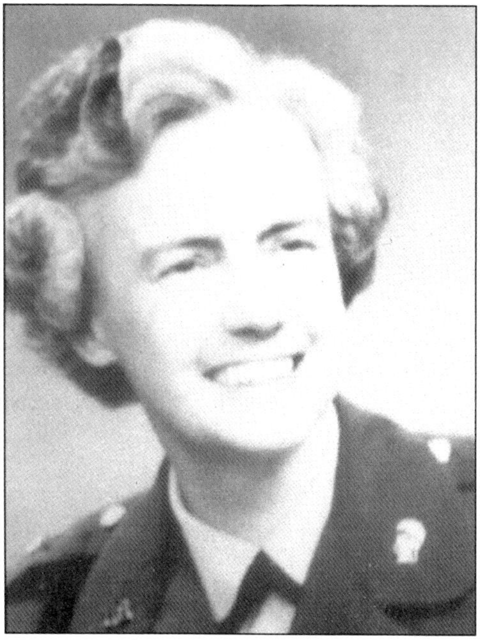

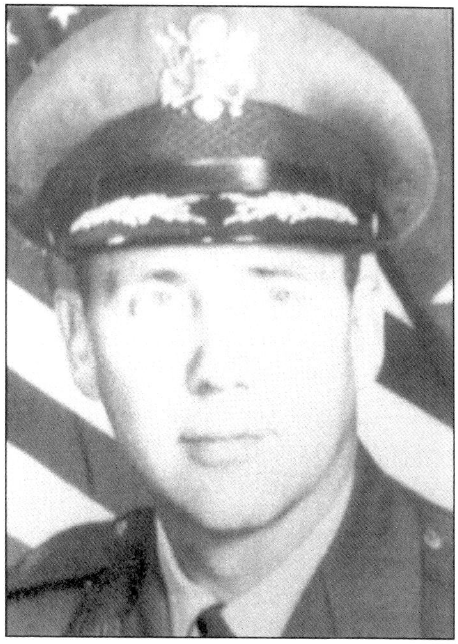

In 1930, Col. Gregory Hoisington Sr. was stationed at Madison Barracks. Two of his children, Elizabeth and Perry, attended school in Sackets Harbor. Both became U.S. Army generals, making them the only brother-sister generals in the world. Elizabeth Hoisington, the first female general in the U.S. Army, attained the rank of brigadier general, and Perry Hoisington became a major general.

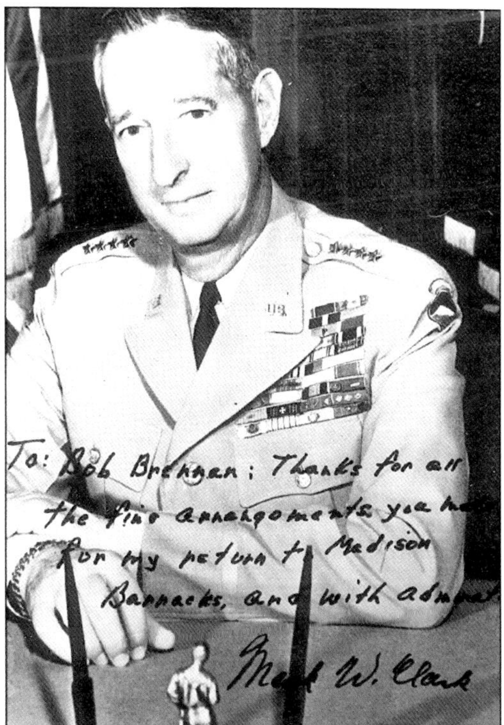

Gen. Mark Clark was born at Madison Barracks on May 1, 1896. A 1917 West Point graduate, Clark had a military career that spanned from World War I to the Korean War. In 1944, as commander of the U.S. 5th Army in Italy, he added the 10th Mountain Division to his forces.

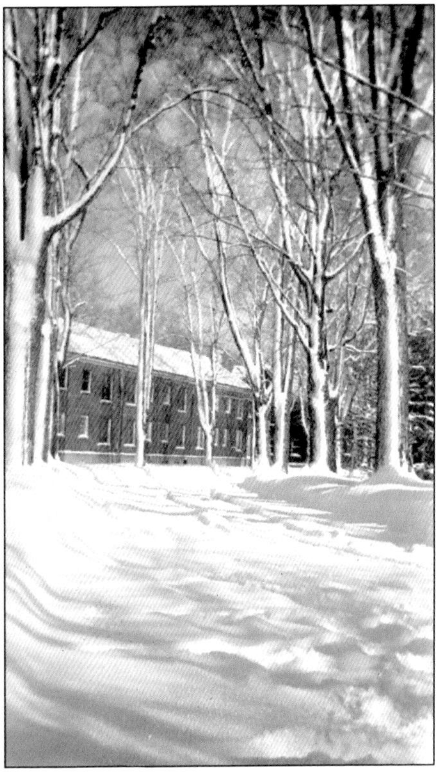

Madison Barracks was abandoned in 1945. This placid, snowy scene behind the bachelor officers' quarters was taken in February 1965.

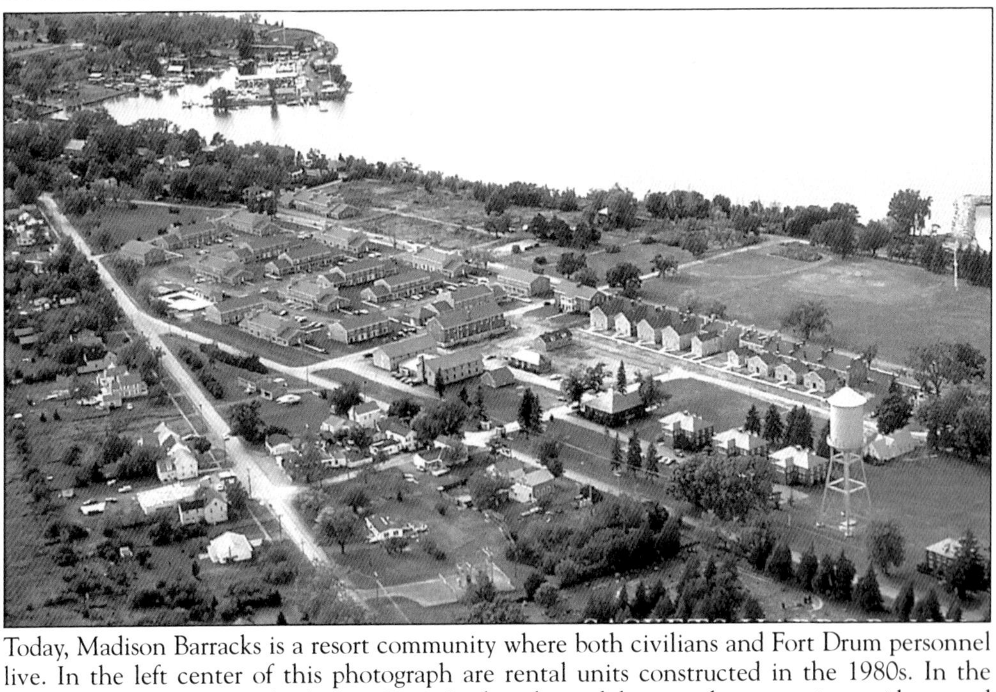

Today, Madison Barracks is a resort community where both civilians and Fort Drum personnel live. In the left center of this photograph are rental units constructed in the 1980s. In the right center is the refurbished Stone Row. In this planned, historical community, residents and tourists have access to community shopping, a marina, a health club, a swimming pool, tennis courts, an inn, restaurants, jogging, and cross-country ski trails.

Two

PINE CAMP-CAMP DRUM

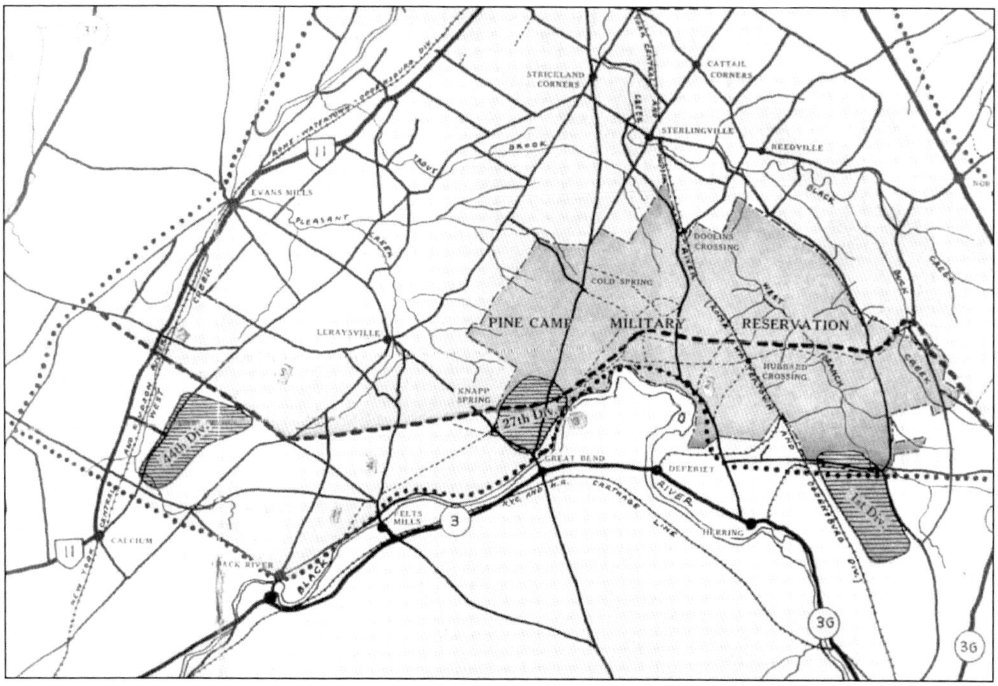

This map earmarks the area named Pine Plains along Black River in Jefferson County. Artillery training was not possible at Madison Barracks in Sackets Harbor, so this site was chosen for summer training. In 1907, Camp Hughes was established opposite the village of Felts Mills on a former Methodist Church meeting ground site. In the next year, a short distance away, Pine Camp was established east of an elevated sand dune area called Hog's Back. In 1951, Pine Camp was renamed Camp Drum. During World War II, Camp Drum expanded between the villages of Black River and Great Bend on the north side of the river. In 1974, Camp Drum became Fort Drum. Fort Drum is a modern military post situated northwest of the former Camp Drum site.

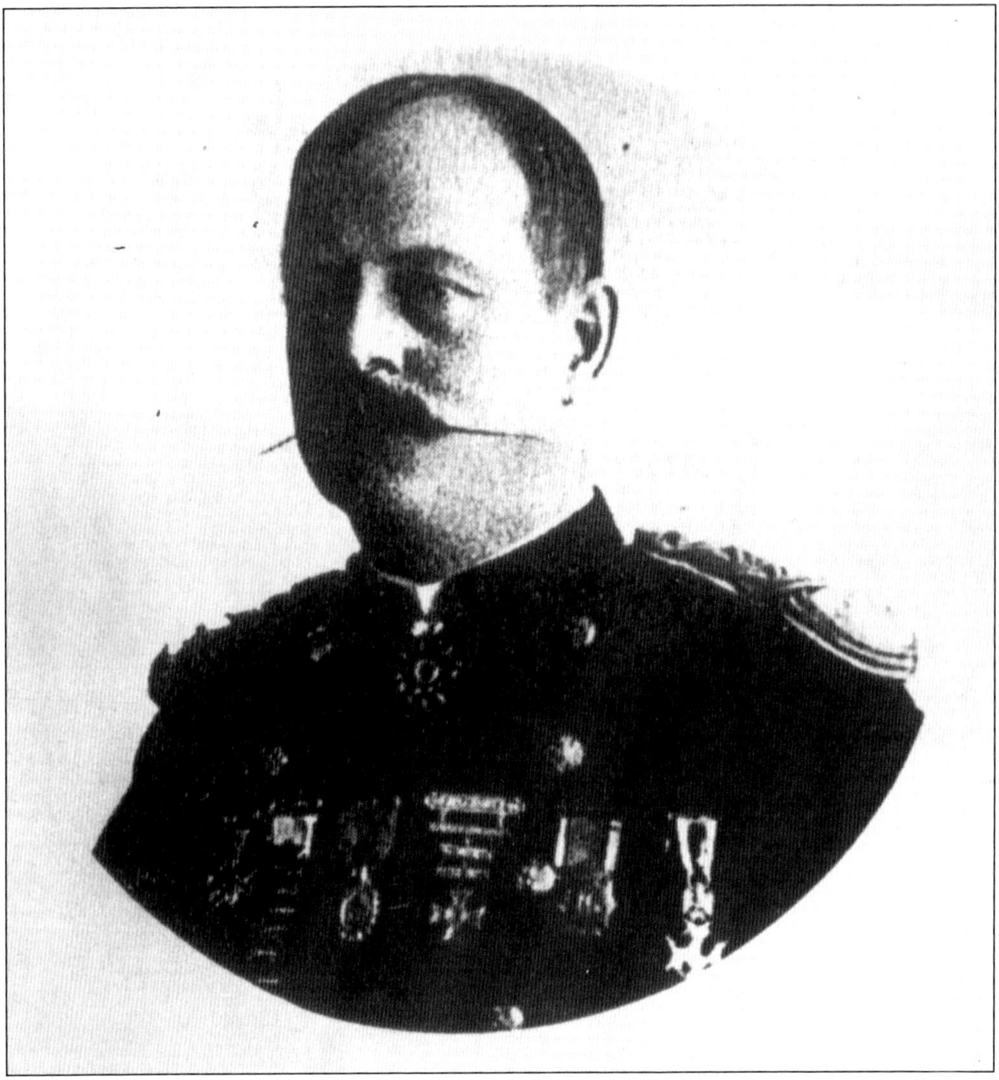

In 1906, Col. Philip Reade of the 23rd Infantry, stationed at Madison Barracks, was directed by Pres. Theodore Roosevelt to select a site for a "concentration" camp (concentrating regular troops with the National Guard) suitable for National Guard and regular troop maneuvers. One of six sites, Pine Plains was chosen for its varied terrain, diverse weather conditions, adequate water supply, and available transportation facilities.

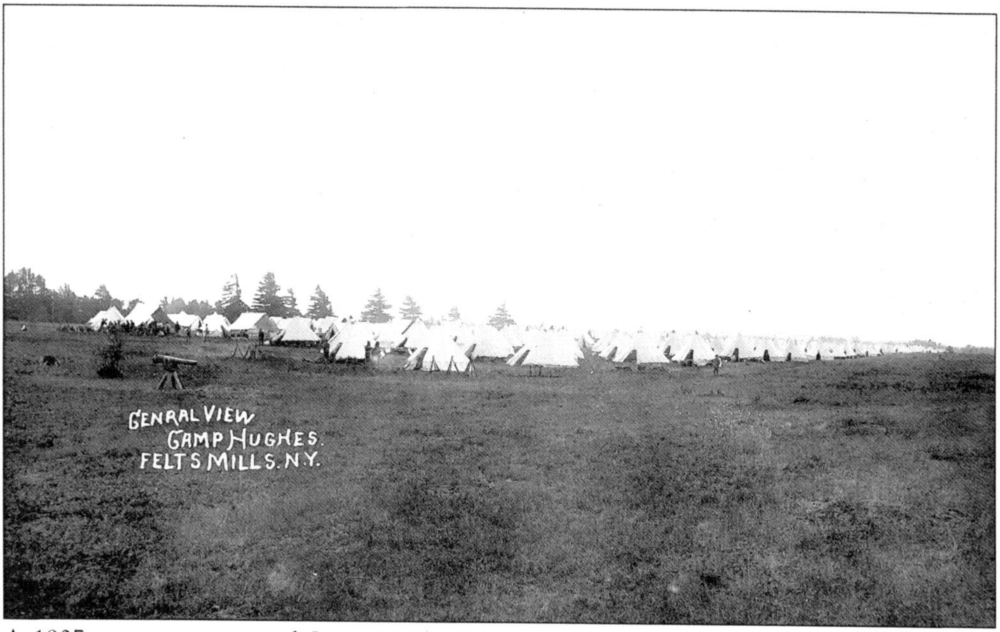

A 1907 panoramic view of Camp Hughes shows numerous tents used by a National Guard brigade of 5,500 men during summer maneuvers. Trains from southeast New York State brought troops to disembark at the Felts Mills train station.

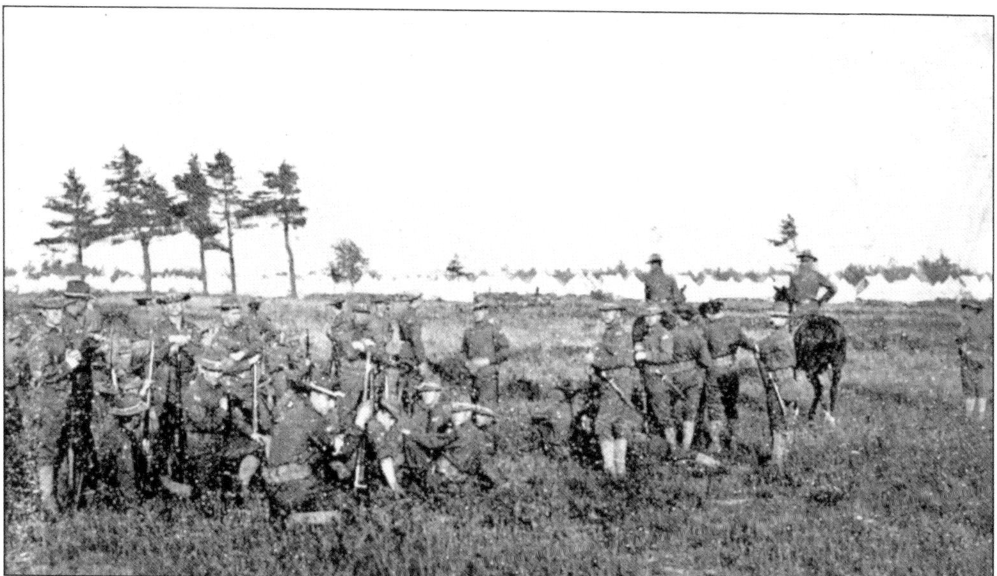

The first camp used for summer maneuvers in 1907 at Pine Plains was named Camp Hughes in honor of New York Gov. Charles Hughes. National Guard units underwent training.

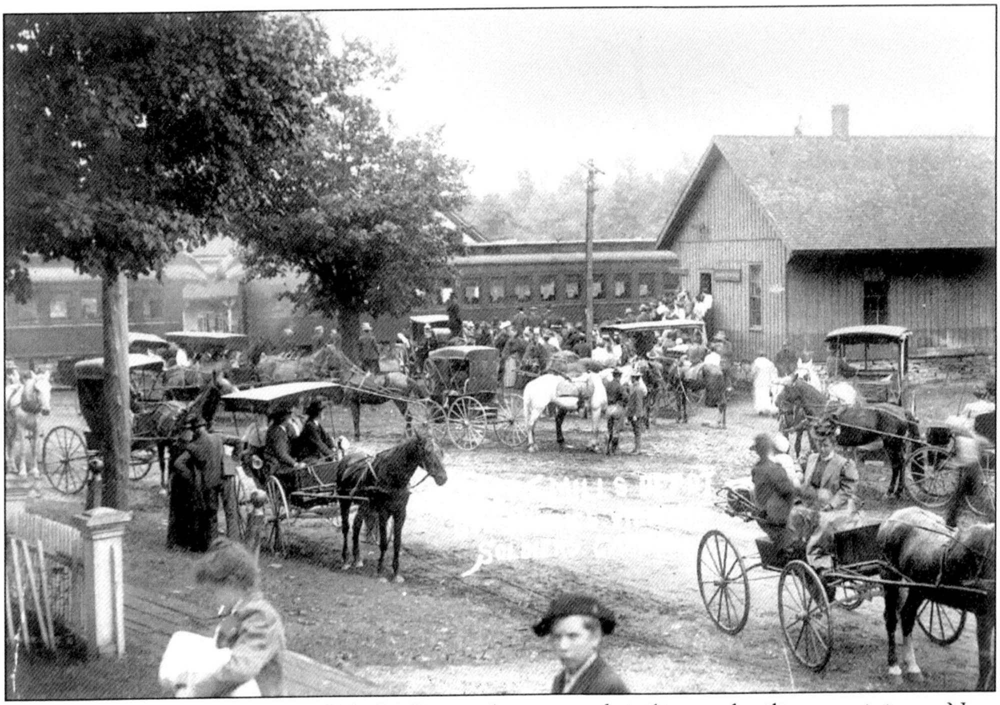

In 1907, the railroad station at Felts Mills was the scene of civilian and military activity, as New York Gov. Charles Hughes arrived to visit Pine Plains and inspect the troops.

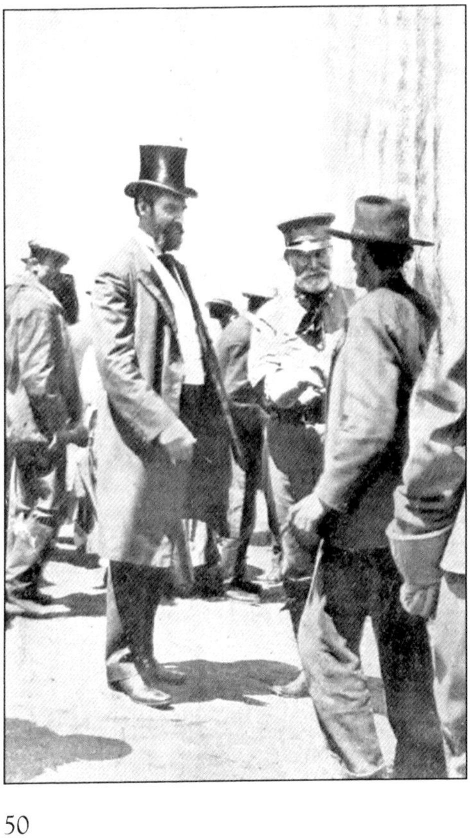

Gov. Charles Hughes arrived at Pine Camp on June 20, 1908. He was greeted by Gen. Frederick Grant, son of Pres. Ulysses S. Grant. The two men pose, surrounded by spectators.

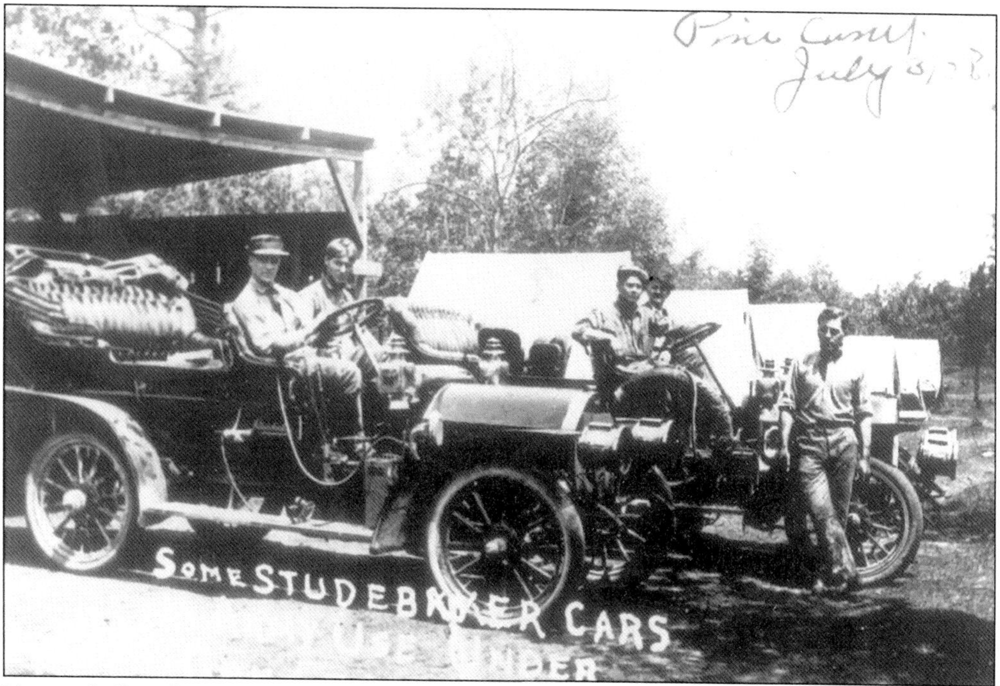

National Guard reserve officers travel to Pine Camp in their Studebaker touring cars. The officers are seen here in civilian clothing before participating in the 1908–1910 army maneuvers.

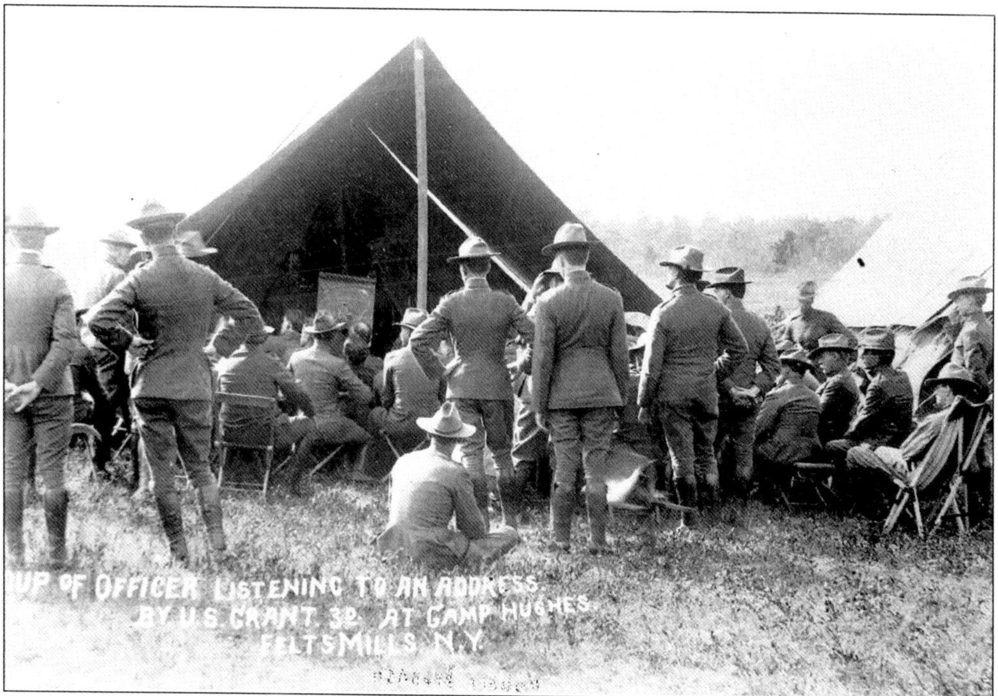

At Camp Hughes in 1907, National Guard officers gather outside a tent to hear an address by Gen. Frederick Grant.

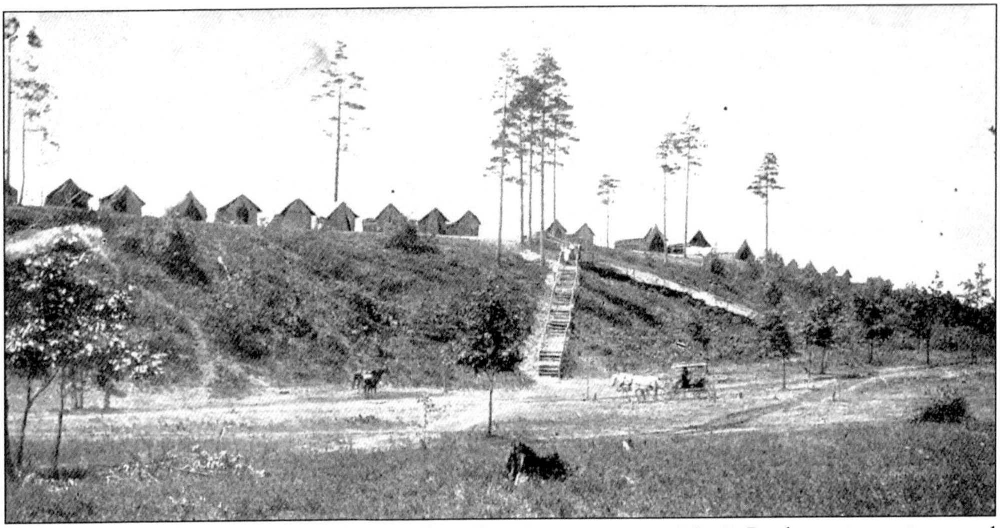

During the war games of 1908, the site for officer's quarters was Hog's Back, an imposing sand dune located at the northern tip of the great bend in Black River. Long, steep, temporary stairs led from the level below to the tents where officers were billeted.

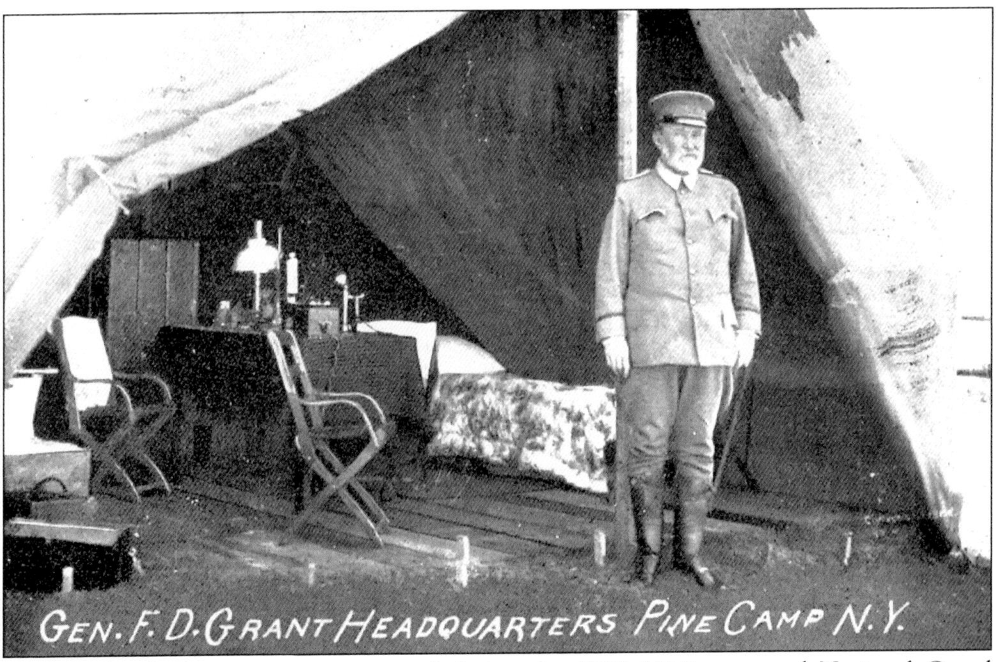

Gen. Frederick Grant was in command during the 1908–1910 army and National Guard maneuvers at Pine Plains. His tent accommodations were on Hog's Back.

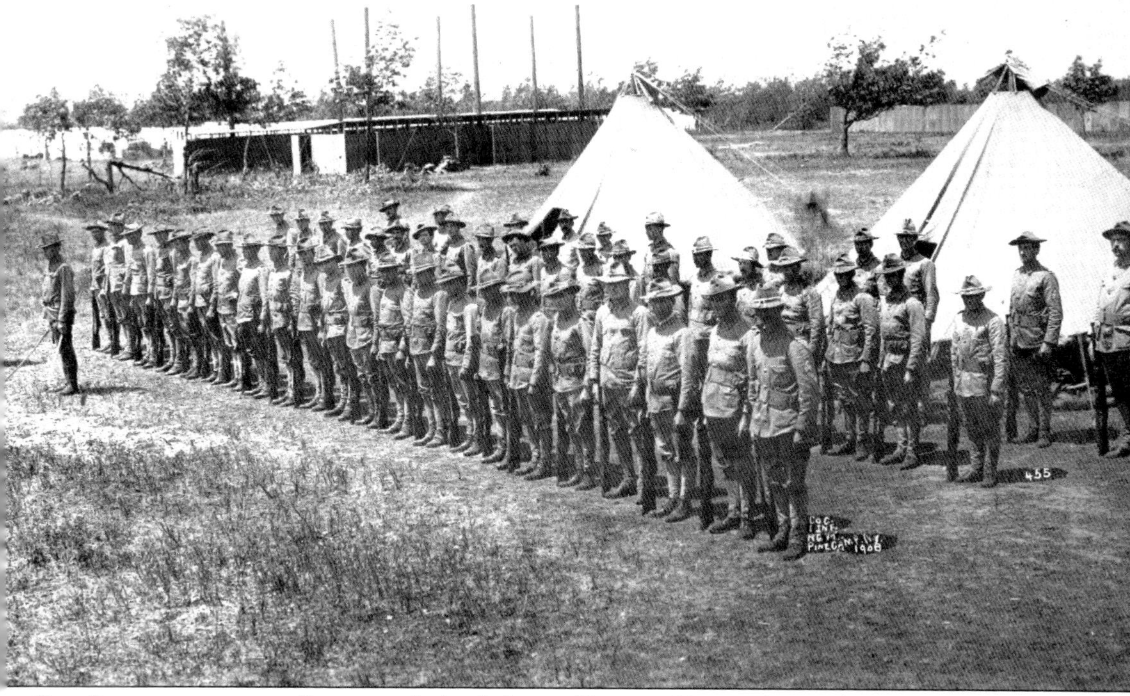

Standing at attention is Company C, 1st Infantry, Vermont National Guard—a unit of 6,000 men, training from June 15 to July 15, 1908. The National Guard's Department of the East assigned infantry, cavalry, and field artillery units to Pine Camp from the states of Maine, New Hampshire, Vermont, Massachusetts, Connecticut, Rhode Island, New York, New Jersey, Pennsylvania, Delaware, Maryland, Virginia, and West Virginia, plus the District of Columbia, Puerto Rico, and adjoining islands.

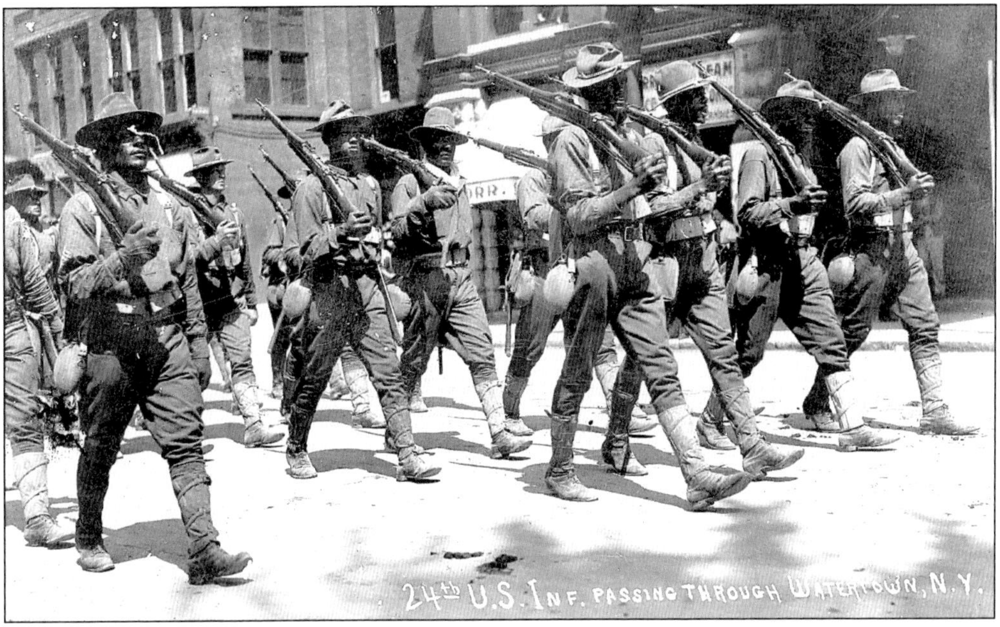

Marching through Watertown on June 13, 1910, the 24th Infantry of Madison Barracks arrived at Pine Camp to set up summer camp for federal troops and National Guard units arriving for training.

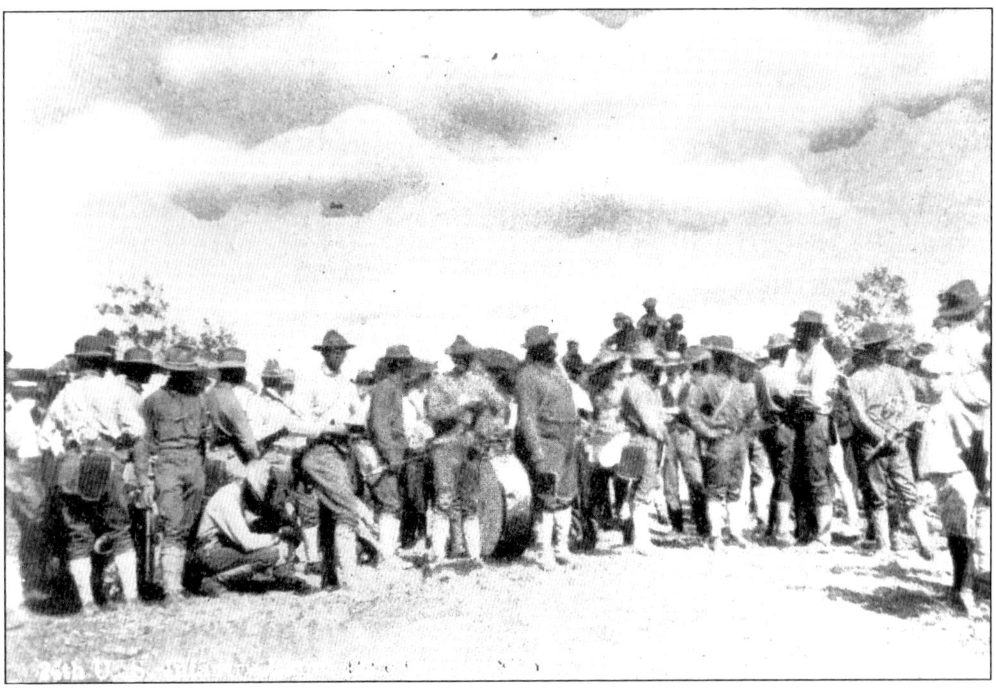

On August 31, 1910, the 24th Infantry stationed at Madison Barracks marched 20 miles from Sackets Harbor to the area named Pine Camp for their assignment to guard general government stores.

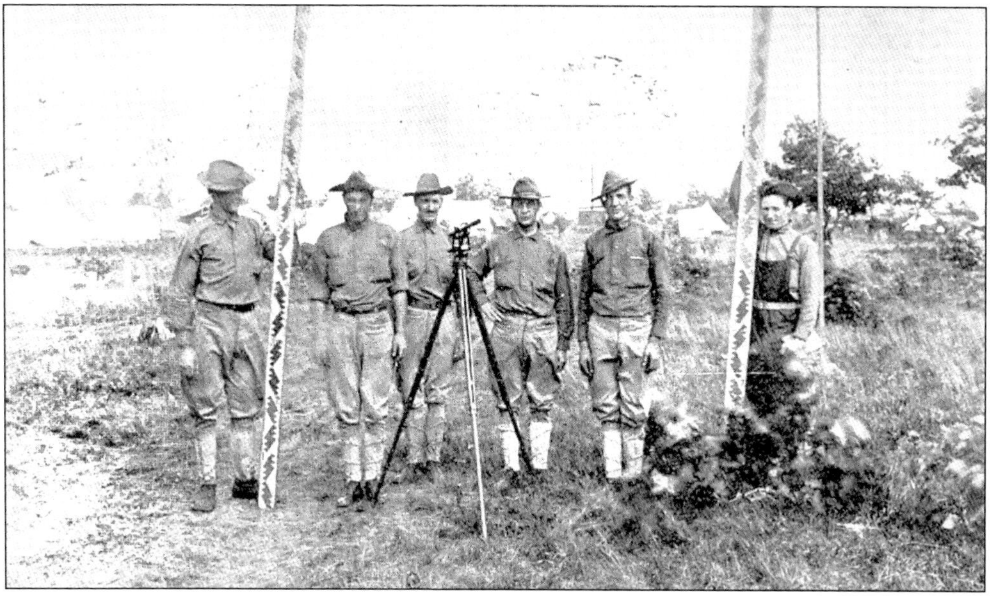

For the 1908–1910 army and National Guard maneuvers, members of the regular U.S. Army Engineer Corps pose with their field survey equipment. The engineers laid out streets and encampments before the troops arrived.

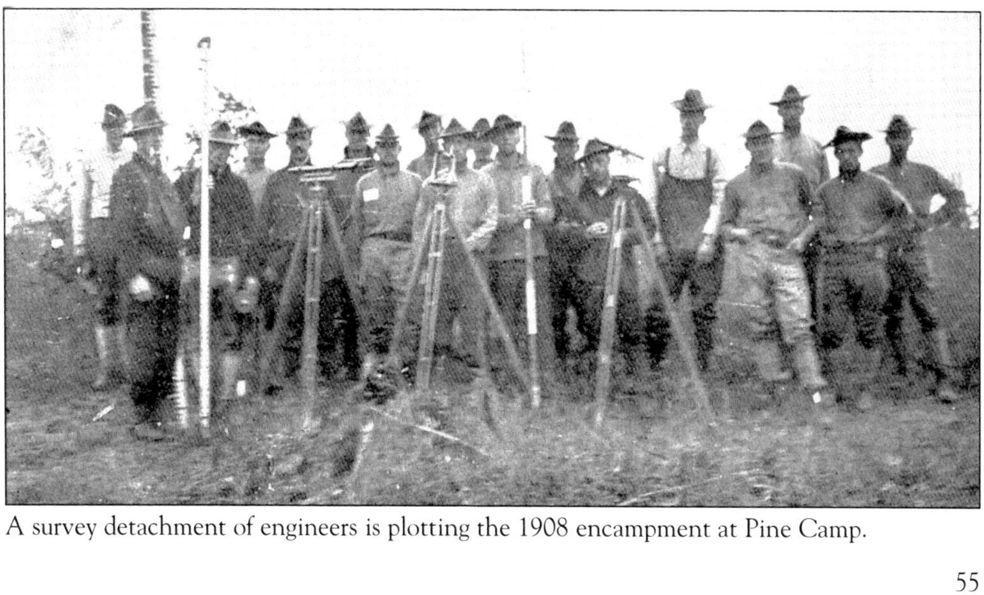

A survey detachment of engineers is plotting the 1908 encampment at Pine Camp.

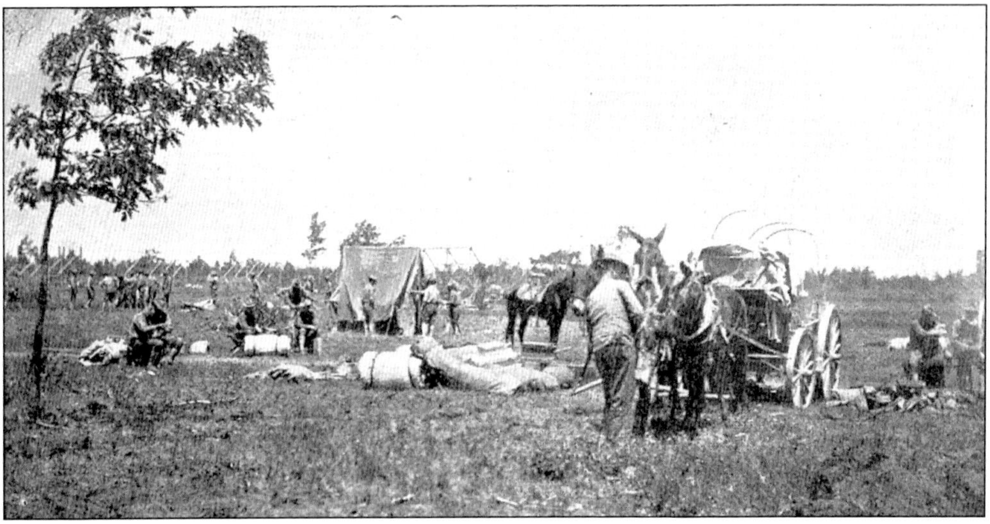

After arriving at Pine Camp, soldiers from an artillery battery prepare to set up camp. Wooden crates contained equipment, and footlockers held personal gear. In the background are Sibley tents.

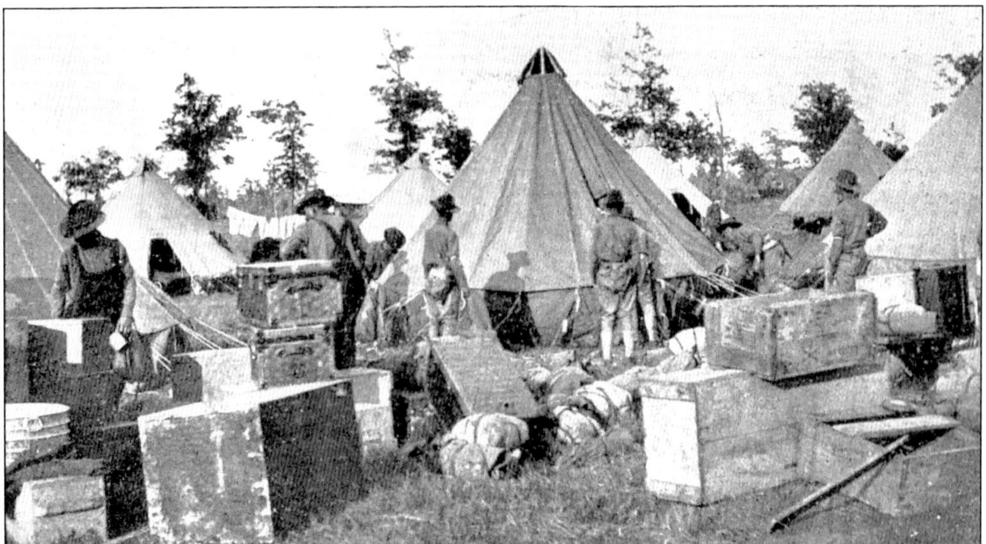

A newly arrived cavalry unit is setting up tents, removing equipment from the horse-drawn wagons, and tending to the horses.

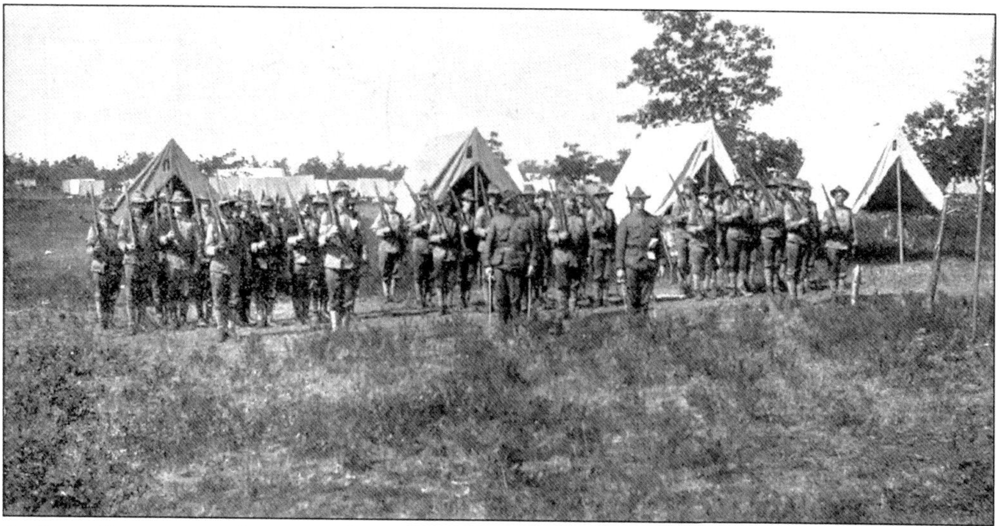

At Pine Camp, a guard mount of the 6th Regiment, Massachusetts National Guard, stands for inspection before reporting for guard duty.

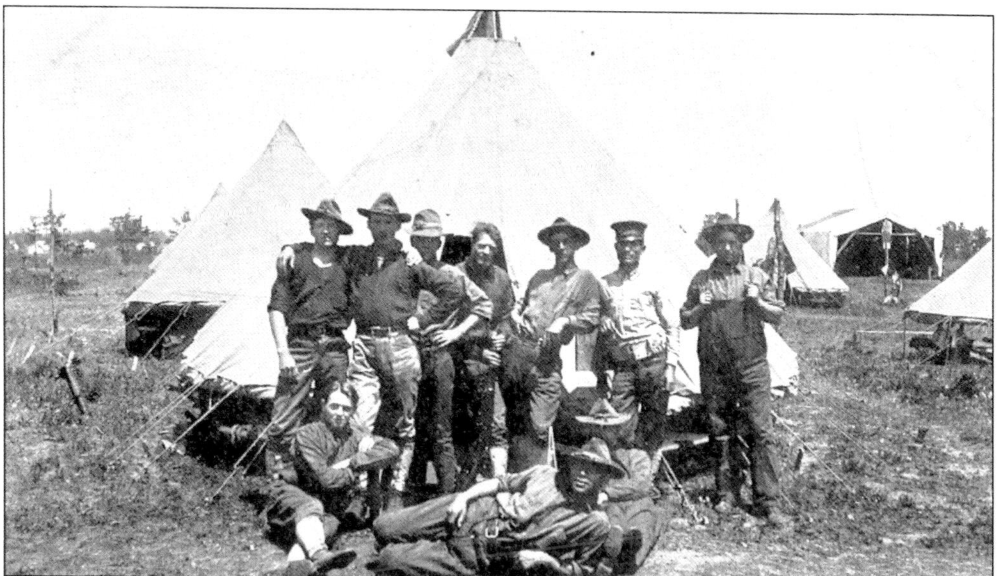

Grouped in front of their tents after the serious work of the day, soldiers indulge in good-natured raillery.

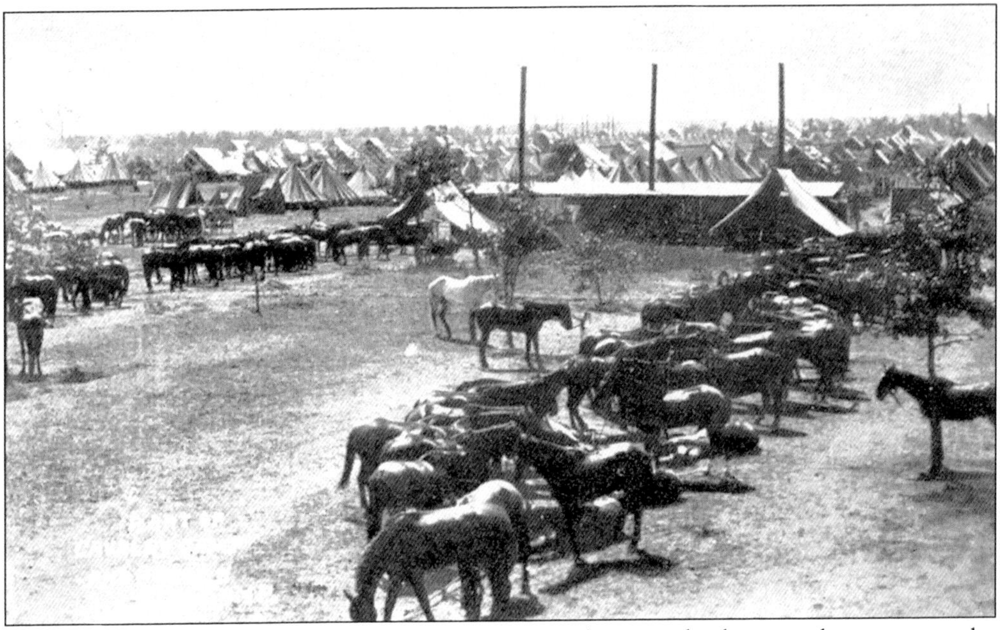

A multitude of cavalry horses and Sibley tents stretching to the horizon demonstrates the extent of the Department of the East's 1910 maneuvers.

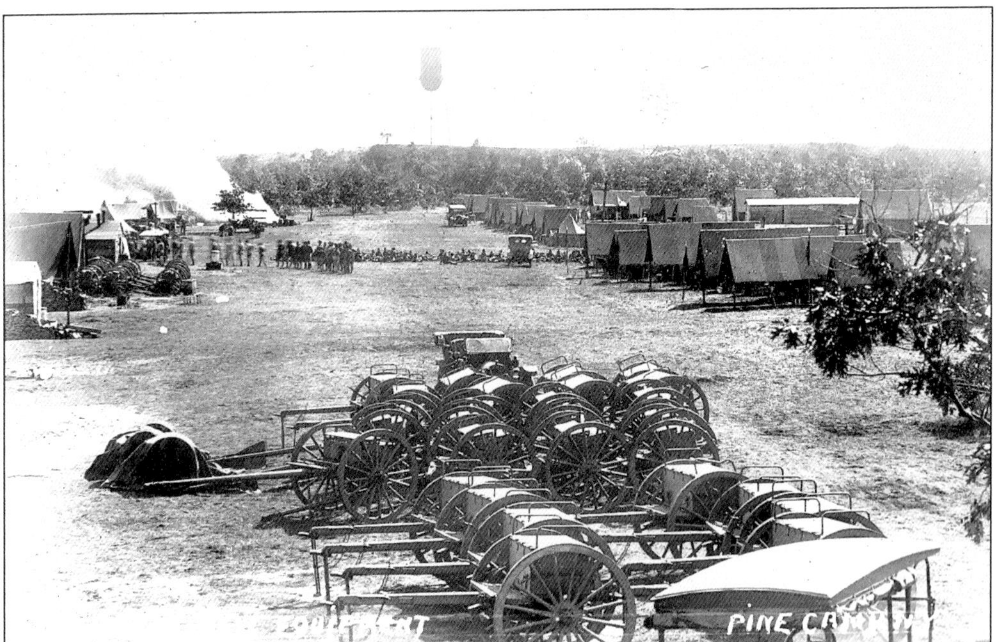

On the fields in front of Hog's Back are rows of caissons. To the right are officers' tents, and in the background is a chow line in front of a kitchen tent.

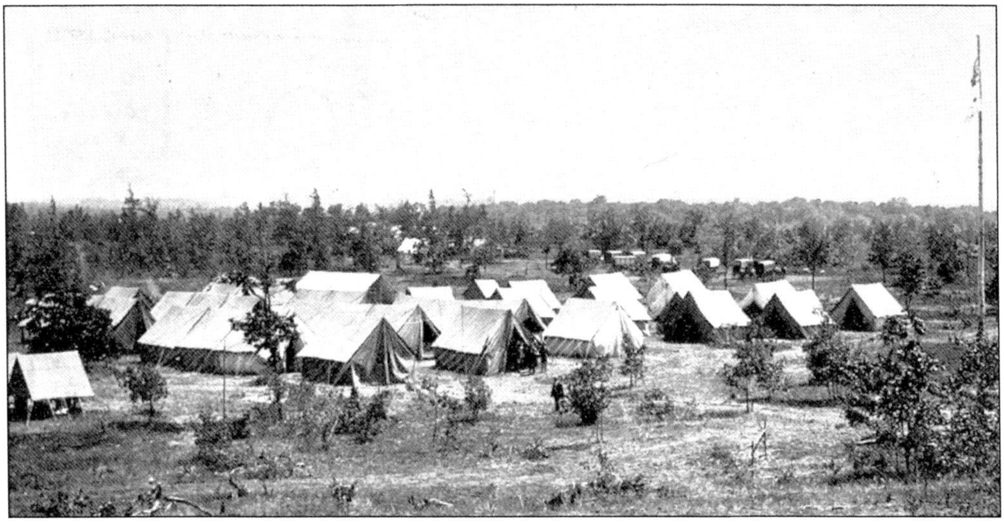

At the 1910 summer maneuvers, a New York National Guard general field hospital provided first aid.

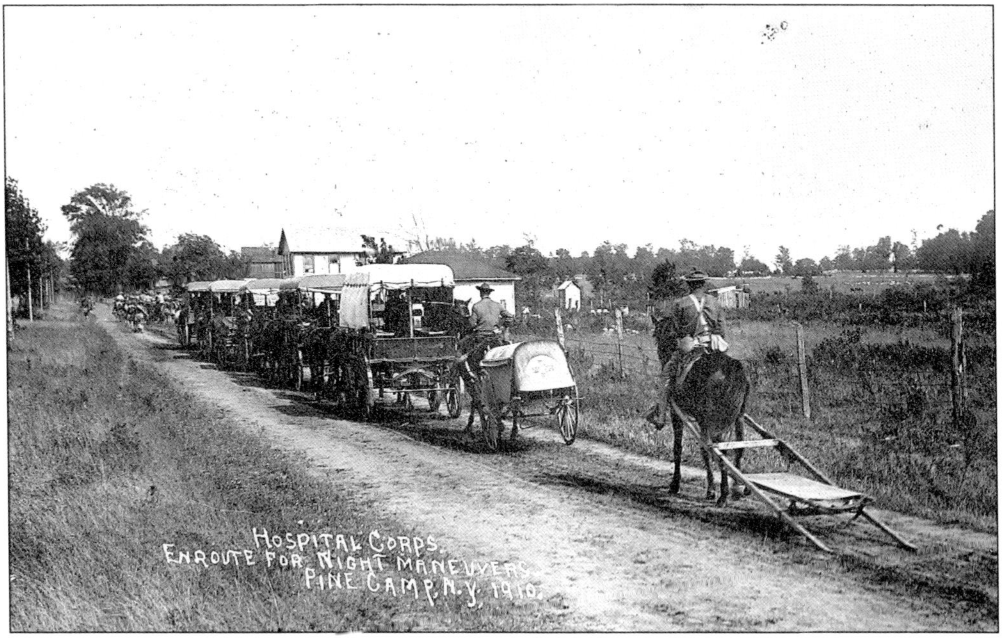

With ambulances and wagons carrying medical supplies, a hospital corps leaves Pine Camp for night practice maneuvers. Travois were used to transport simulated casualties from the field.

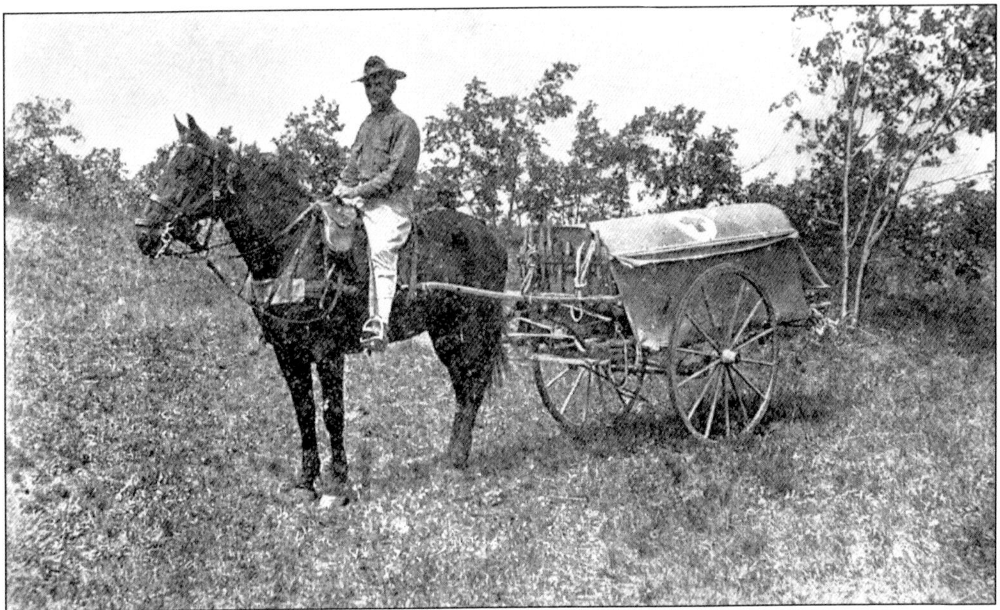

During the 1910 army and National Guard maneuvers and field training, the field ambulance corps used lightweight wooden wagons pulled by horses. (Courtesy Jefferson County Historical Society.)

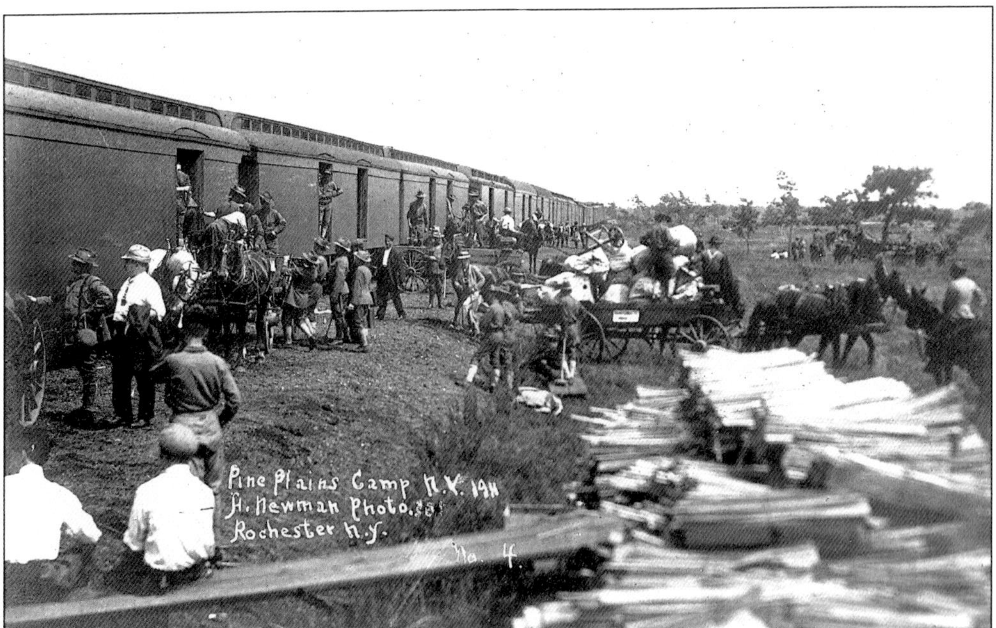

By 1911, the New York Central Railroad spur connected the north boundary of Pine Plains to within one mile of Hog's Back. On August 5, opening day of summer maneuvers, 15 troop trains arrived.

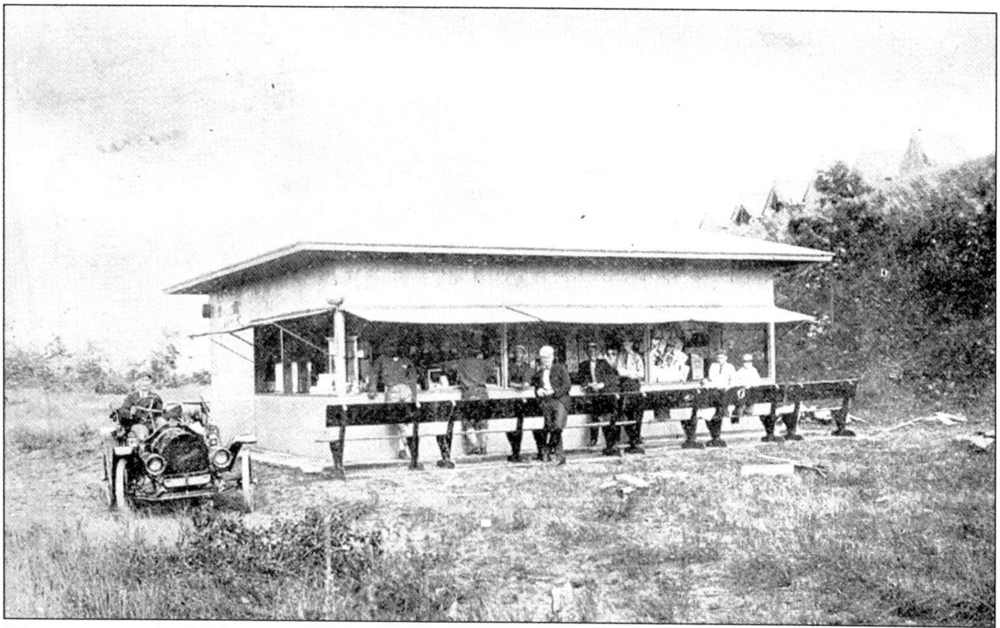

This version of a U.S. post office was used during the war games of 1908–1910. The structure was located at the base of Hog's Back headquarters for troop maneuvers.

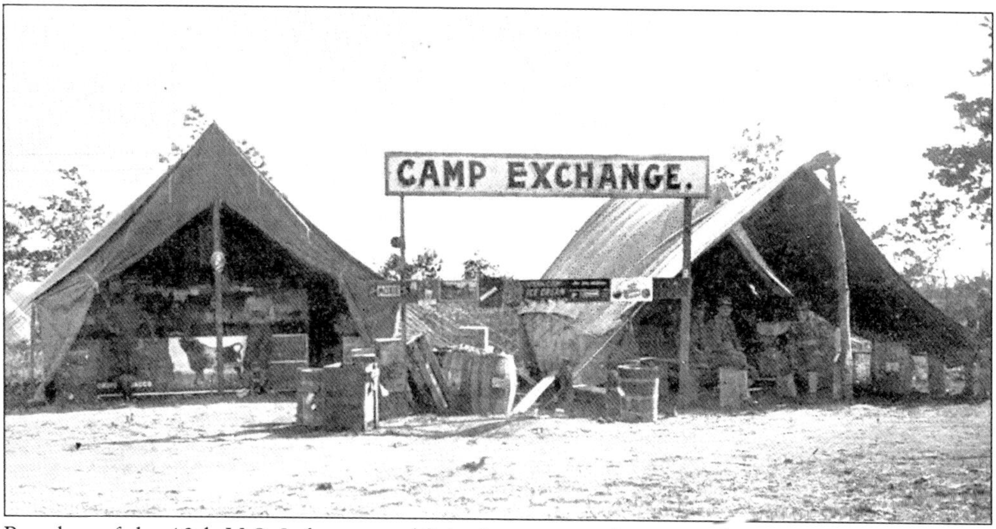

Regulars of the 12th U.S. Infantry established a camp exchange in the vicinity of Hog's Back. Items for sale—such as toiletries, towels, gun oil, shoelaces, souvenirs, bandages, handkerchiefs, tobacco, cigars, and matches—were placed on counters at the front of the tent. The proprietor's living quarters were in a tent at the rear.

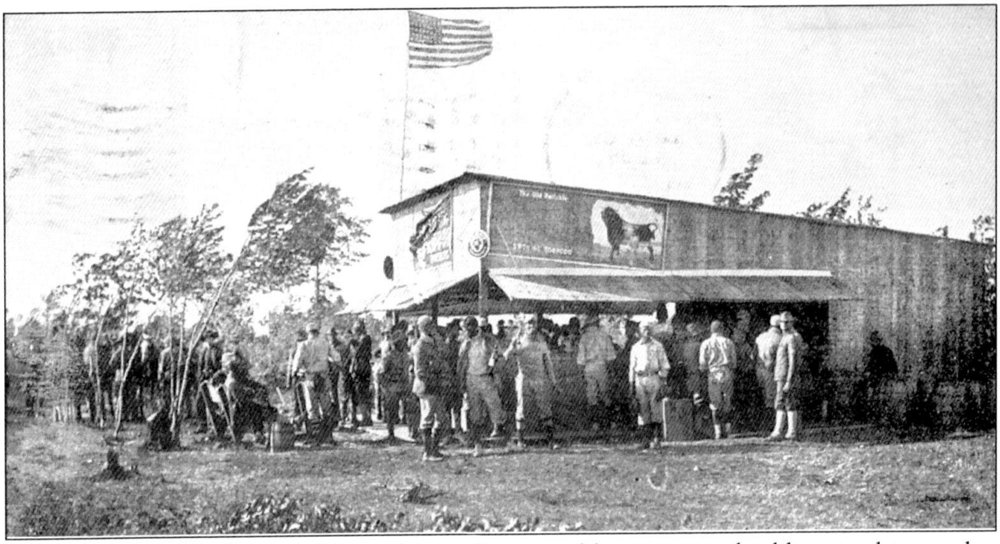

Advertisements for Old Reliable smoking tobacco and beer attracted soldiers to this wooden store outside the confines of the cantonment.

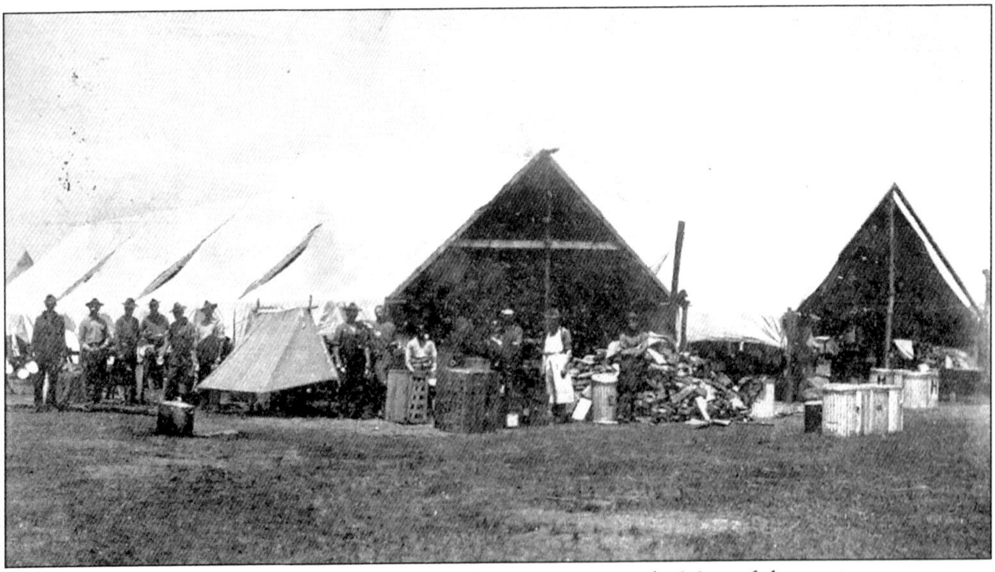

Mess sergeants and helpers set up field tents for preparing meals. Men of the engineer corps are waiting in a chow line.

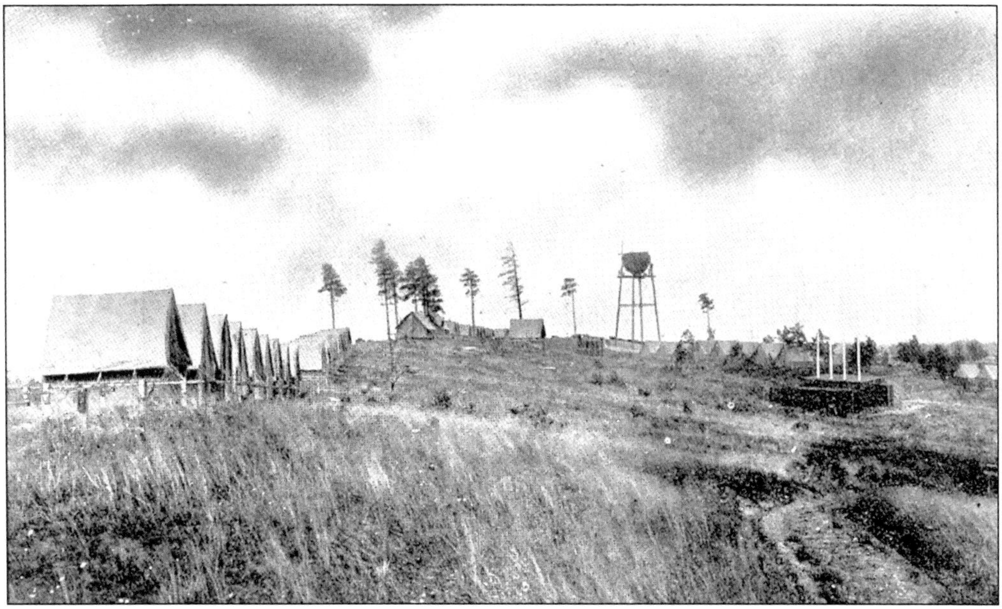

In 1910, a 60,000-gallon steel water tower was erected on Hog's Back. A pumping station, located 1,500 yards from the railroad spur, pumped water from Black Creek to the tank and then distributed water through pipes to the encampment facilities on the lower fields.

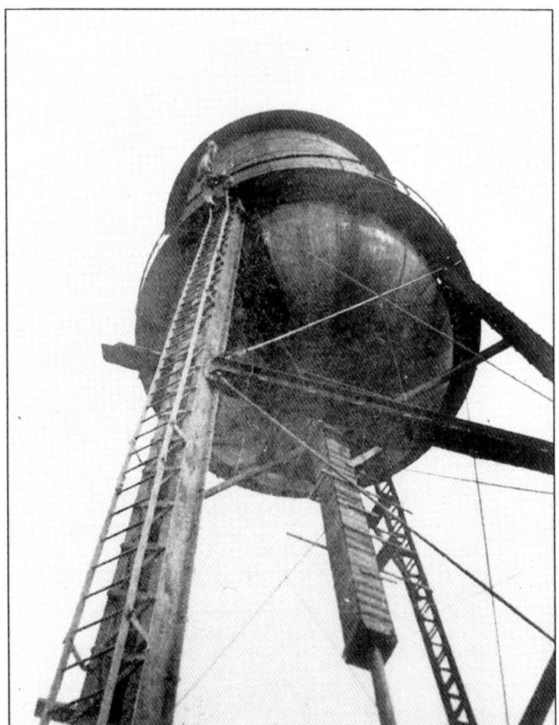

The steel water tank and a wooden observation tower remained Pine Camp landmarks until they were demolished after World War II.

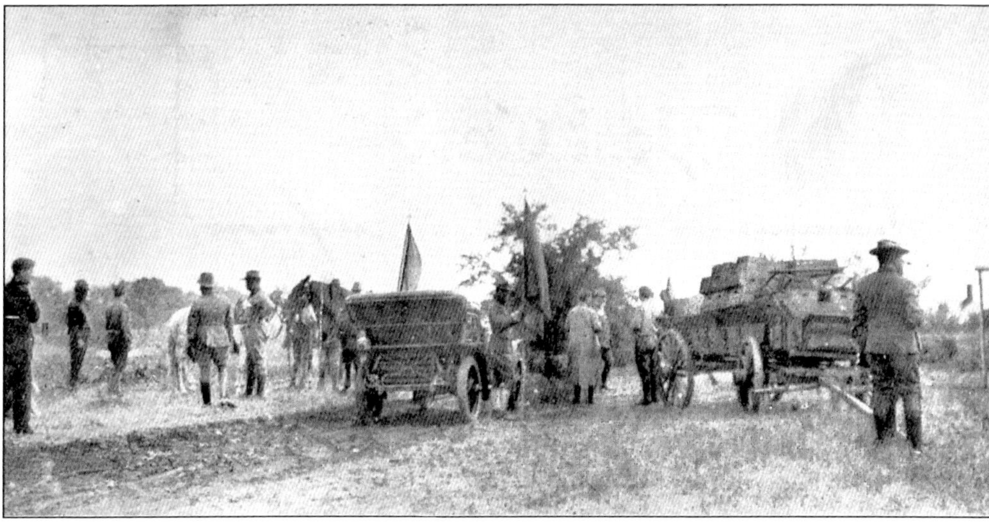

Gen. Frederick Grant and Col. E.N. Glenn, chief umpire of maneuvers, observe troops in action. Note both the motorized vehicle and the horse-drawn wagon.

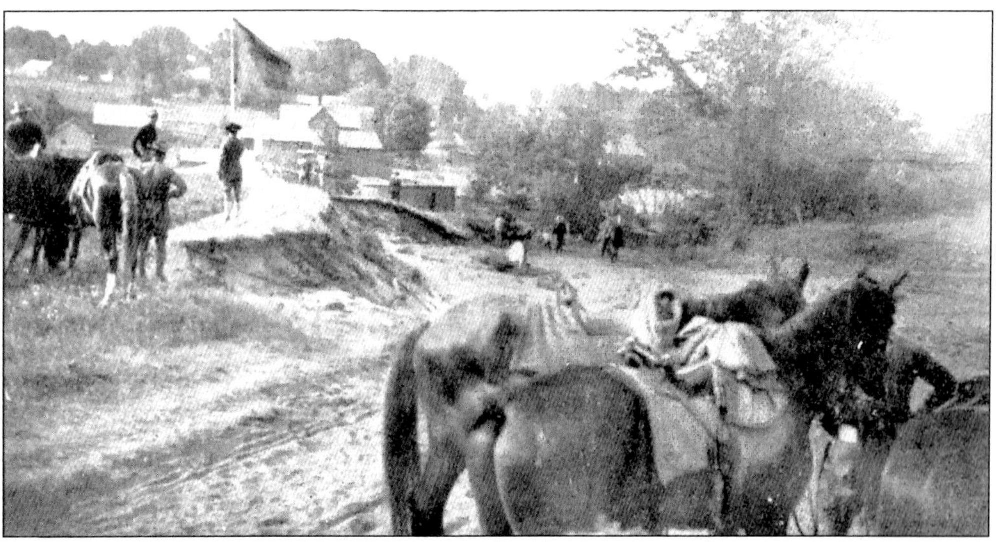

A bridge at the village of Great Bend became the objective target during the 1908–1910 army and National Guard maneuvers. The flag in the left foreground indicated Gen. Frederick Grant was in command. (Courtesy Jefferson County Historical Society.)

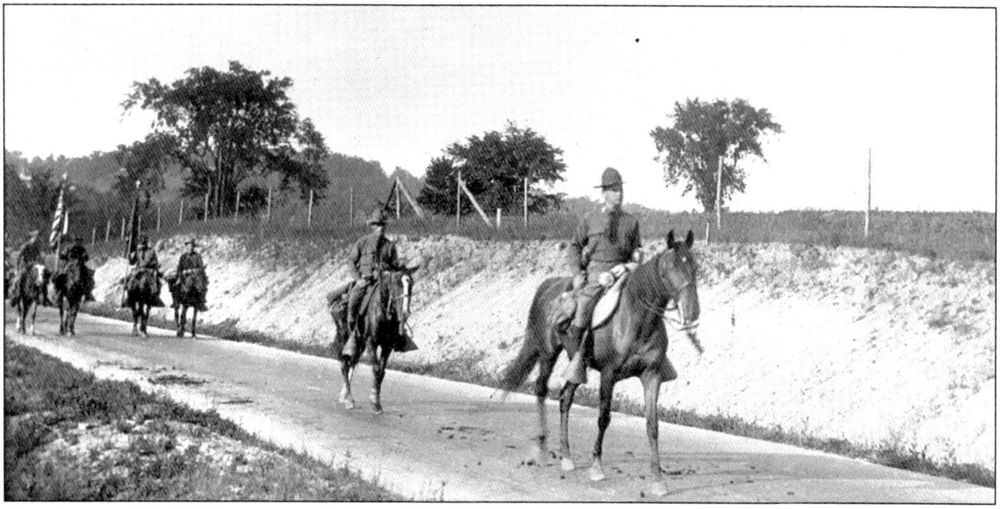

On August 15, 1917, troops of the 4th Field Artillery National Guard, stationed at Madison Barracks, are en route to Pine Camp. The head of the column is approaching Eastern Boulevard in Watertown.

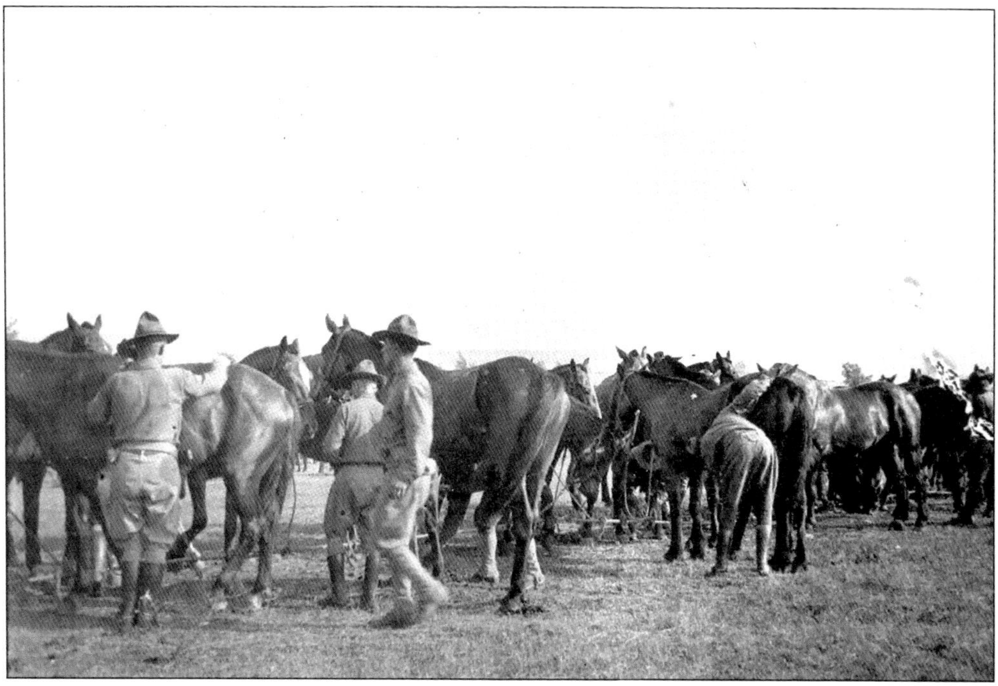

After a 23-mile ride from Madison Barracks to Pine Camp, troops of the National Guard 4th Field Artillery care for their horses.

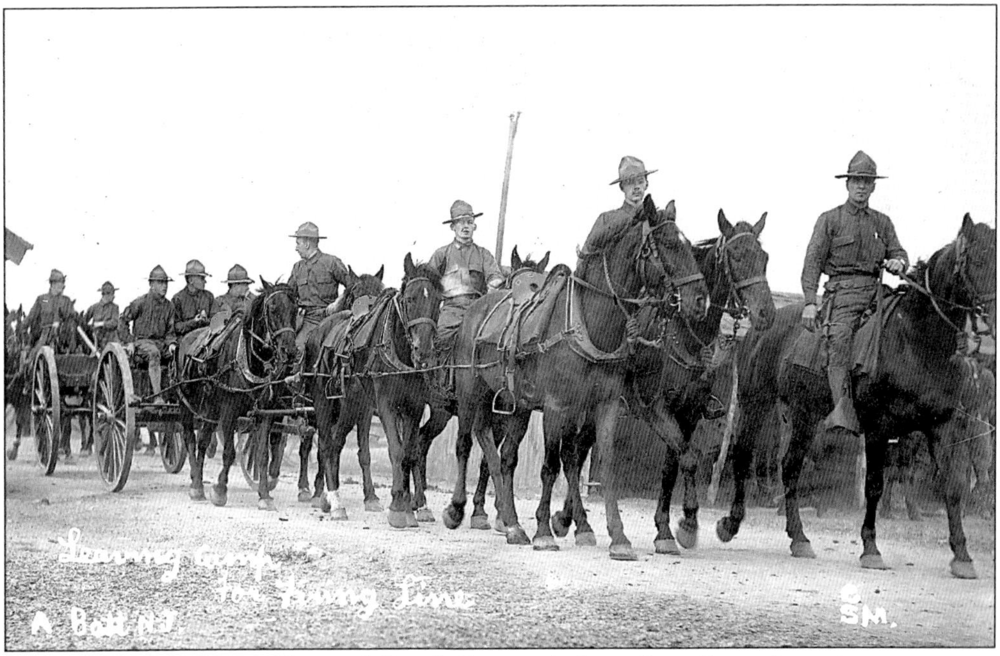

Troops of the New Jersey National Guard, Battery A, leave Pine Camp for an impact area on the firing line.

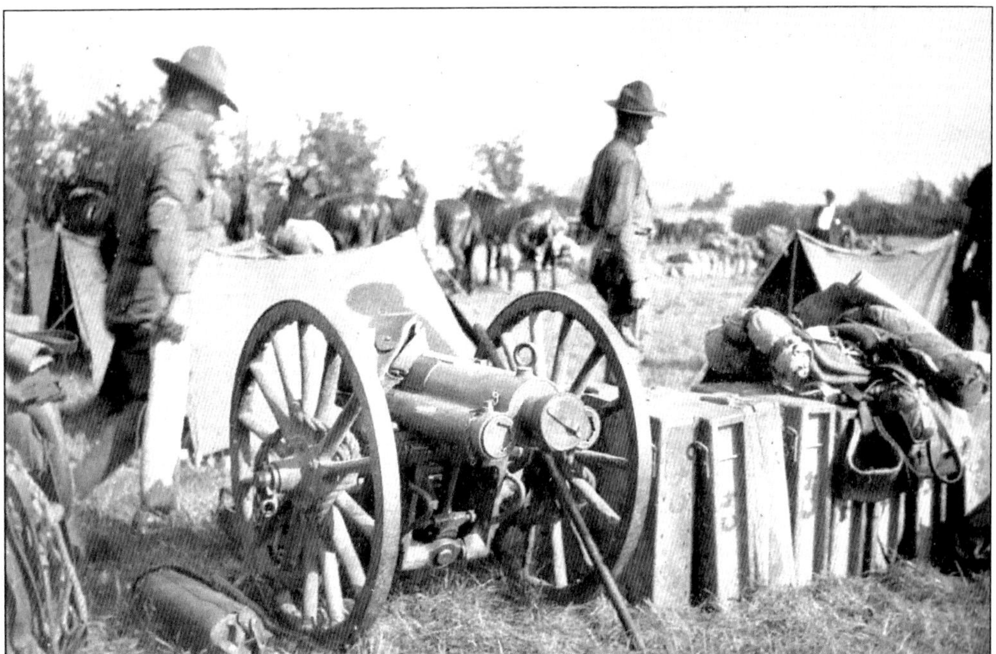
On August 17, 1917, the 4th Field Artillery positions one of the four 3.95-millimeter field pieces assigned to each battery.

Near the beginning of the 20th century, Charles R. Sherman, better known as "Huckleberry Charlie," was a familiar figure around Pine Plains. He claimed Pine Plains was "good only to raise h_ _ _ and huckleberries." Charlie sold his huckleberries in Watertown around Public Square, where merchants gave him unsold clothing from their stores. At the end of his tour around the square, he would be dressed in the colors of the rainbow.

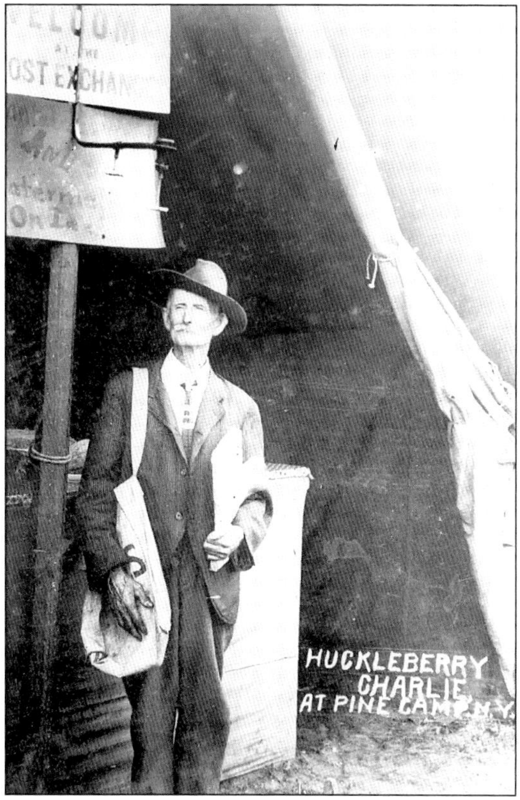

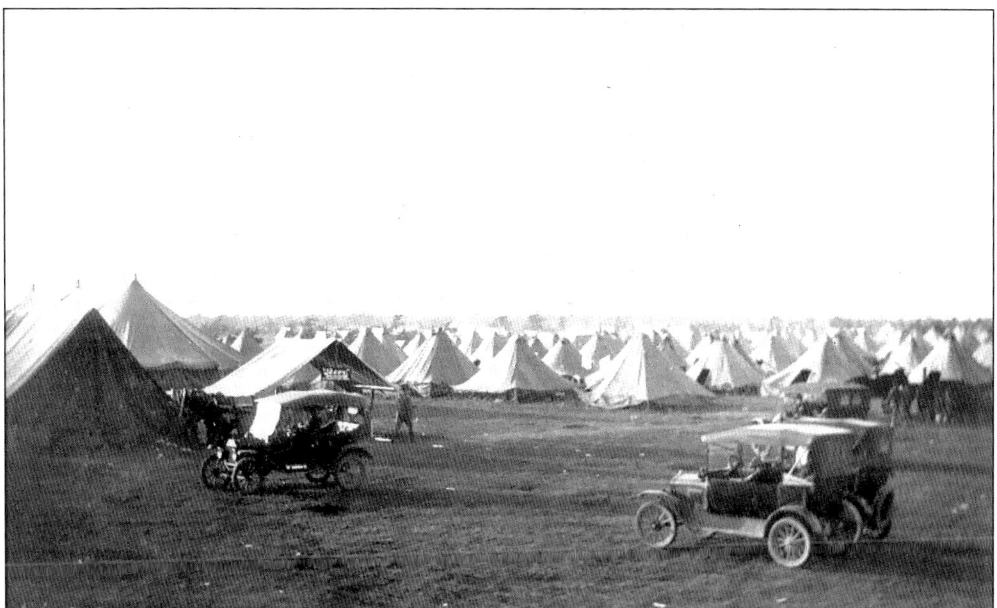

On September 15, 1917, rows of Sibley tents mark the location of the New York City National Guard 4th Field Artillery encampment at Pine Camp.

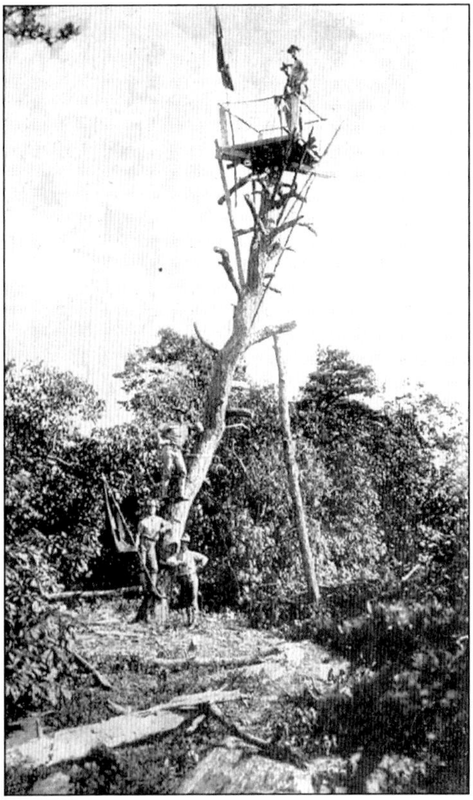

During the 1908–1910 training maneuvers, the signal corps station's observation tower shows an example of Yankee ingenuity. By 1920, a more stable tower was constructed.

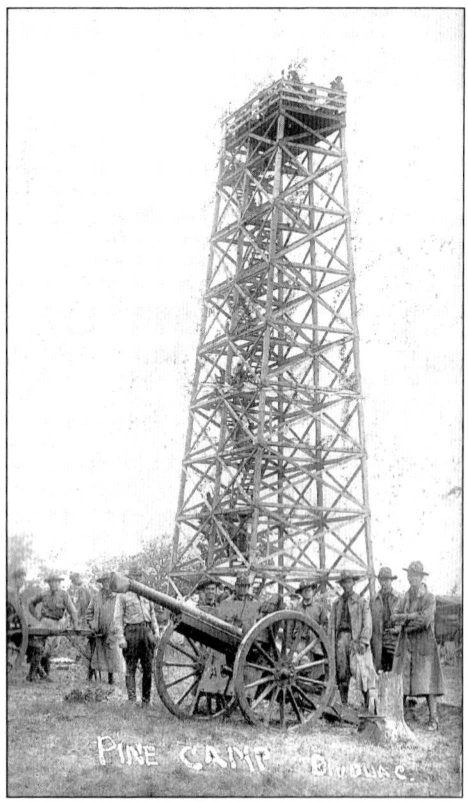

The new observation tower with an enlarged platform allowed more than one umpire to observe maneuvers.

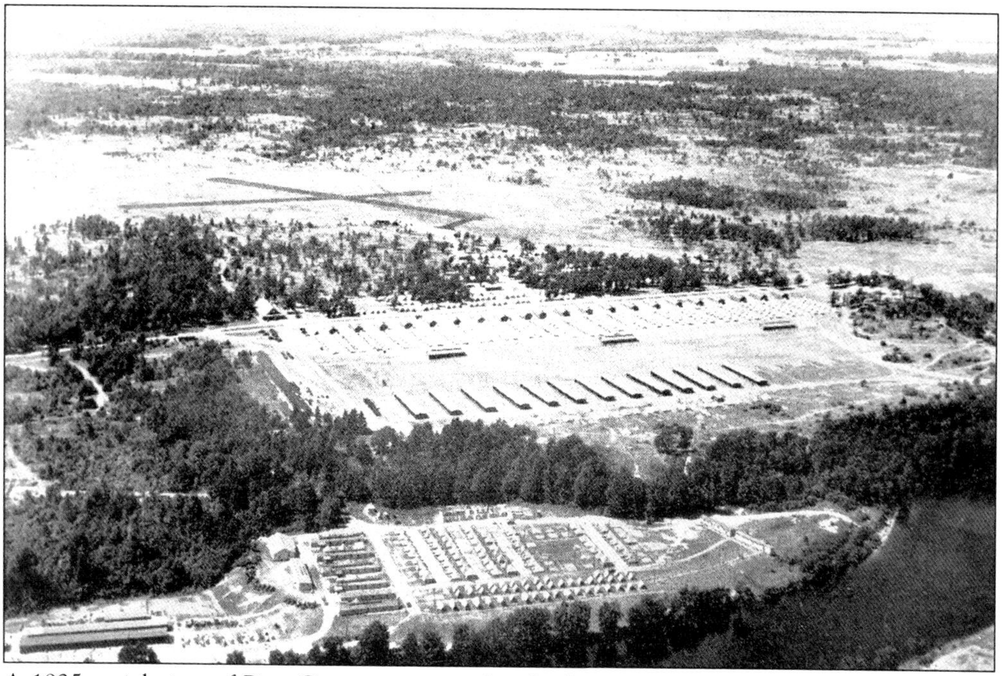

A 1925 aerial view of Pine Camp pinpoints the third cantonment, located between the Pine Camp airfield and the village of Great Bend. In the foreground is the Madison Barracks summer camp for the artillery units. In the center is the National Guard cantonment, with gun sheds, mess halls, and latrines. In the background are officers' tents and the airfield runways.

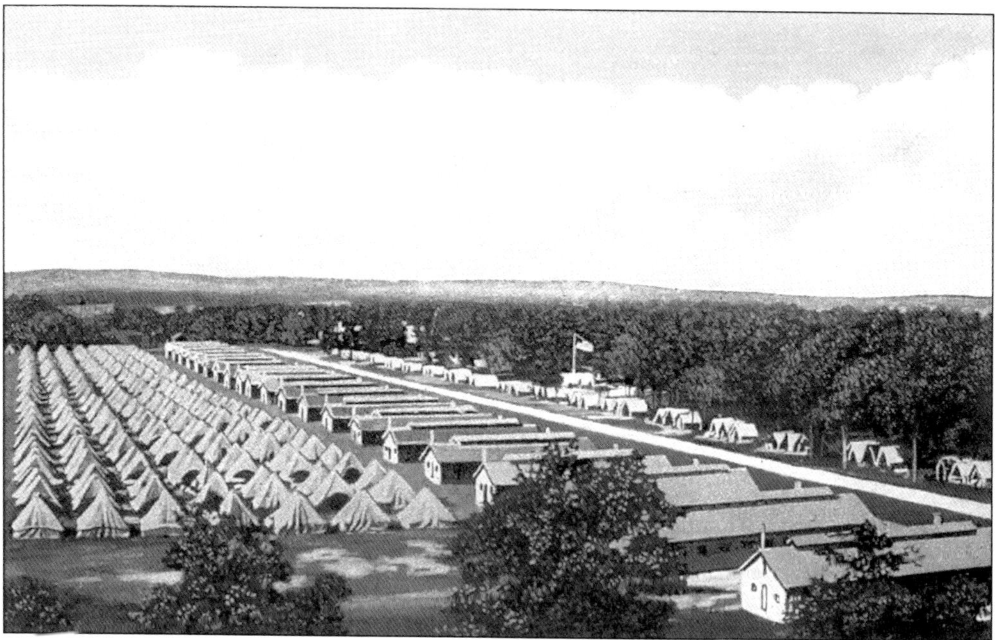

This photograph shows in more detail the National Guard summer encampment. Permanent wooden buildings served as mess halls and latrines. Guardsmen lived in pyramid tents.

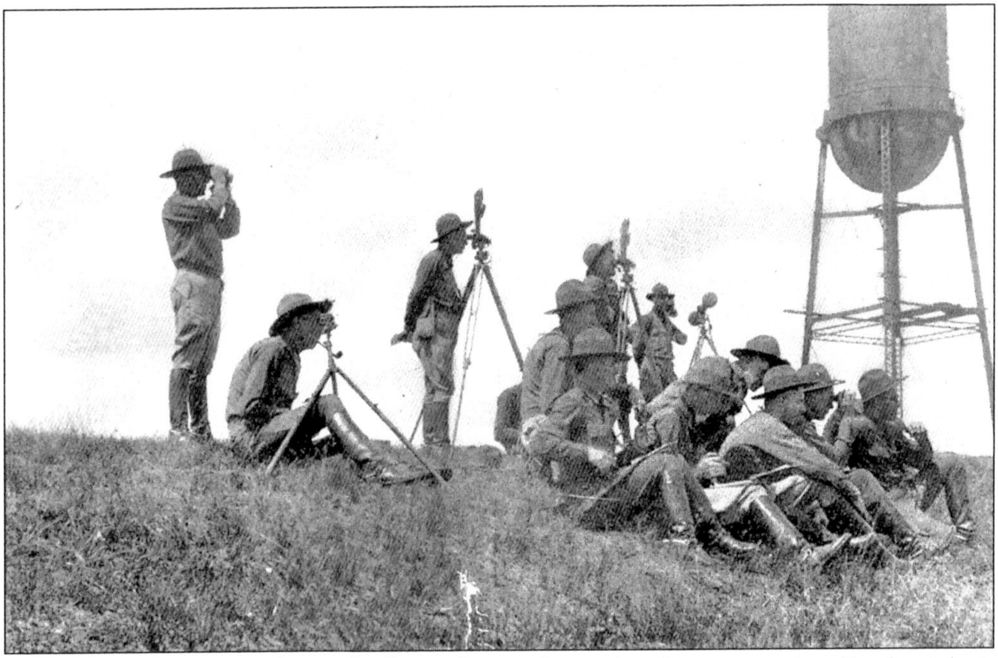

Atop Hog's Back, National Guard officers observe the results of target practice. On the right is the steel water tower constructed to supply water during the maneuvers.

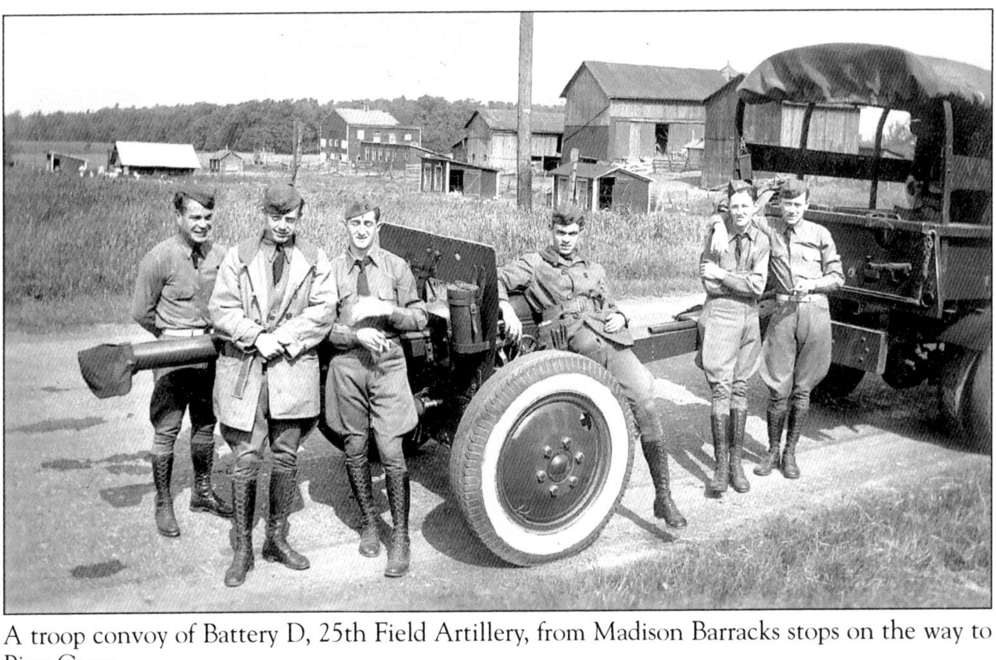

A troop convoy of Battery D, 25th Field Artillery, from Madison Barracks stops on the way to Pine Camp.

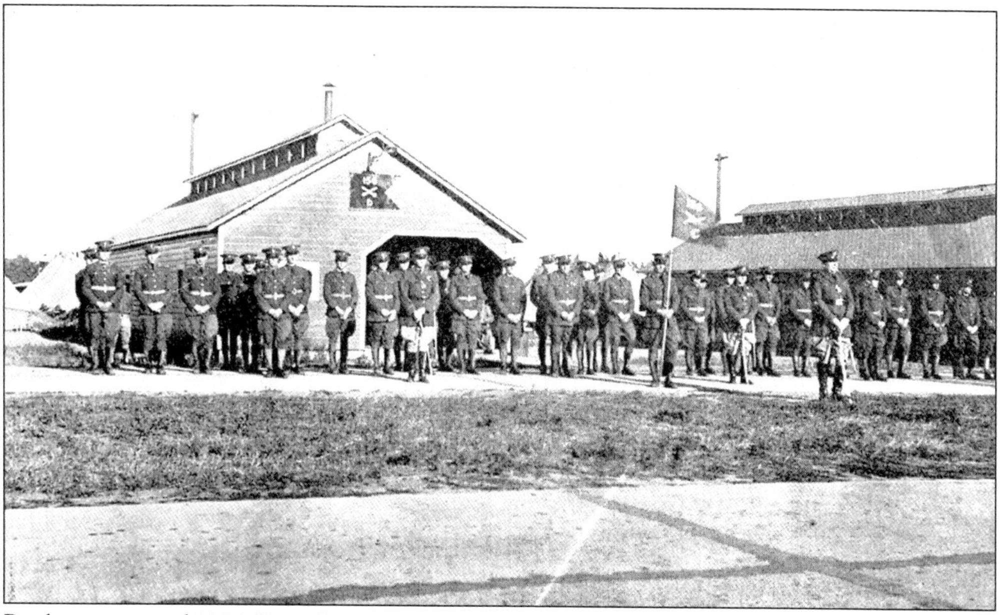

By the summer of 1924, Pine Camp at Great Bend was termed a model camp. It was the largest artillery training camp in New York State. Officers of the 7th Field Artillery, stationed at Madison Barracks under the command of Col. William Harts, instructed units of the National Guard Reserve Officer Training Camp and Civilian Military Training Camp. On August 7, 1924, this parade formation of Battery D, 156th National Guard, waits to pass in review. (Courtesy of Santway Photocraft Company.)

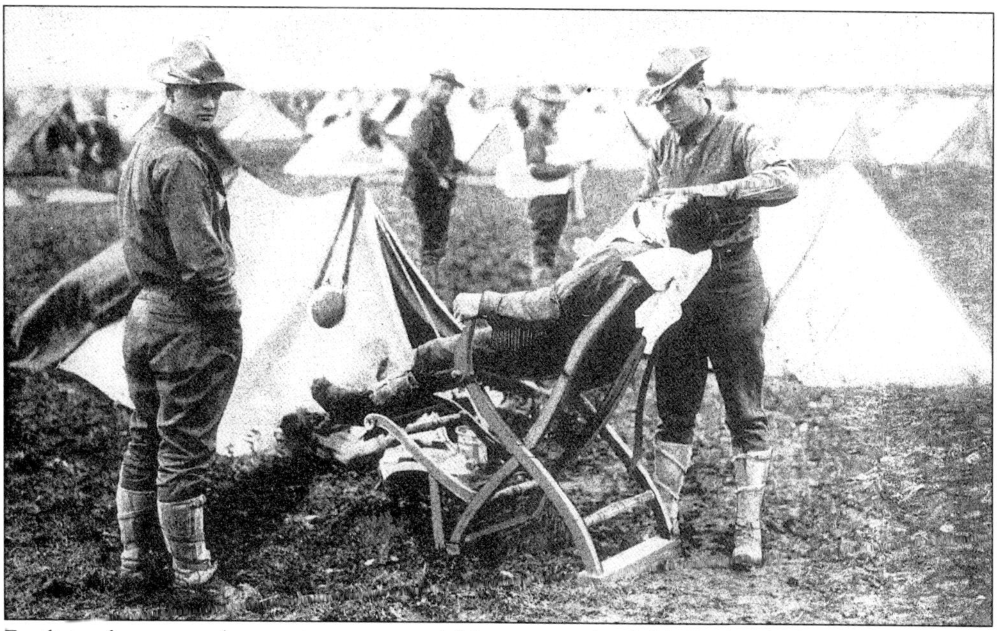

Facilities for personal grooming were available even in the field. With a barber in the group, a shave and a haircut were possible.

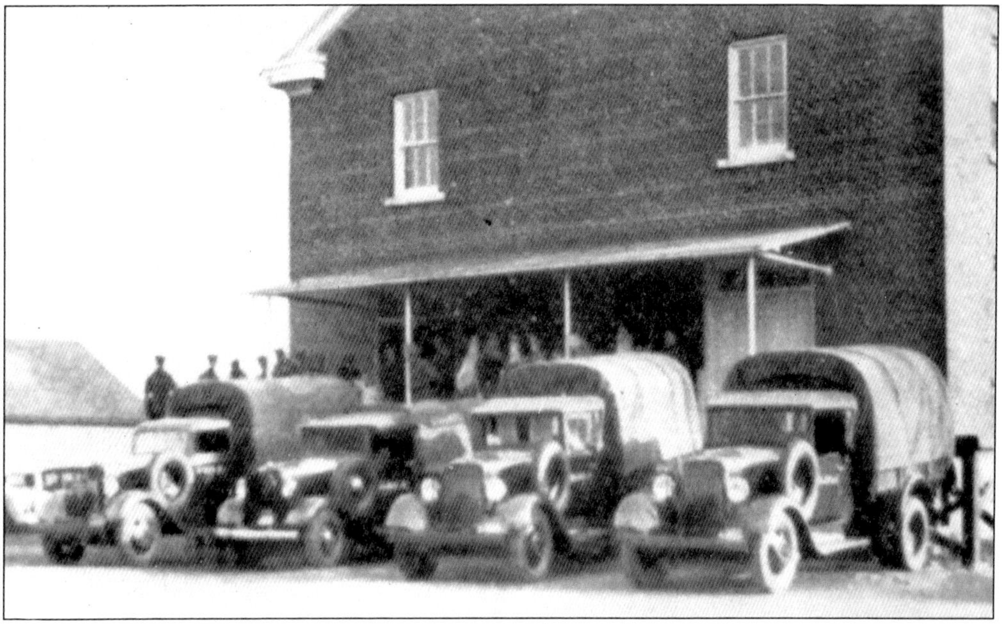

For the summer of 1935 maneuvers at Pine Camp, the regular army depot at Madison Barracks served the regular army, and the army depot in Watertown served the National Guard units. The photograph shows a fleet of trucks loading supplies at the Madison Barracks commissary for distribution to field units. (Courtesy of Santway Photocraft Company.)

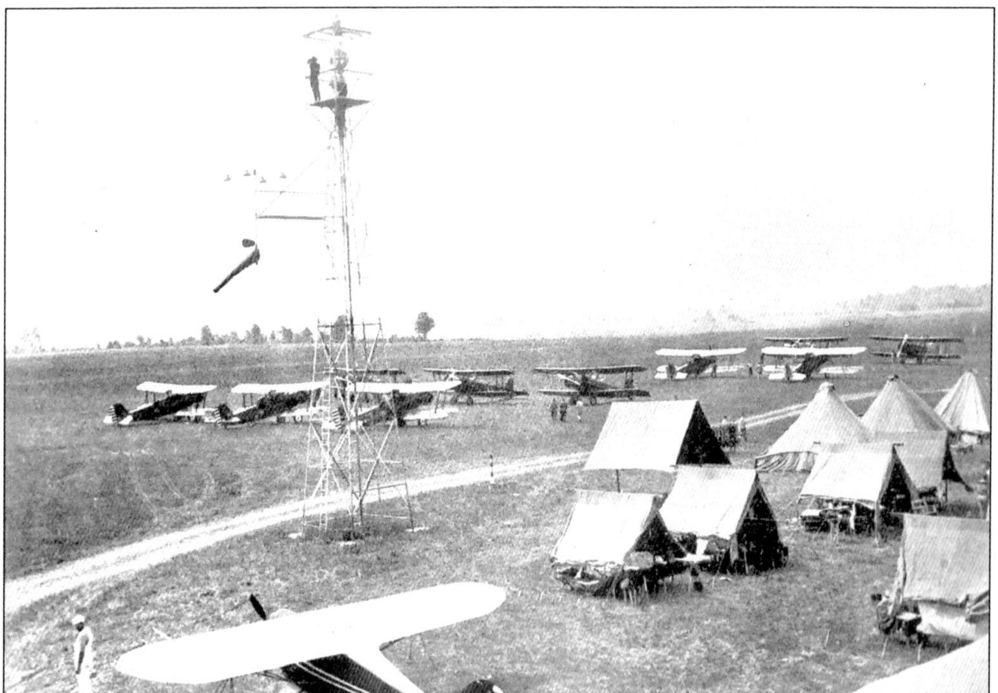

Observation planes and smoke-laying planes used in the 1935 maneuvers are assembled at the Watertown airport, located 16 miles from Pine Camp. (Courtesy of Santway Photocraft Company.)

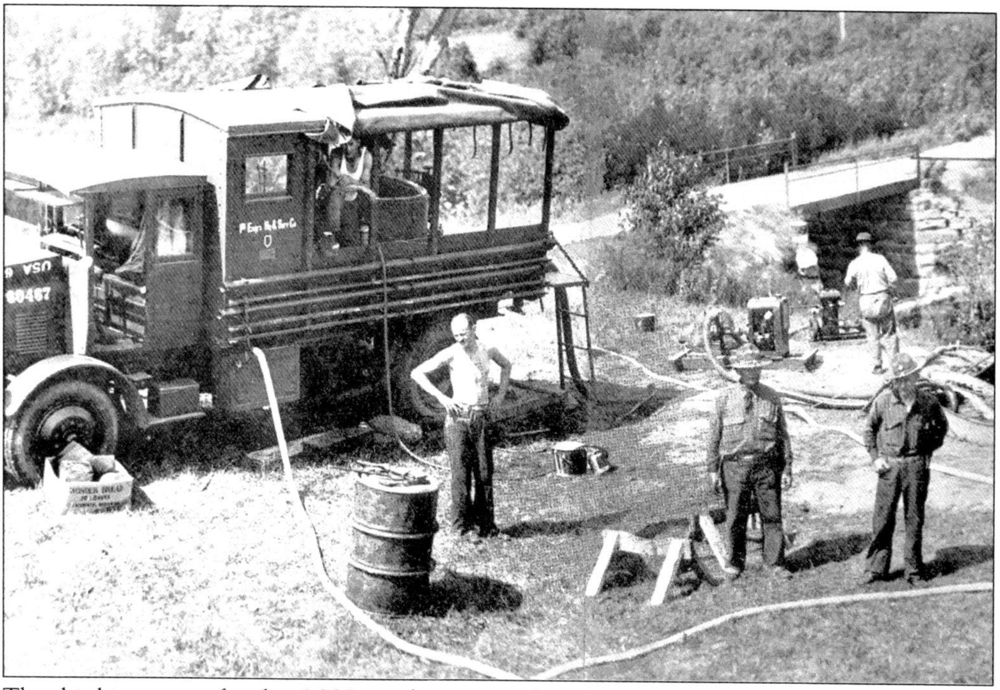

The drinking water for the 6,000 regulars engaged in the 1935 war games was obtained from Black Creek, east of Hog's Back. A filtration plant and chemical laboratory mounted on trucks turned creek water into pure drinking water. (Courtesy of Santway Photocraft Company.)

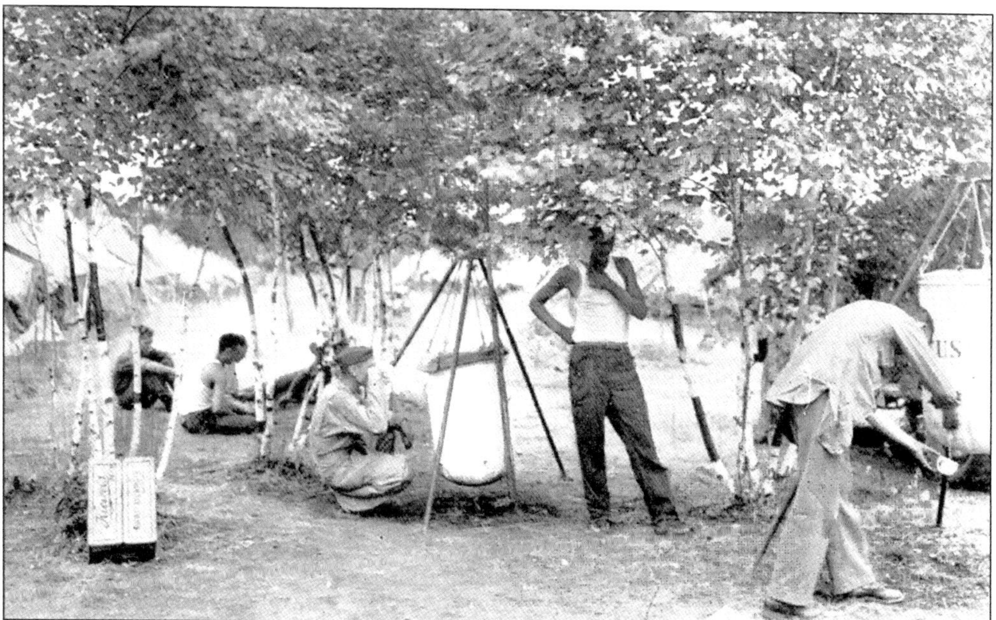

Out in the field, the drinking water was stored in Lister bags suspended on tripods.

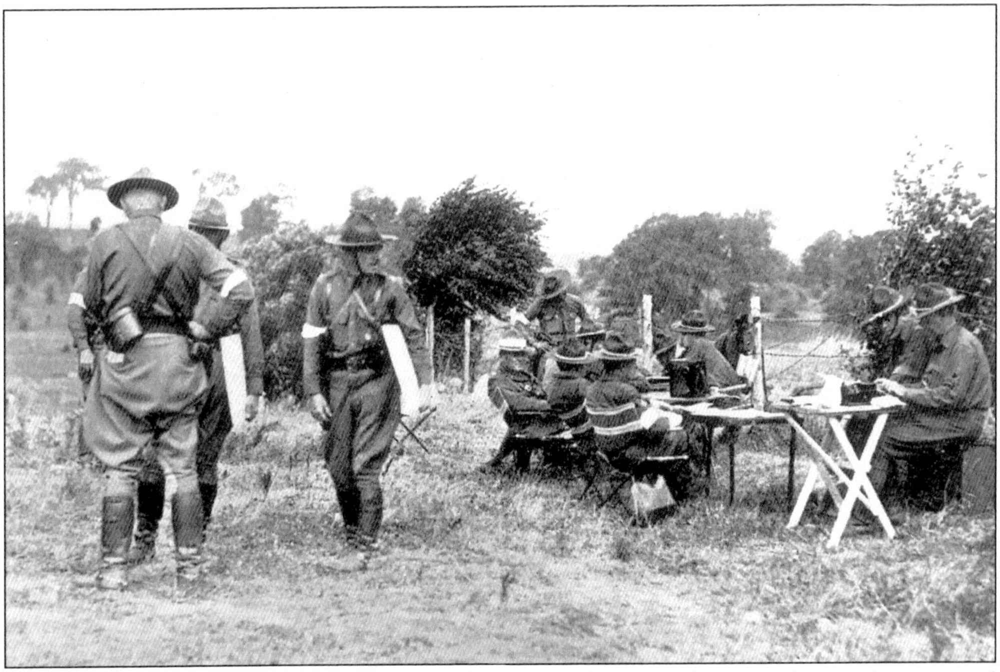

A typical communications center handled all messages between the firing line and regimental headquarters. Telephones and field radios enabled the artillery to report the enemy's location throughout the 1935 maneuvers. (Courtesy Santway Photocraft Company.)

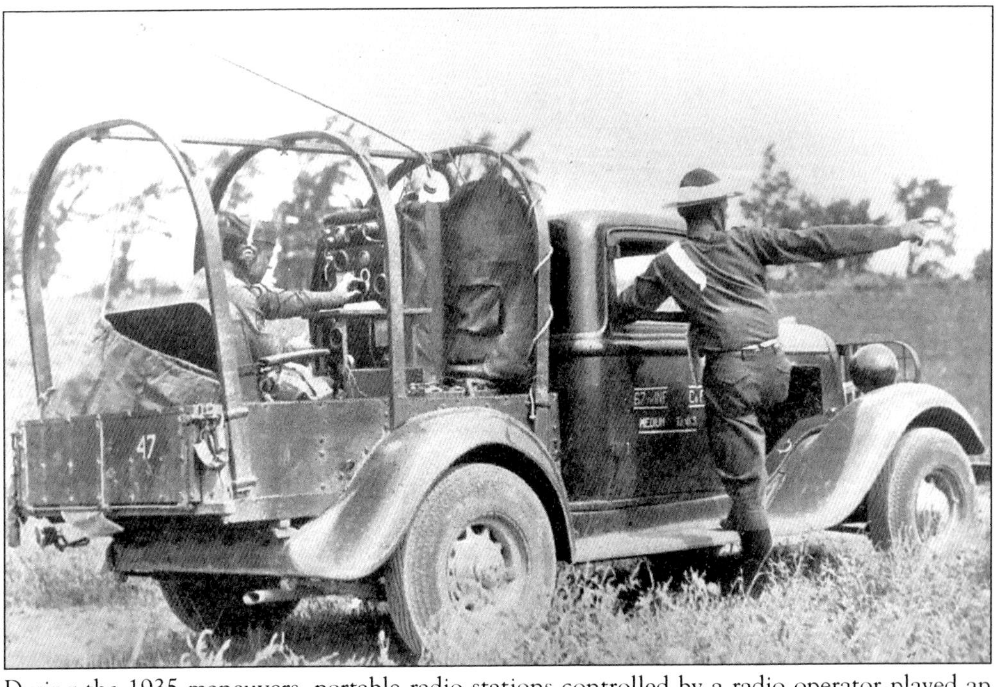

During the 1935 maneuvers, portable radio stations controlled by a radio operator played an important role in the communication system. (Courtesy Santway Photocraft Company.)

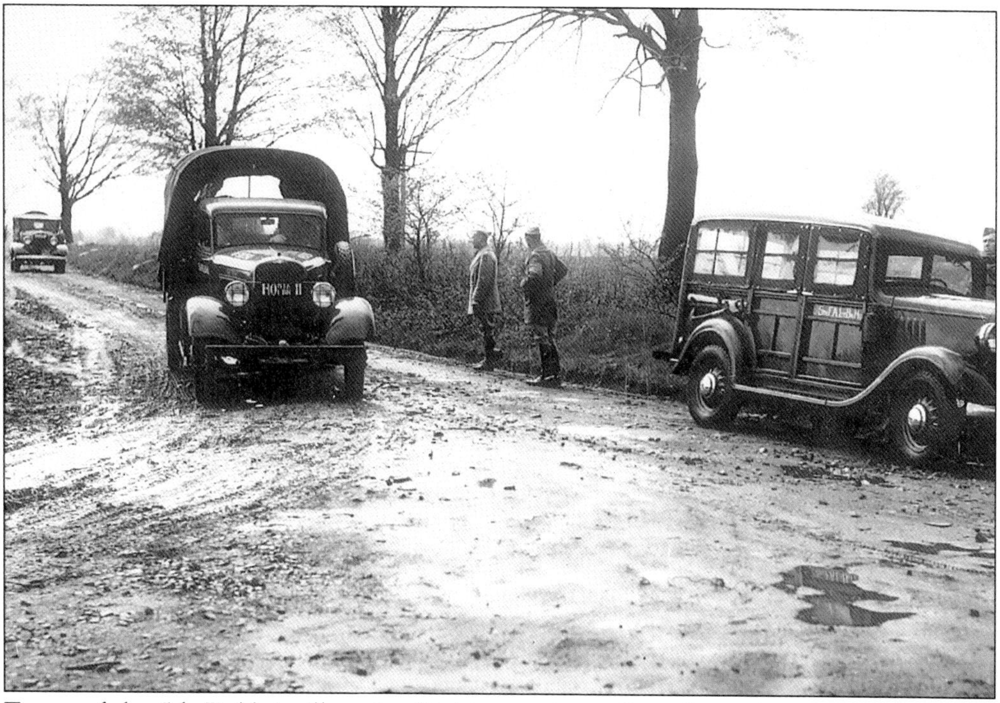

Troops of the 5th Field Artillery, 1st Division, arrive at Pine Camp for a training exercise. Col. Samuel Hopkins is standing behind a reconnaissance vehicle.

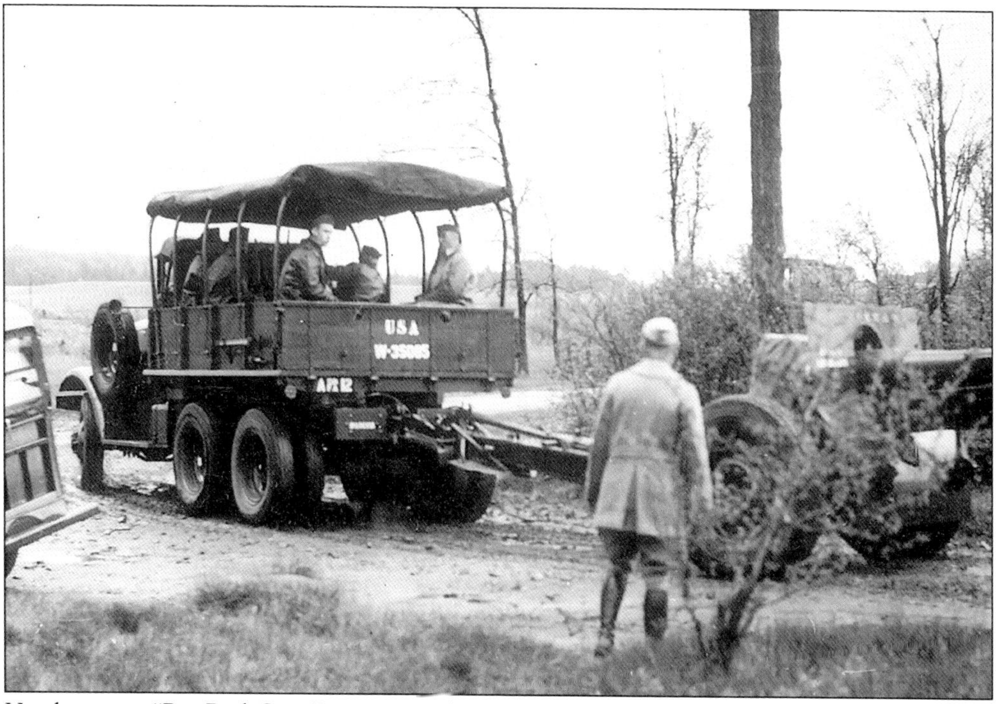

Headquarters "Big Red One Division," 5th Field Artillery, from Madison Barracks arrives at Pine Camp. Col. Samuel Hopkins, commanding officer, watches as a 155-millimeter artillery piece is hauled onto the firing line.

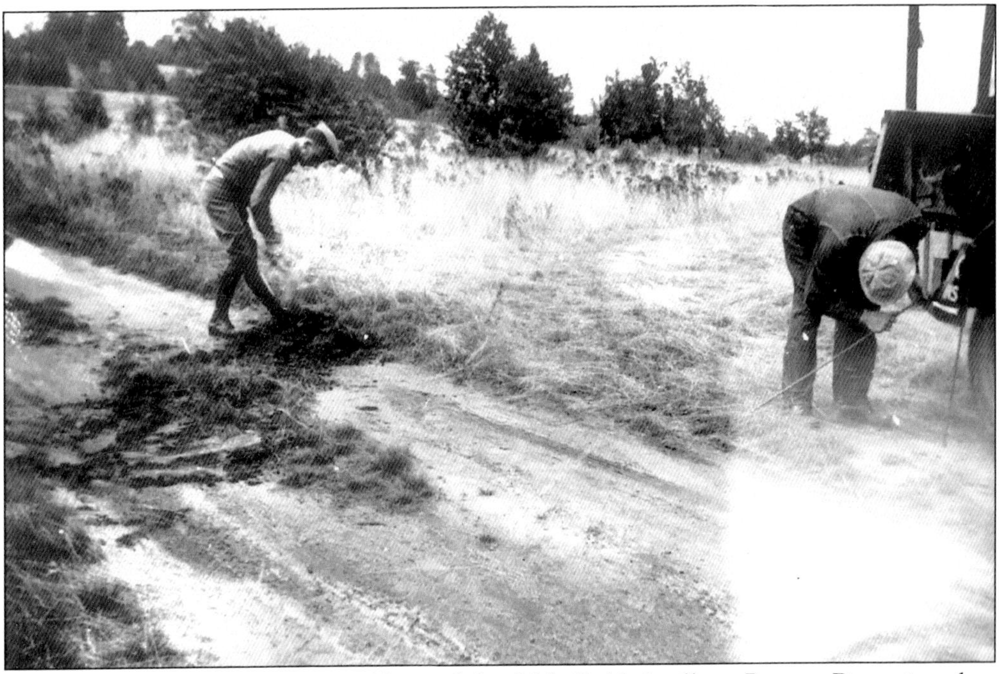

For the 1938 summer training, soldiers of the 25th Field Artillery, Battery D, stationed at Madison Barracks, dig trenches to lay telephone lines under a road at Pine Camp. Chief of the signal section, Sgt. Mc Cune and Pfc. Fisher, were in charge of the detail.

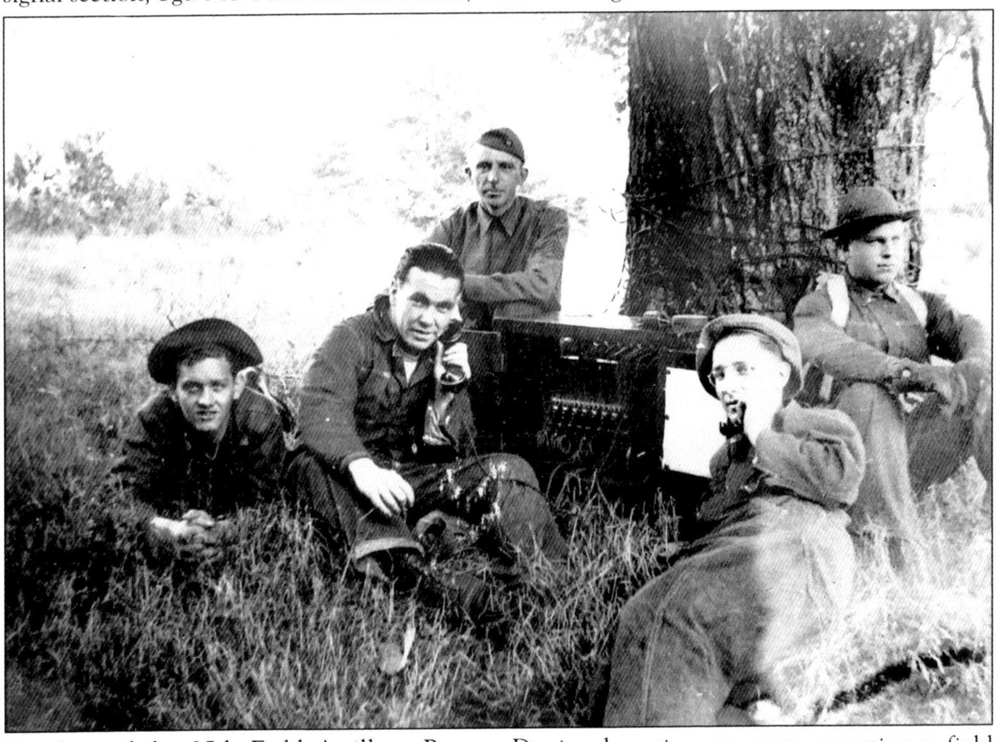

Members of the 25th Field Artillery, Battery D, signal section are seen operating a field switchboard at Pine Camp.

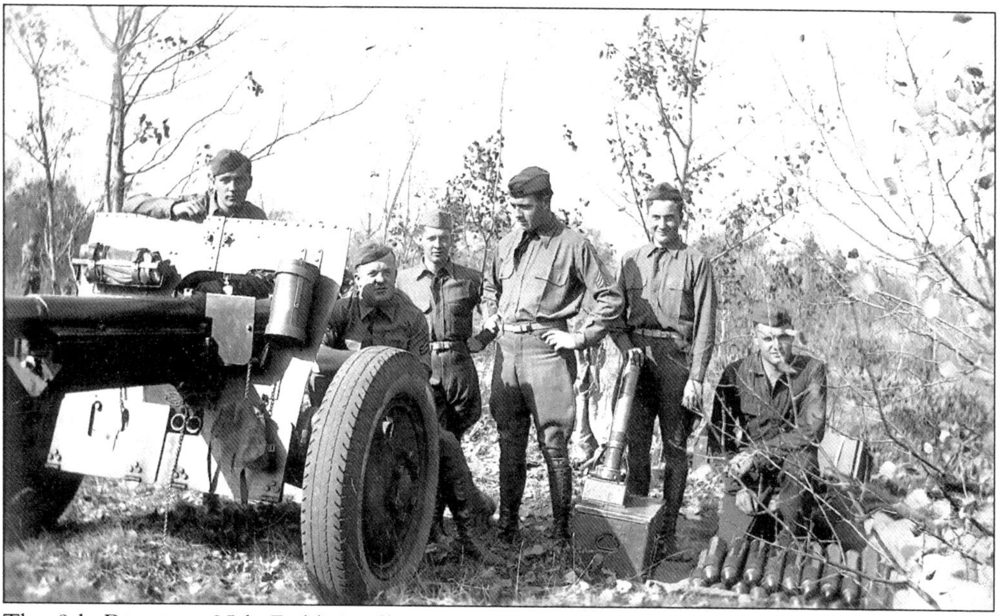

The 9th Division, 25th Field Artillery, stationed at Madison Barracks from 1935 to 1940, travels to Pine Camp for artillery practice. Battery D positions a 75-millimeter artillery piece on the firing range.

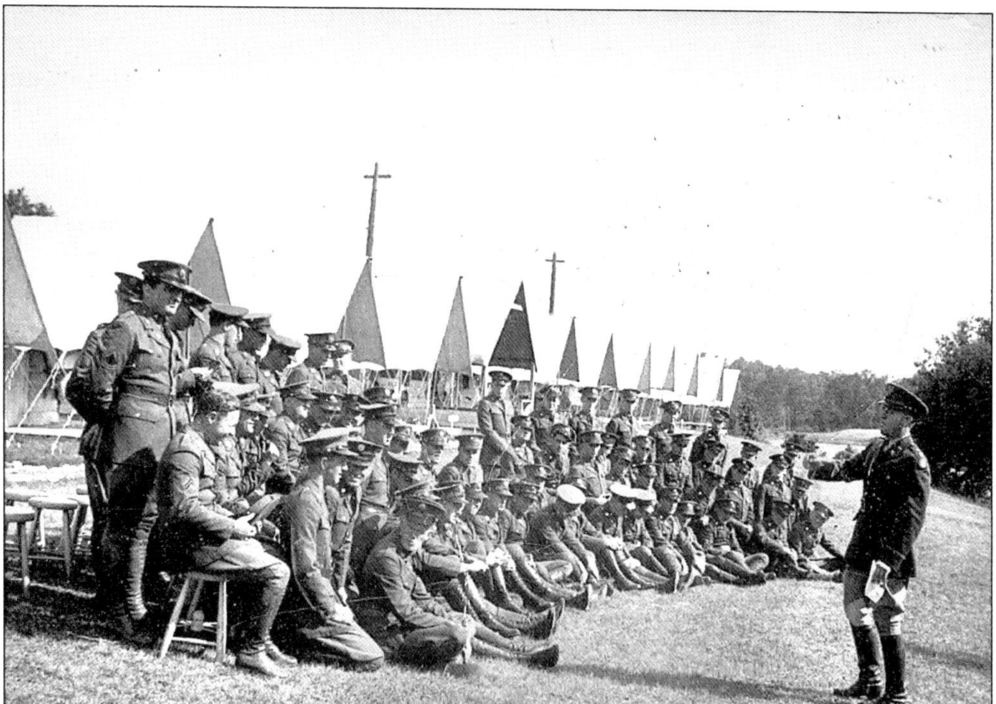

Capt. Lindsey Winfield, commanding officer of Battery E, 25th Field Artillery, addresses a group of enlisted men during a training session at Pine Camp.

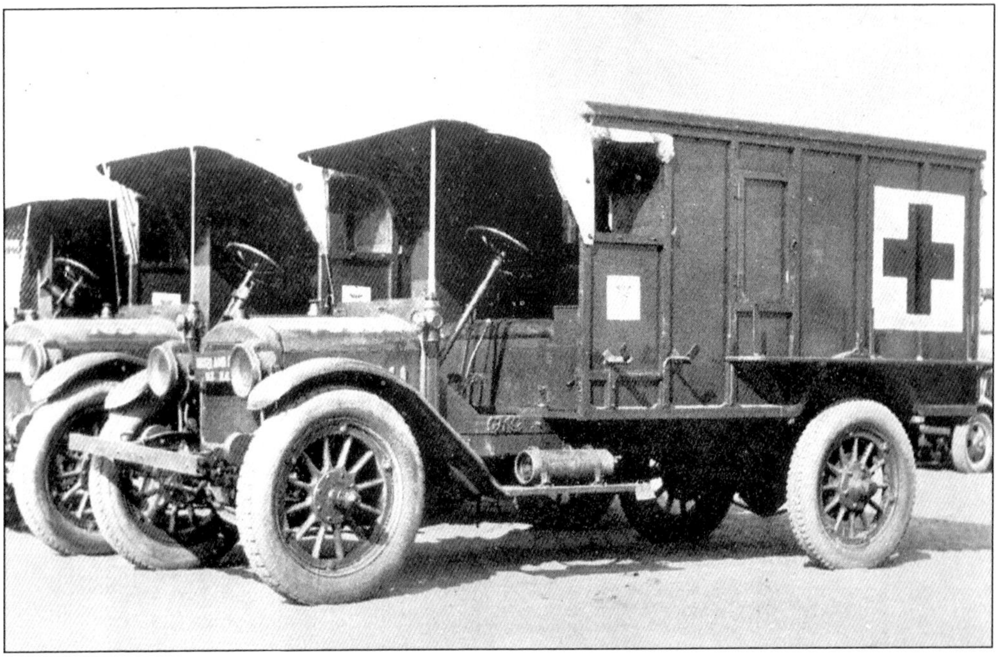

Red Cross ambulances of World War I vintage are lined up for use during the 1935 maneuvers at Pine Camp.

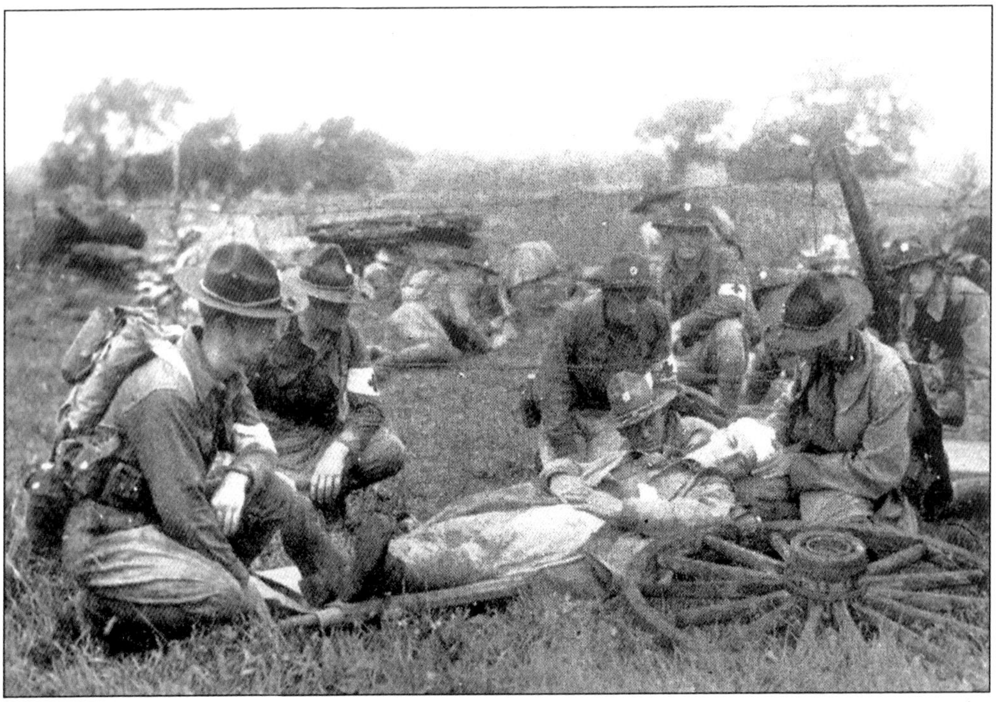

During the war games, a practice exercise gives stretcher-bearers experience in caring for casualties. Real casualties were treated at the Madison Barracks base hospital.

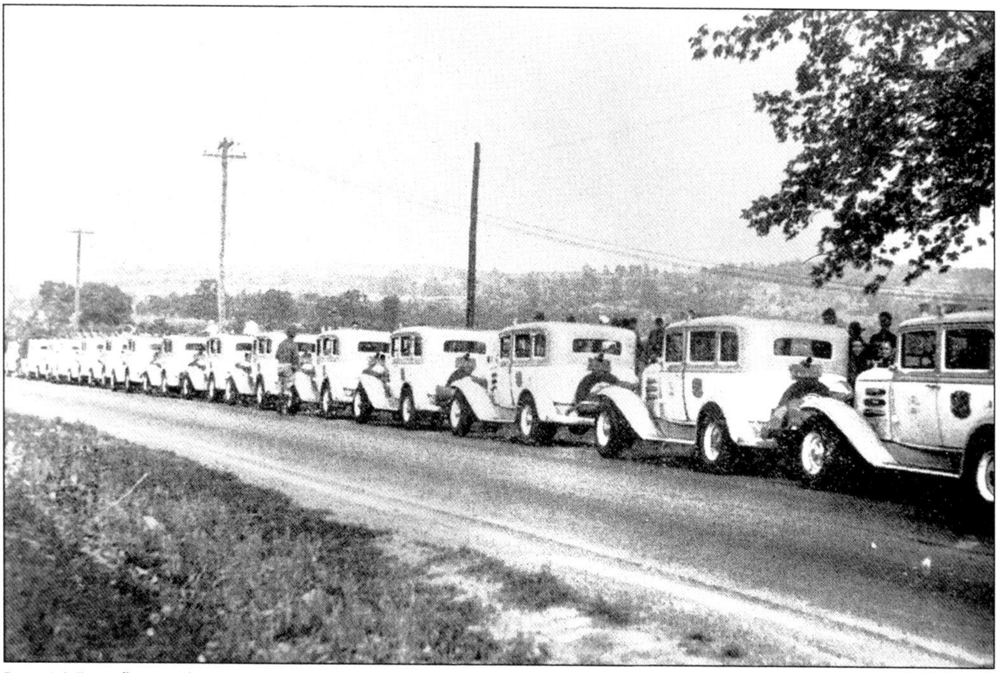

In 1935, a fleet of taxis from New York City transported the 106th Field Artillery from Buffalo to the village of Great Bend. (Courtesy of Santway Photocraft Company.)

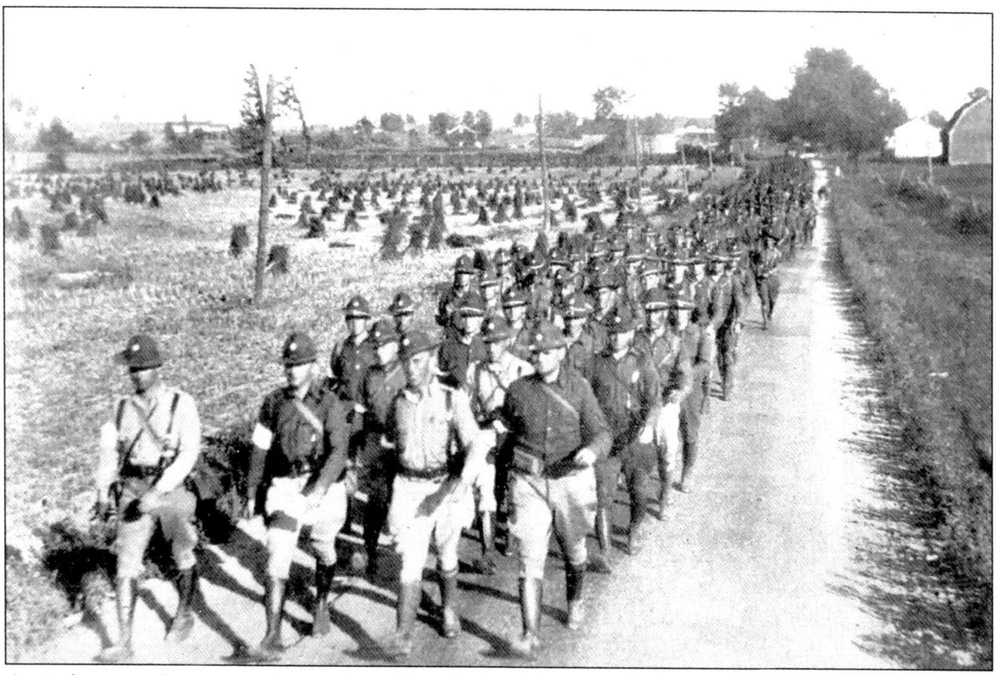

An infantry column marches back to Pine Camp after an engagement. Well-trained guardsmen withstood exhaustion from arduous operations and intense heat during the 1935 maneuvers.

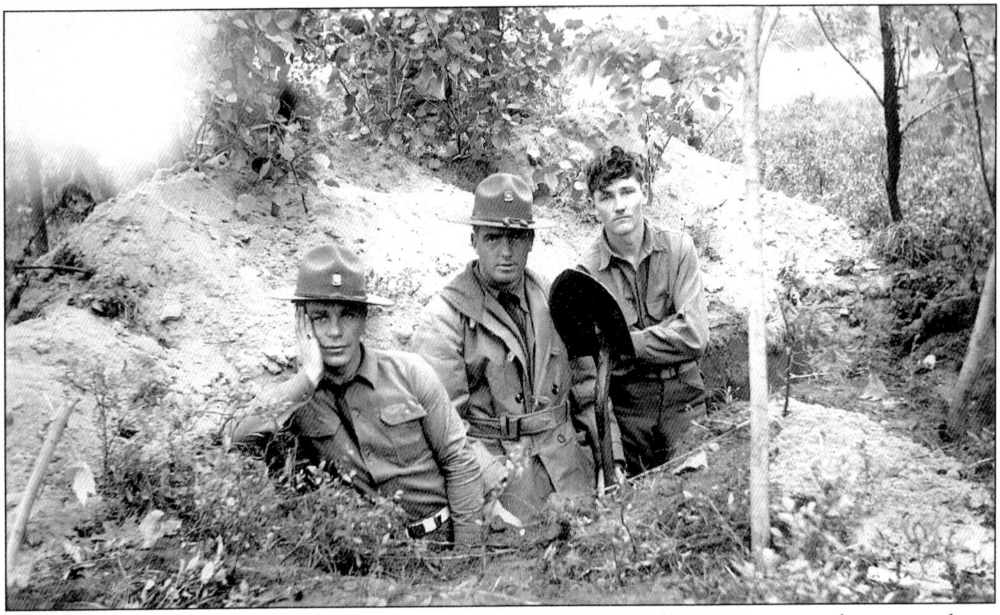

Madison Barracks soldiers from D Battery, 25th Field Artillery, pause in their trench at Pine Camp.

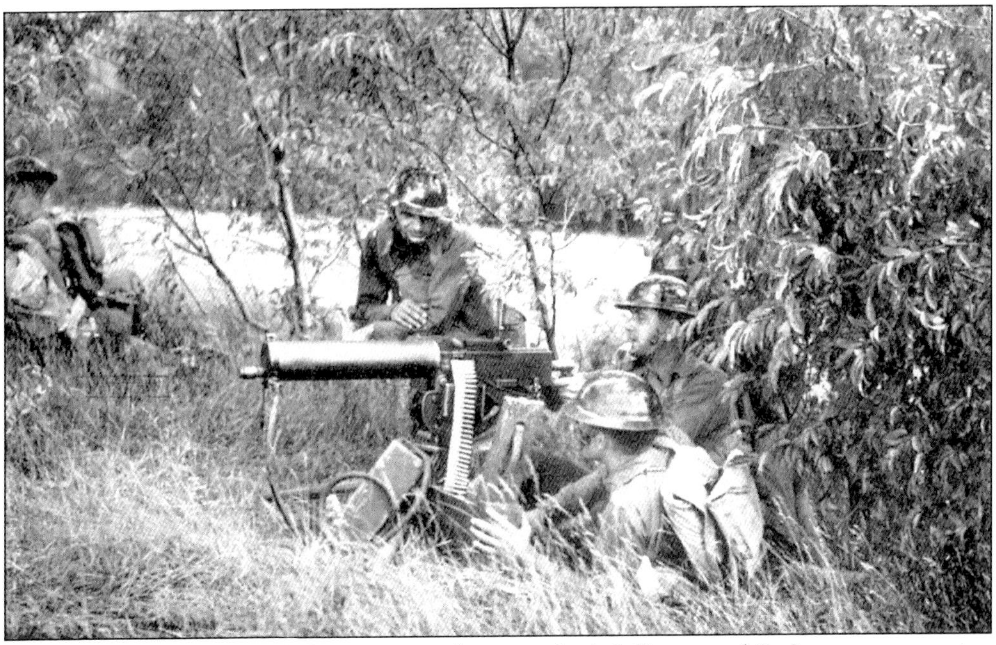

First Army maneuvers in 1940 encompassed areas in both Jefferson and St. Lawrence counties. A machine-gun crew awaits action from the enemy.

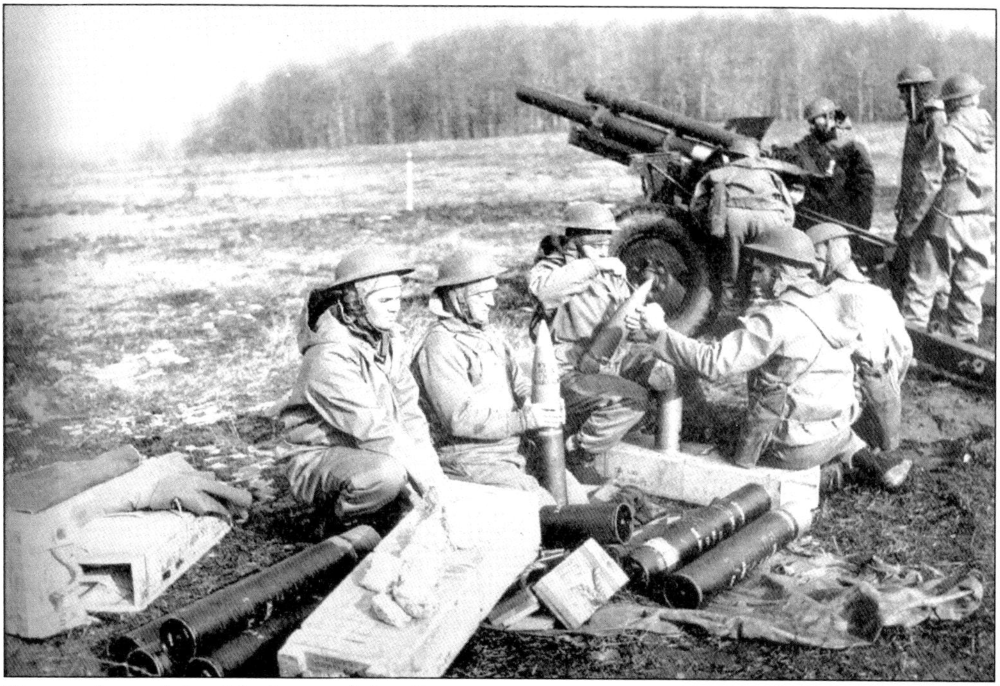

Six members of the 4th Armored Artillery nine-man gun crew prepare shells to be fired from a 105-millimeter howitzer.

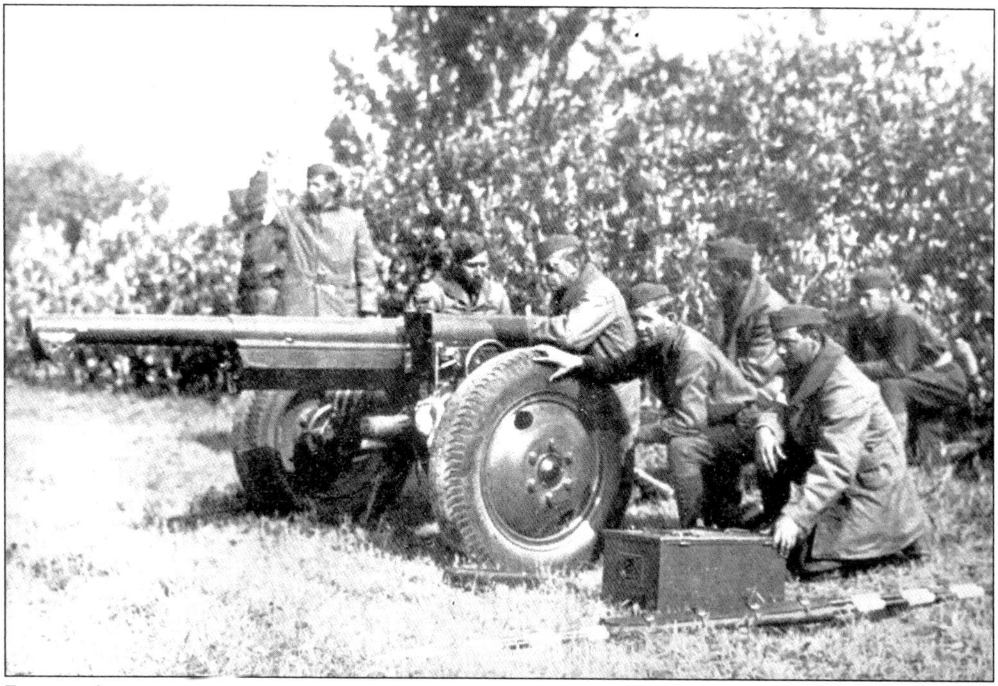

During the 1935 maneuvers, a 75-millimeter piece is set in position by a field artillery crew. Balloon tires were a motorized innovation. Ammunition was carried by trucks. Overseas caps were worn by several units.

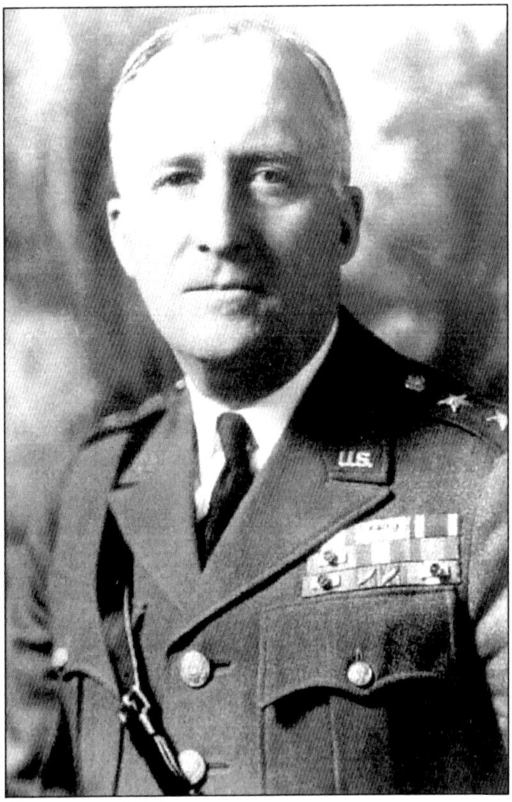

Lt. Gen. Hugh A. Drum served as a captain with the 23rd Infantry stationed at Madison Barracks from 1905 to 1908. In 1940, he was appointed lieutenant general of the New York National Guard. In 1950, Pine Camp was renamed Camp Drum in his honor. In 1974, Camp Drum was upgraded to Fort Drum.

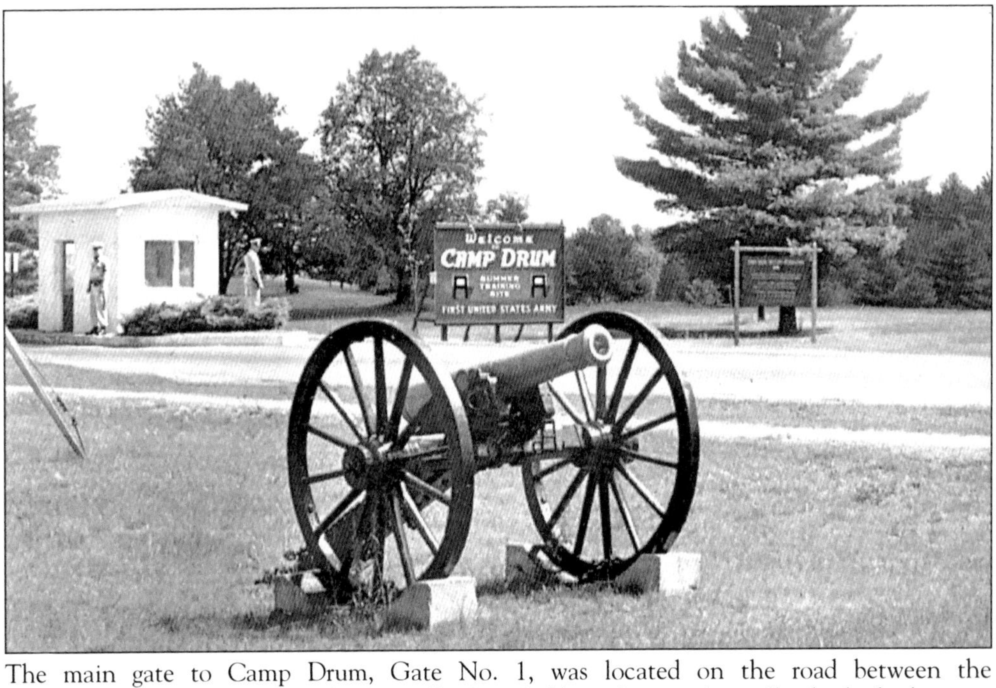

The main gate to Camp Drum, Gate No. 1, was located on the road between the communities of Black River and Felts Mills. Guarded by military police, all vehicles had to stop for identification.

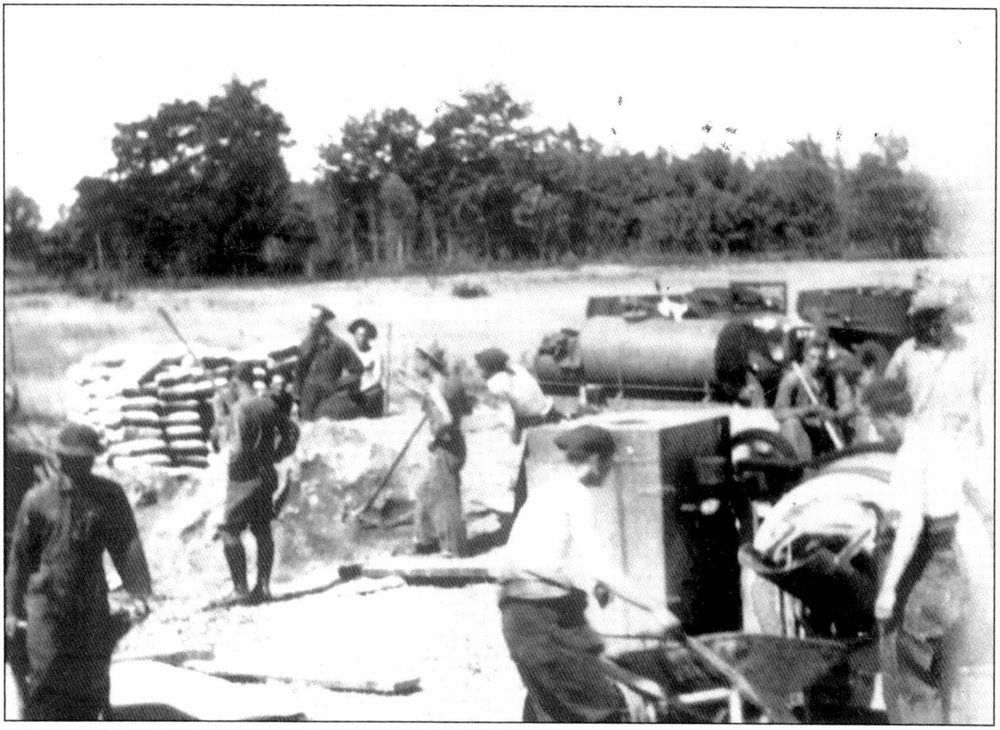

When public funds were no longer available, from 1935 to 1940, soldiers at Pine Camp were called upon to complete construction projects started under the Works Project Administration.

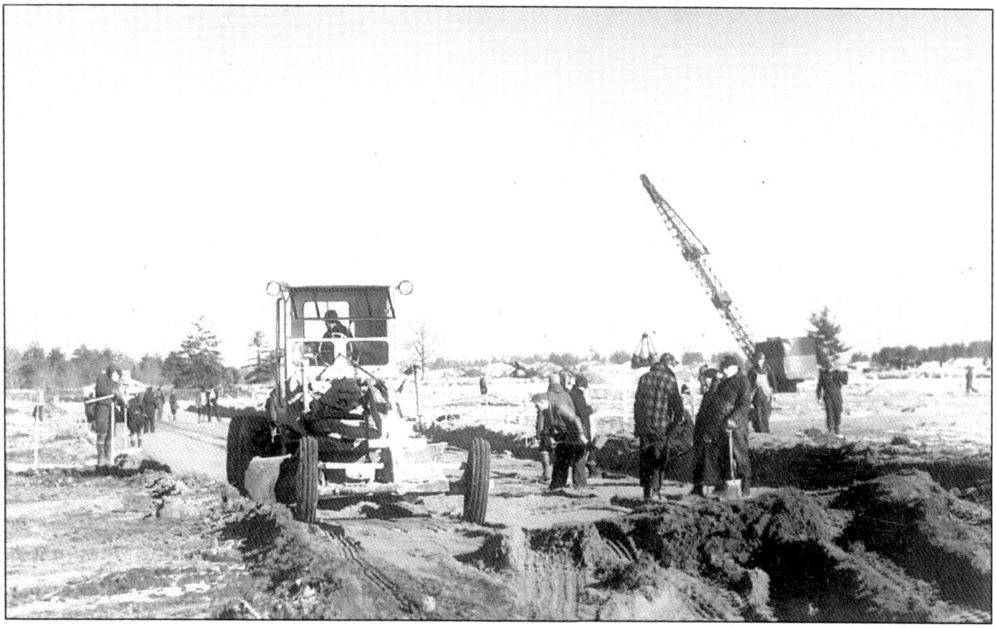

In May 1941, contractors hired by the federal government were busy constructing a section of 1,265 miles of highways in preparation for the $7 million expansion project at Pine Camp.

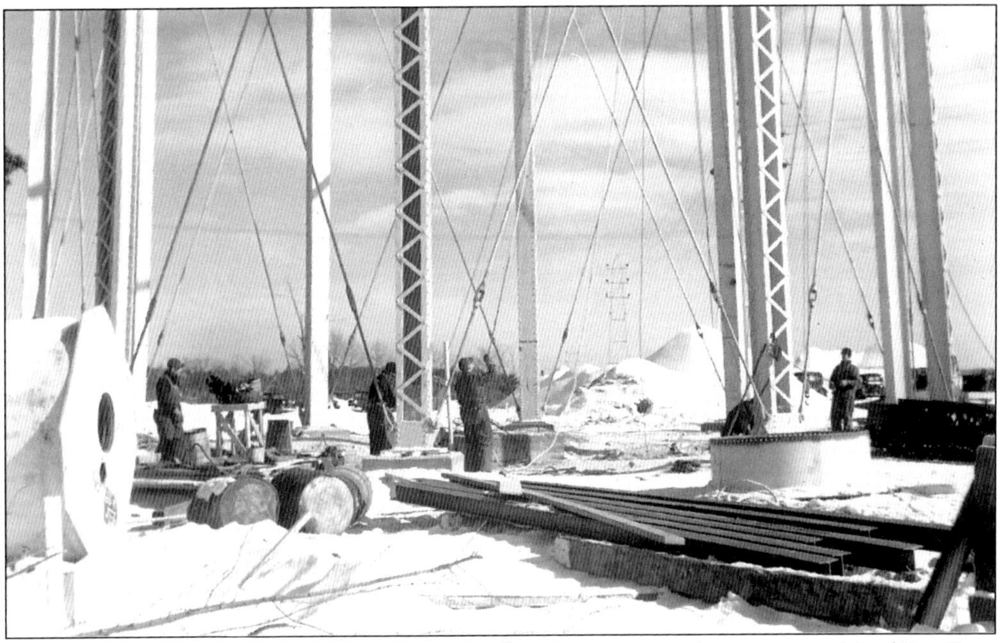

Construction of four water towers to insure an adequate water supply were part of the $7 million expansion project. The completed base of one tower is seen here.

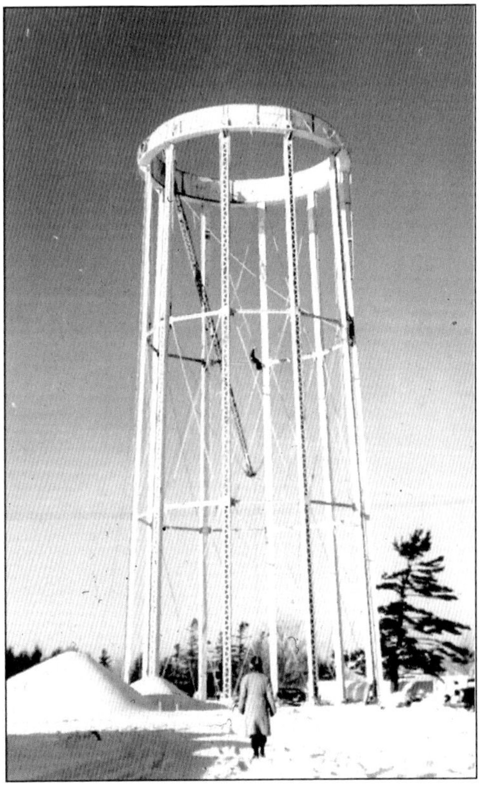

A completed tower stands ready for the 500,000-gallon water tank to be mounted. Ten wells north of the village of Leraysville Road were drilled. Powered by electric pumps, the wells could produce 1,500 gallons of water per minute.

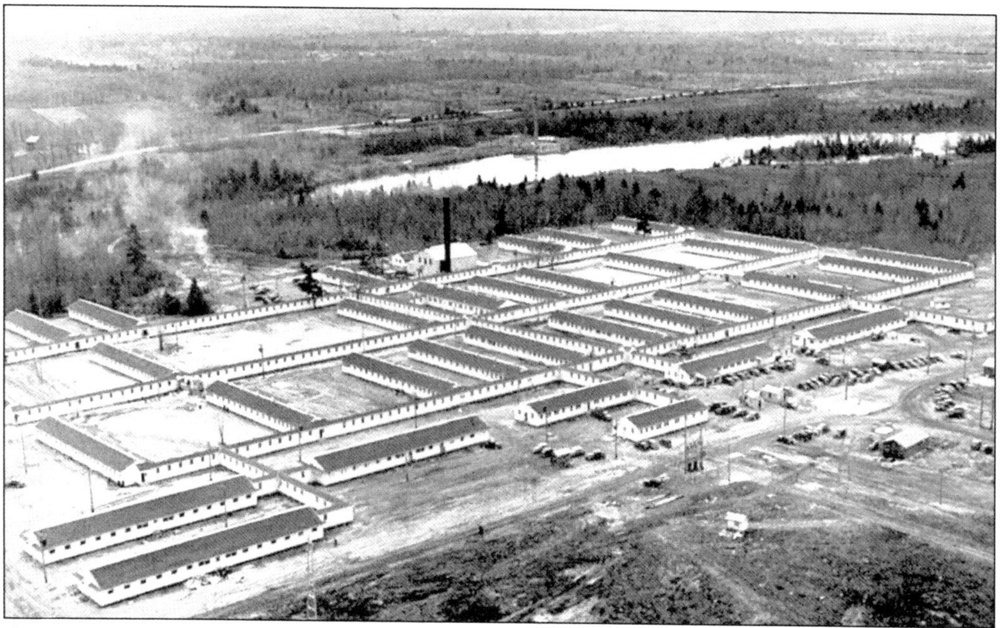

A 1940 aerial view of the Pine Camp hospital unit shows the 40 buildings constructed during the $7 million project. Administration buildings, clinics, nurses' quarters, physicians' quarters, and wards for 550 men were constructed. (Courtesy Santway Photocraft Company.)

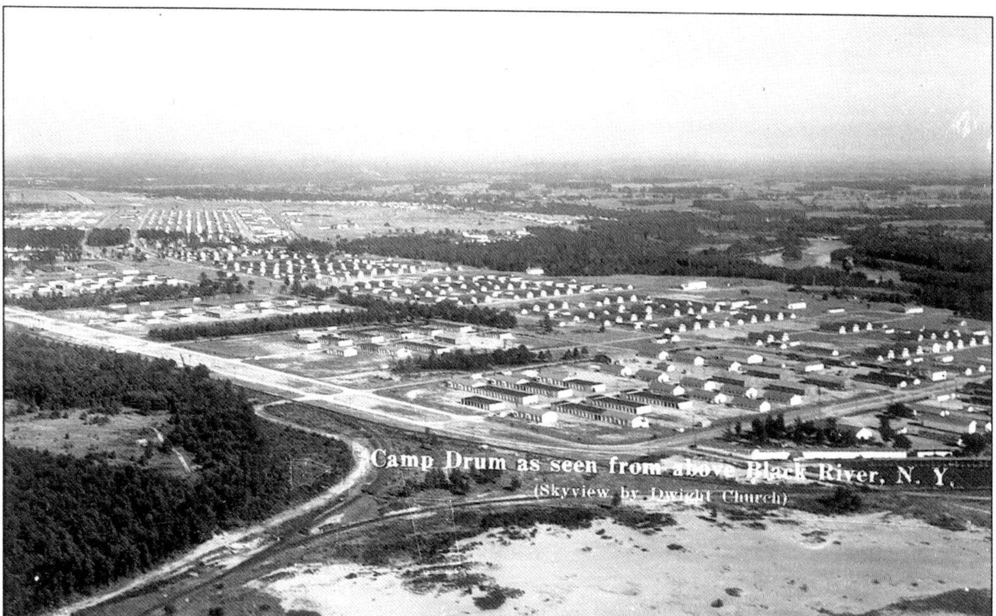

As seen from above Black River, an aerial view of the completed $7 million cantonment looks east. The airport is in the background, and in the foreground is the railroad spur. Gasoline alley, where vehicles line up for fueling, borders on the left.

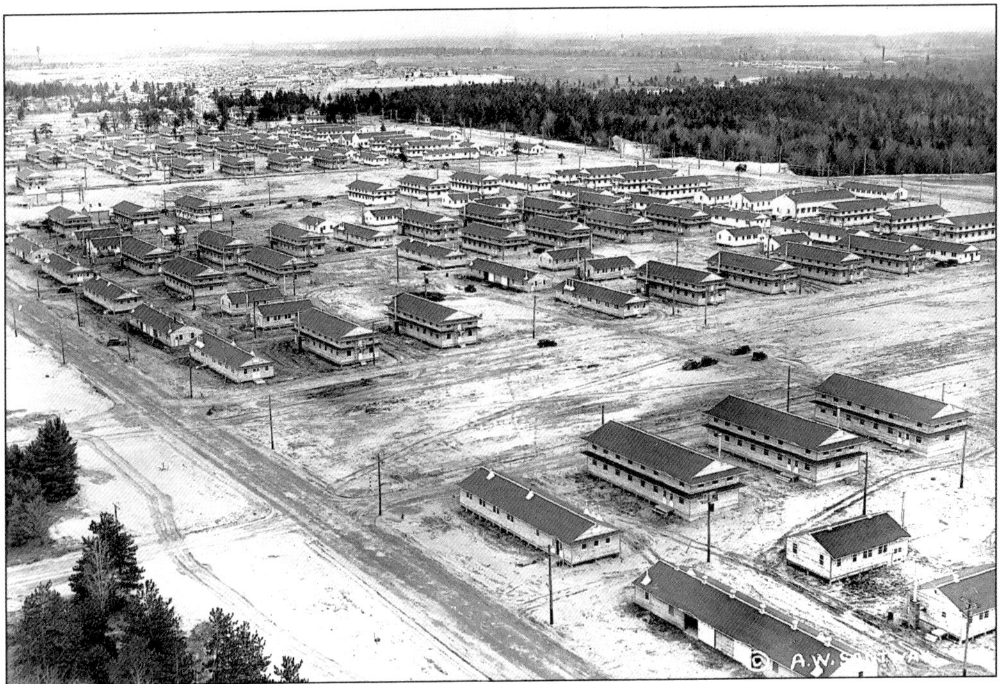

A 1941 aerial view shows the expansion of Pine Camp on the north side of Black River between the villages of Black River and Great Bend. A total of 900 buildings included two-story barracks, supply rooms, mess halls, warehouses, and garages. (Courtesy Jefferson County Historical Society.)

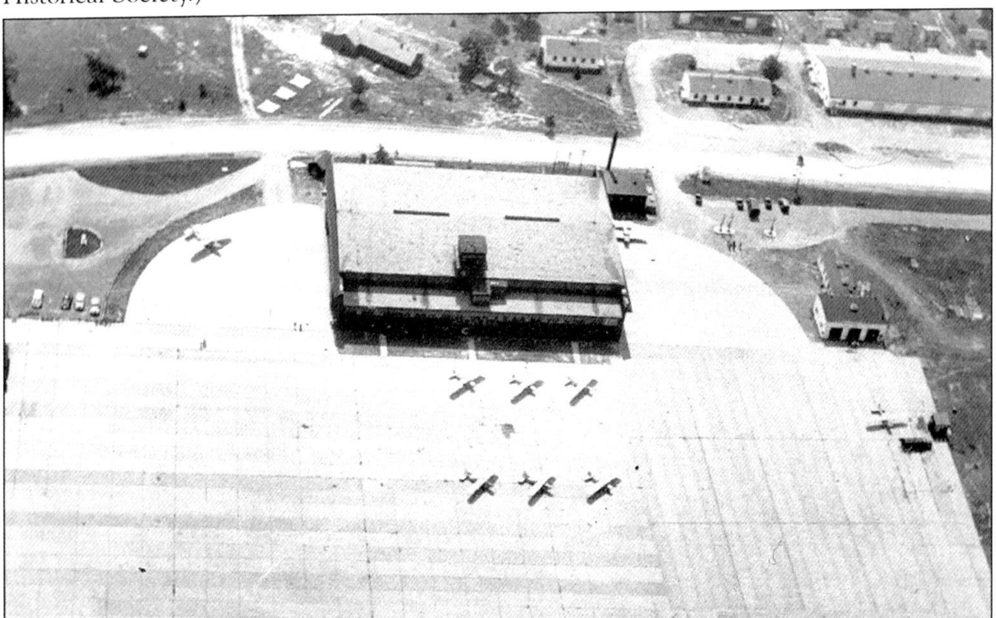

On October 24, 1941, the steel hangar at Pine Camp reservation airport is completed. Construction of the hangar, 200 feet by 161 feet, was started in August by John W. Couper Company. Six observation planes of the 91st Observation Squadron are parked on the 2,200-square-yard concrete apron. (Courtesy Fort Drum Museum.)

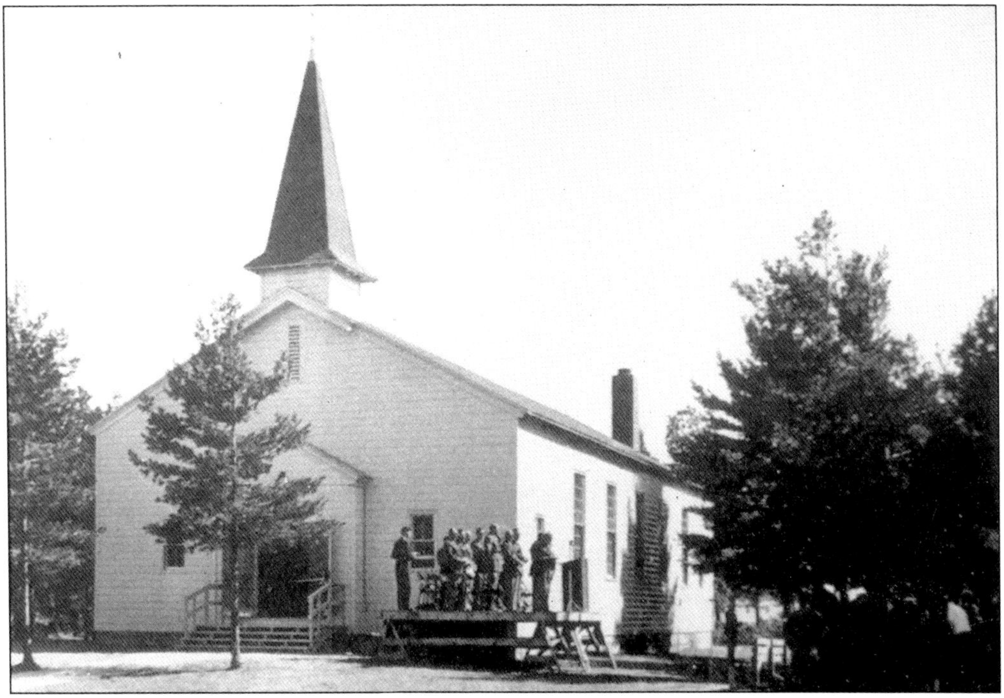

To provide religious services for Pine Camp personnel and families, five chapels were built. Chapel in the Pines, located on Nash Boulevard, was one of the chapels.

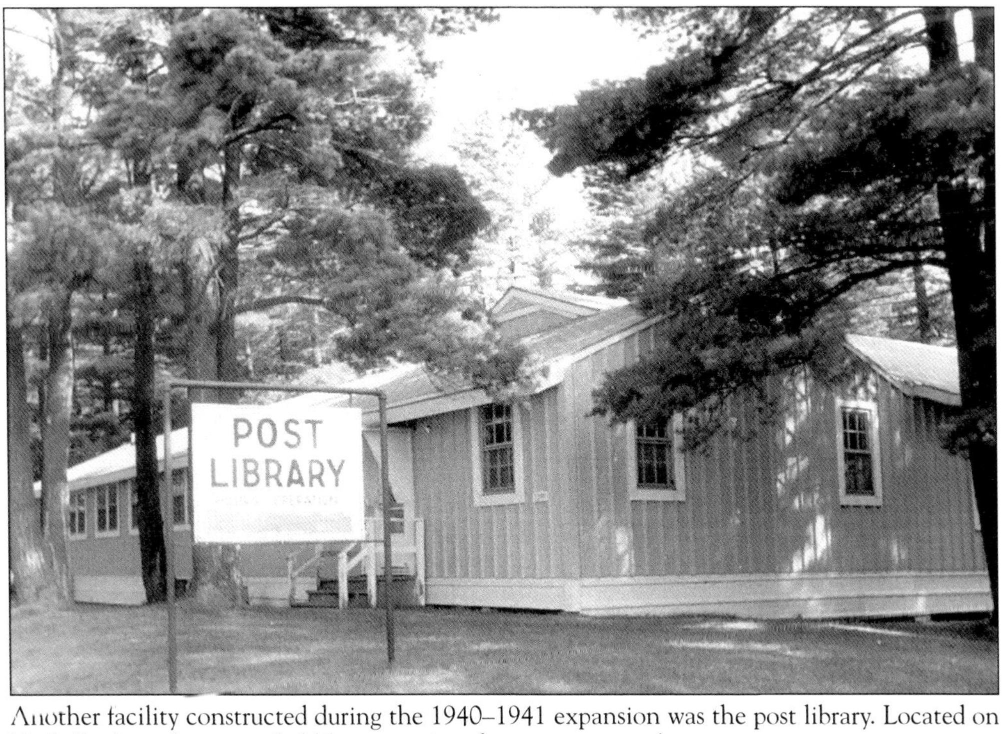

Another facility constructed during the 1940–1941 expansion was the post library. Located on Nash Boulevard, it provided library services for post personnel.

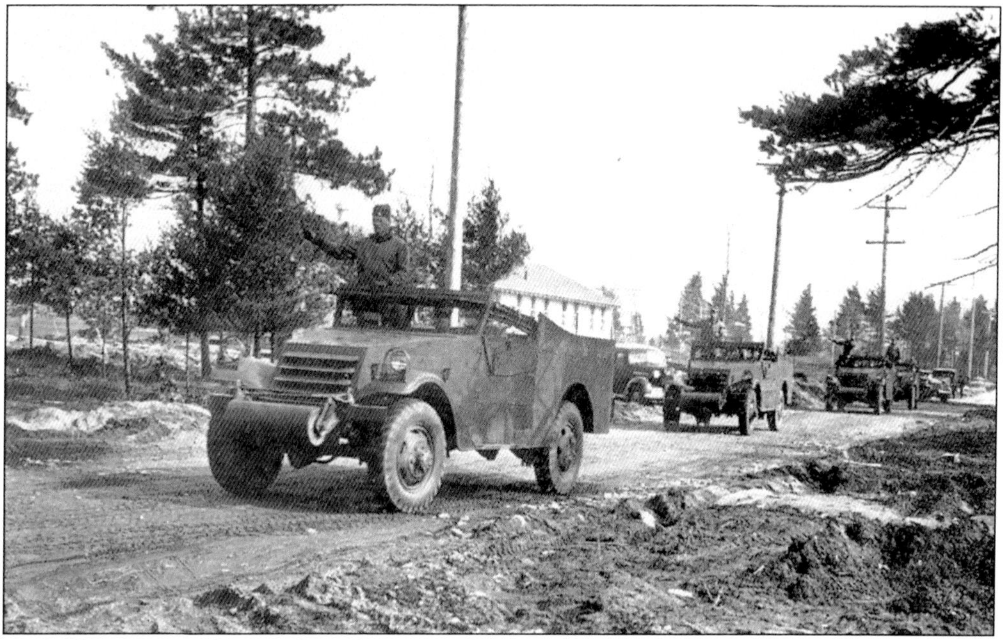

In the late spring of 1941, the 4th Armored Division of Gen. George Patton arrived at Pine Camp. For 17 months, the division trained with tanks before transferring to the 3rd Army in the European theater of operations.

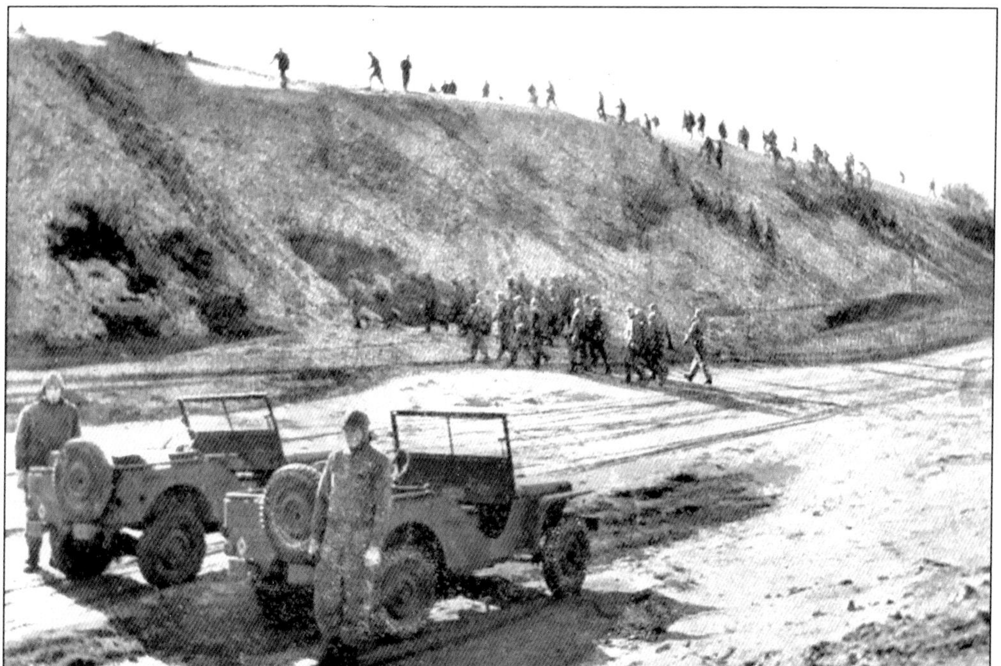

During the 1941–1942 army training exercises, Hog's Back again became the focal point for practice maneuvers.

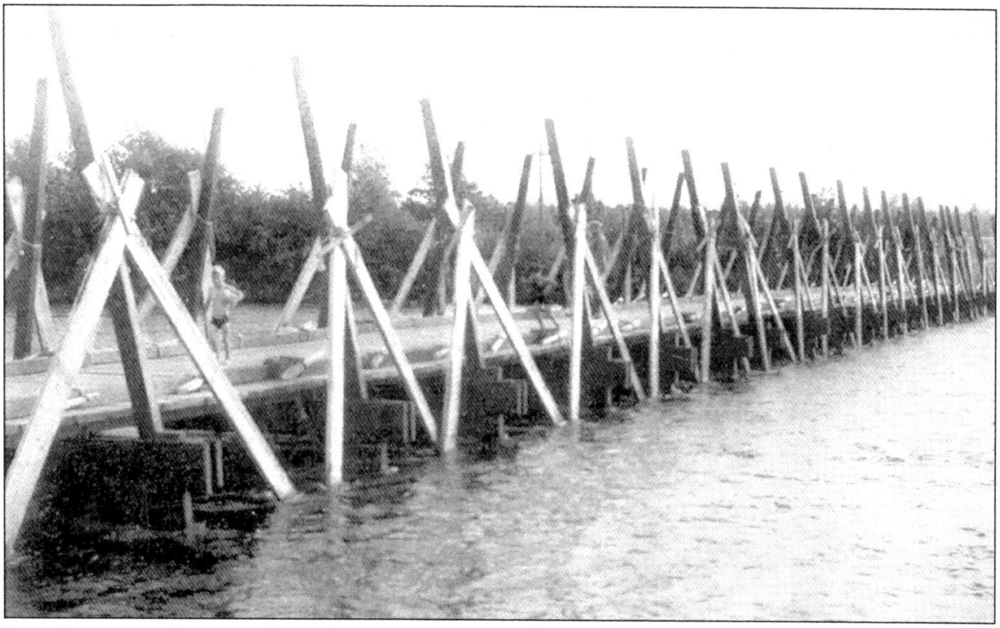

It took army engineers only six hours to construct this timber bridge capable of supporting loads up to 10 tons. Wooden uprights supporting the bridge floor were tied on by rope-bound braces, which guaranteed a girderlike rigidity.

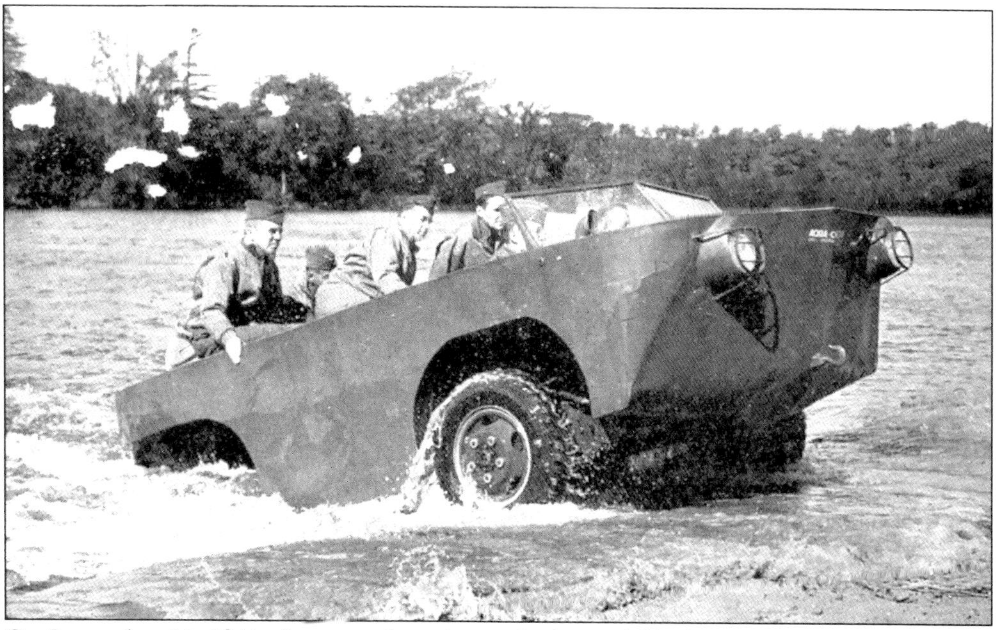

On September 12, 1941, the aqua-cheetah, a vehicle available for use on land and in water, crosses Black River near the 4th Armored Division pontoon school. Maj. Gen. Henry W. Baird and members of his staff are testing its performance.

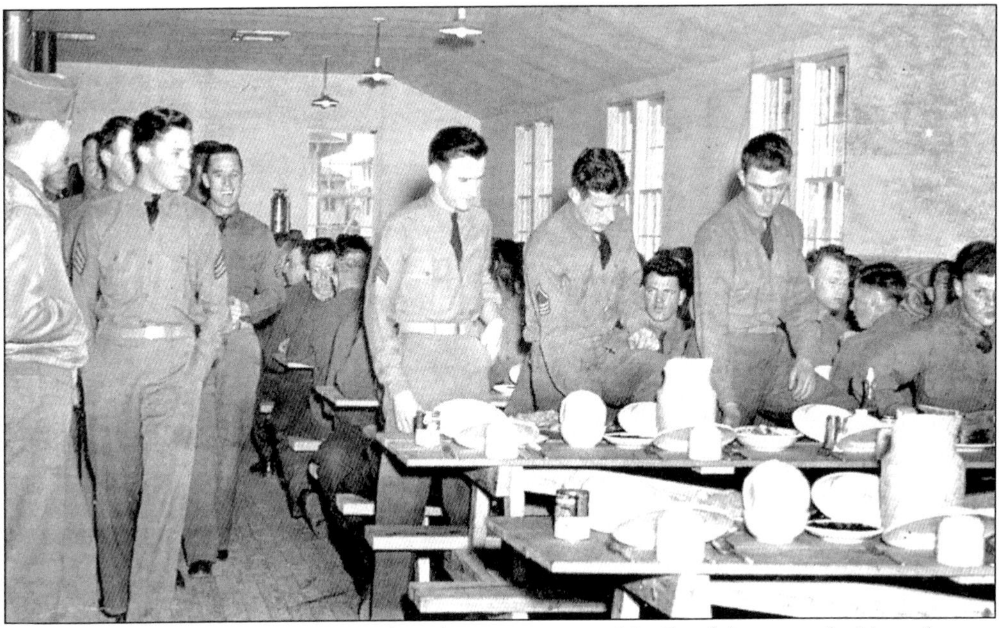

In an area mess hall, soldiers wait in line for seating at a table. Breakfast is ready. Note the can of Carnation milk at the end of the table.

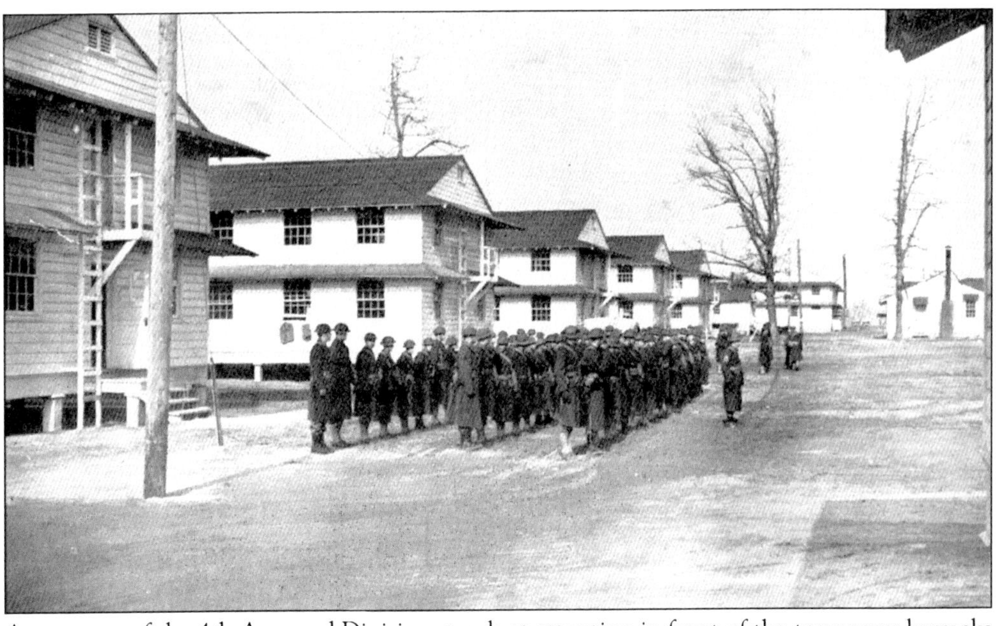

A company of the 4th Armored Division stands at attention in front of the temporary barracks built before World War II.

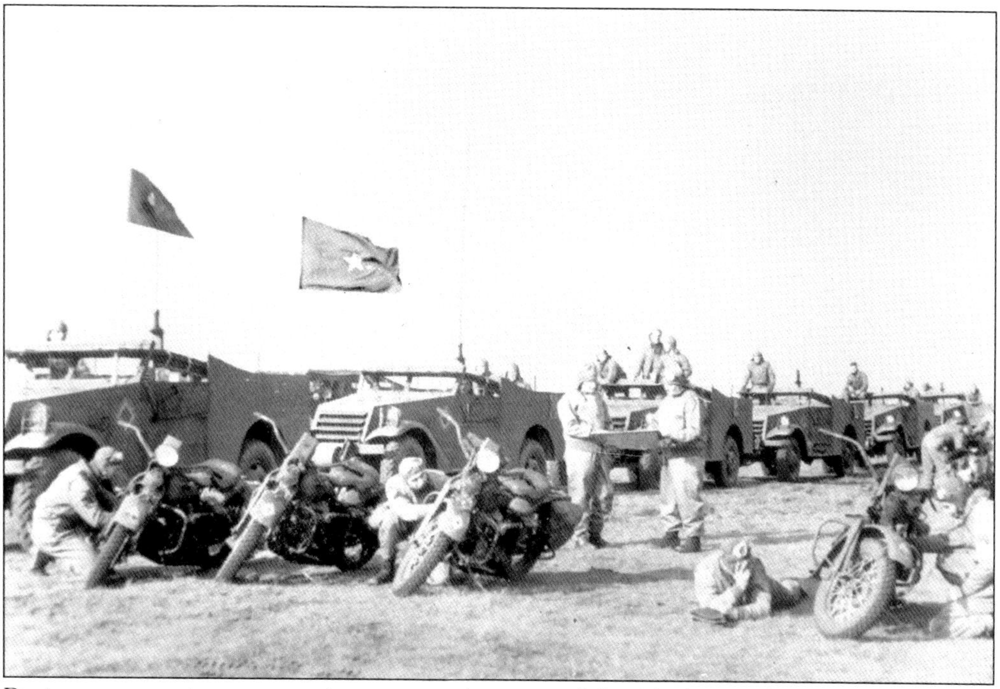

During a reconnaissance exercise, motorcycle troops of the 4th Armored Division assemble at Pine Camp. (Courtesy Jefferson County Historical Society.)

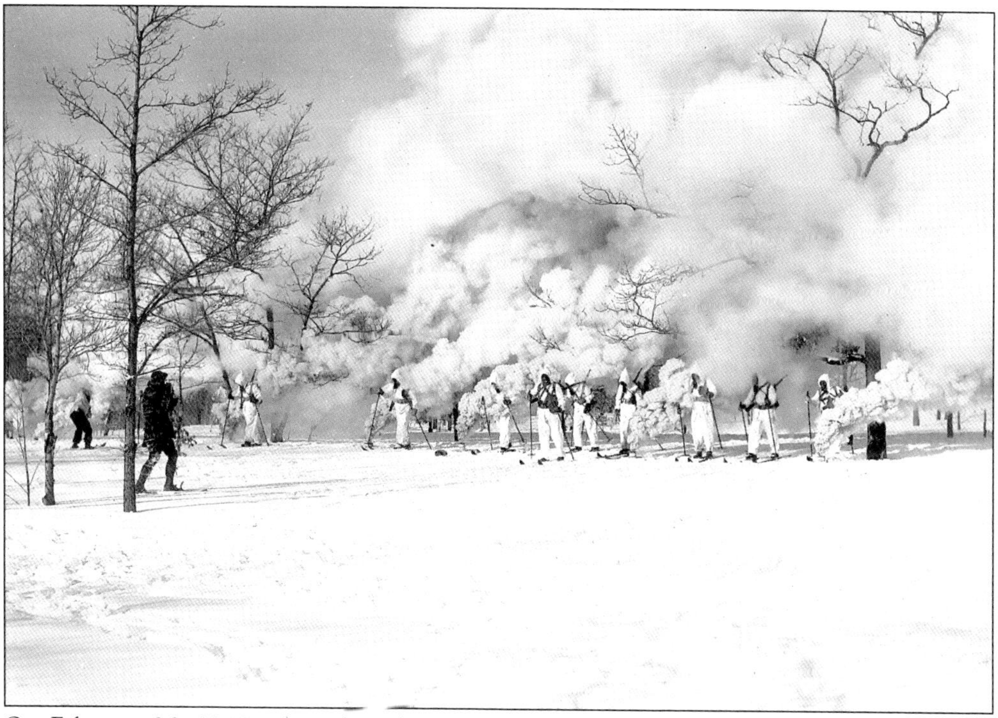

On February 26, 1940, white-shrouded ski troops of Company F, Fort Niagara, under the command of Lt. Robert Lucas, demonstrate their ability to negotiate snow-covered terrain. Equipped with gas masks, they pass through a simulated gas attack toward an imaginary enemy.

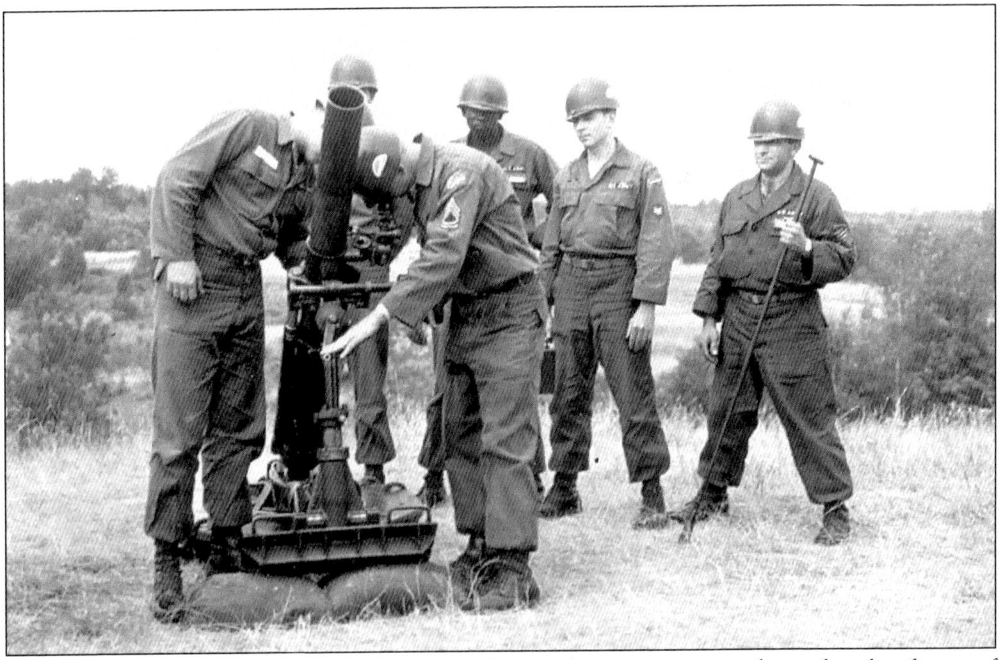

A six-man unit of the New Jersey National Guard practices procedures for the firing of a mortar.

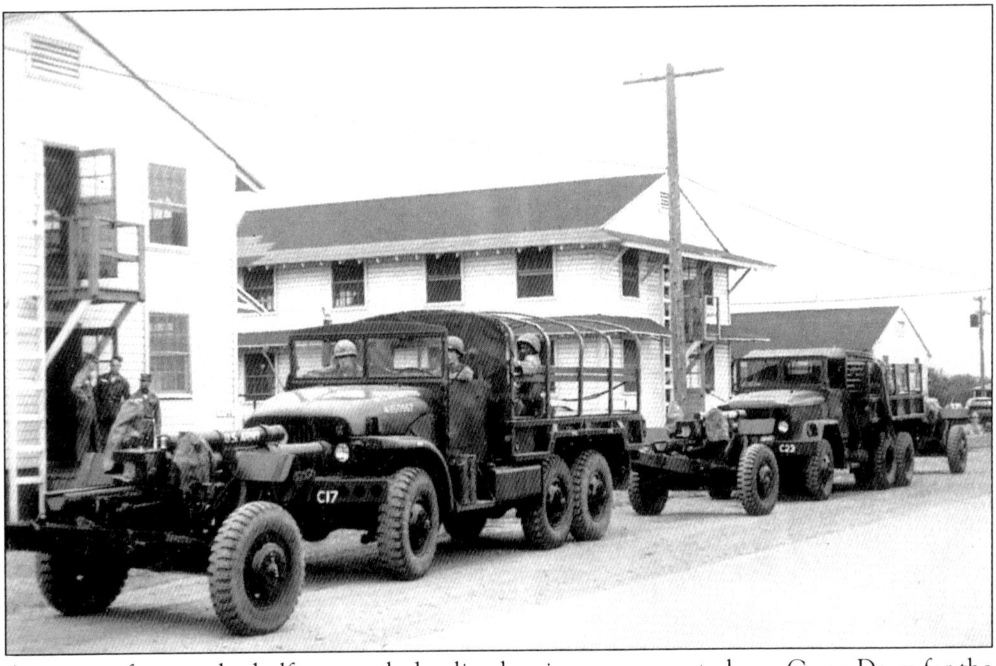

A convoy of two-and-a-half-ton trucks hauling howitzers prepares to leave Camp Drum for the firing range near the village of Antwerp. In the background are World War II barracks, which housed regular troops.

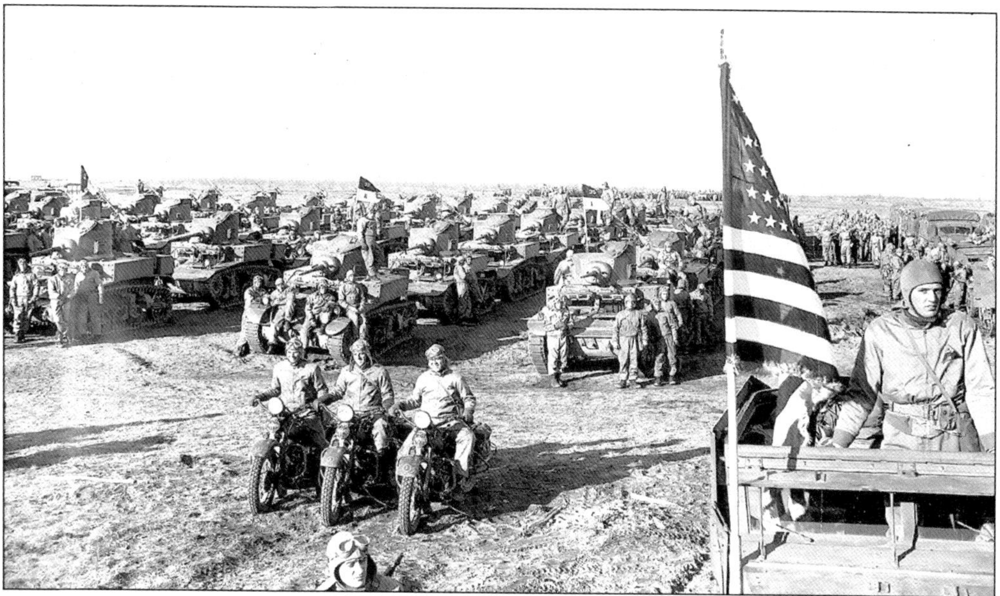

Cyclists of the 35th Armored Regiment, a unit of the 4th Armored Division, and light tanks of the 37th Armored Regiment stand ready in battle formation. (Courtesy Jefferson County Historical Society.)

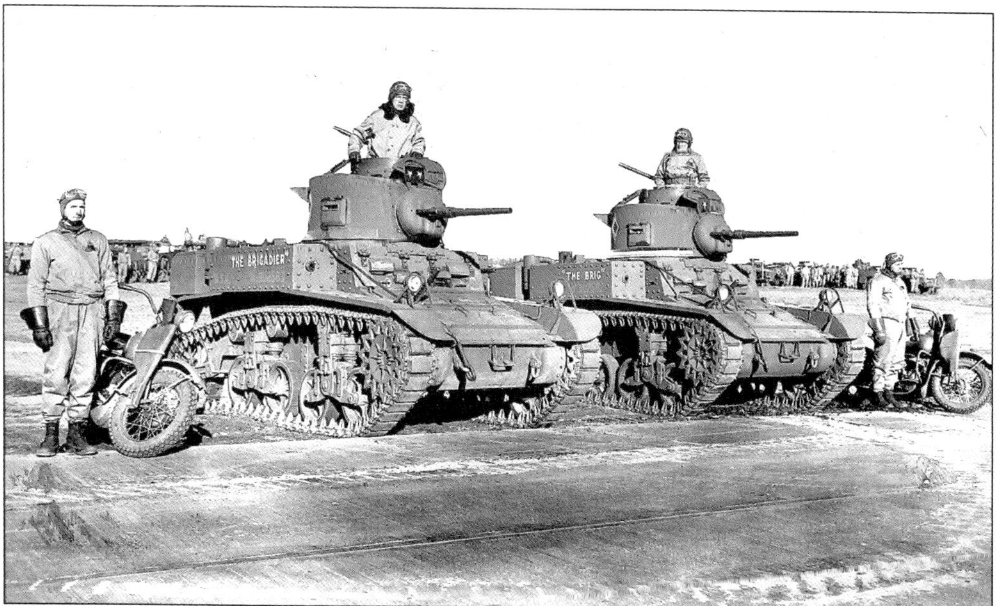

Olive green 13-ton light tanks of the 4th Armored Division replaced obsolete tanks first used in training. The tanks mounted a 37-millimeter gun. (Courtesy Jefferson County Historical Society.)

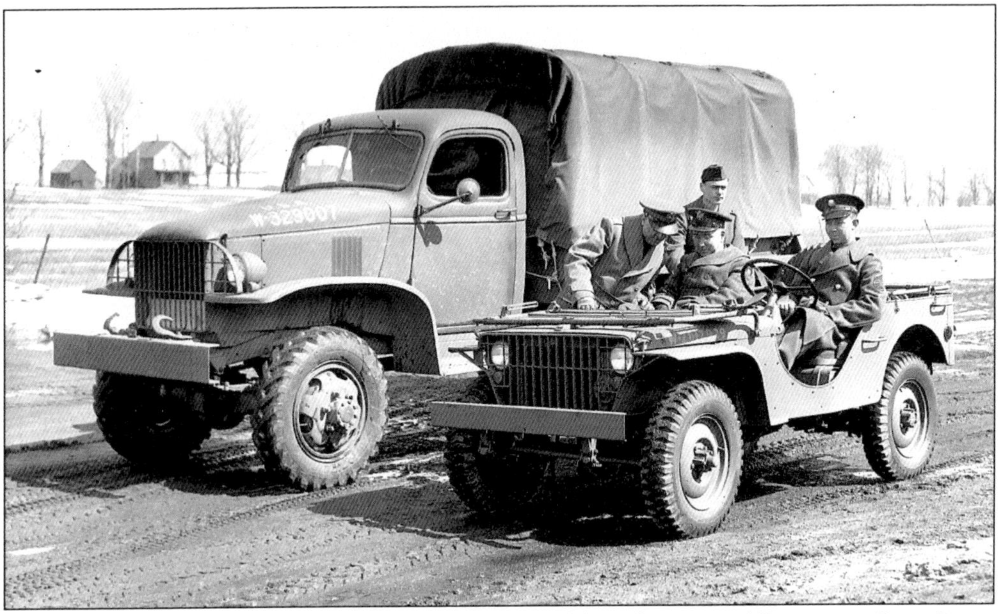

In the early spring of 1941, officers and enlisted men of the 4th Armored Division at Pine Camp tour the reservation. A supply truck and "peep" provide transportation. The peep was a quarter-ton command and reconnaissance car.

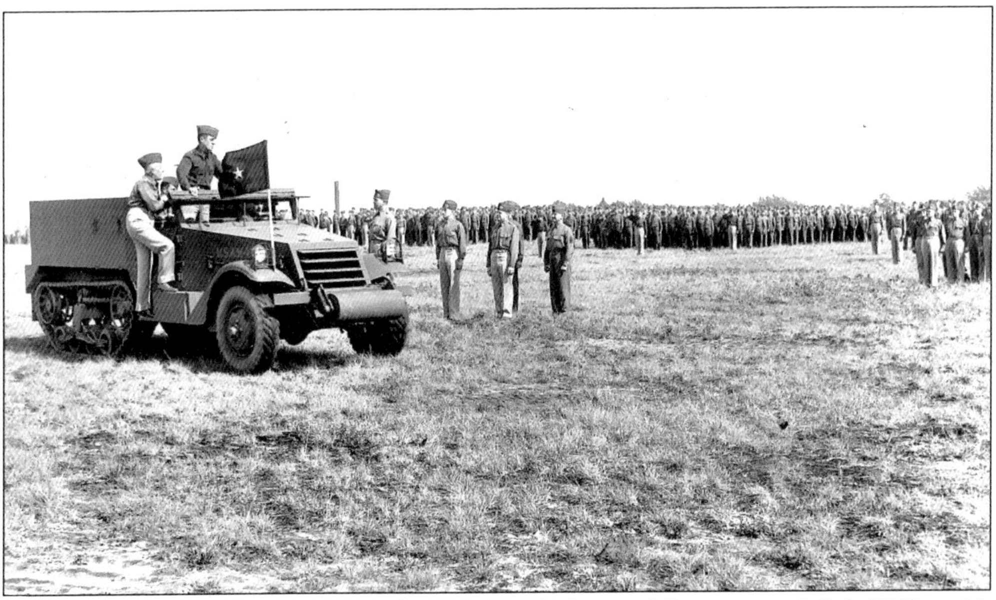

Brig. Gen. Henry W. Baird, commandant of the 4th Armored Division, and Col. William M. Grimes, commander of the 37th Armored Regiment, review the assembled troops. (Courtesy Jefferson County Historical Society.)

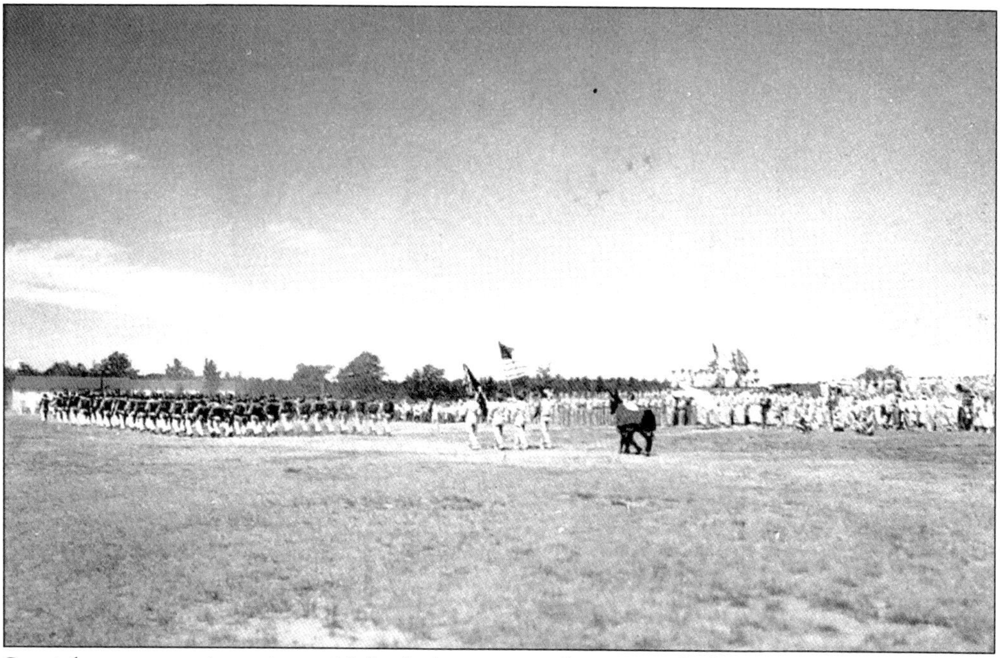

Special troops pass in review, with both the commanding general of Camp Drum and the army mule in attendance. Civilians from surrounding communities were always welcome to attend such special events.

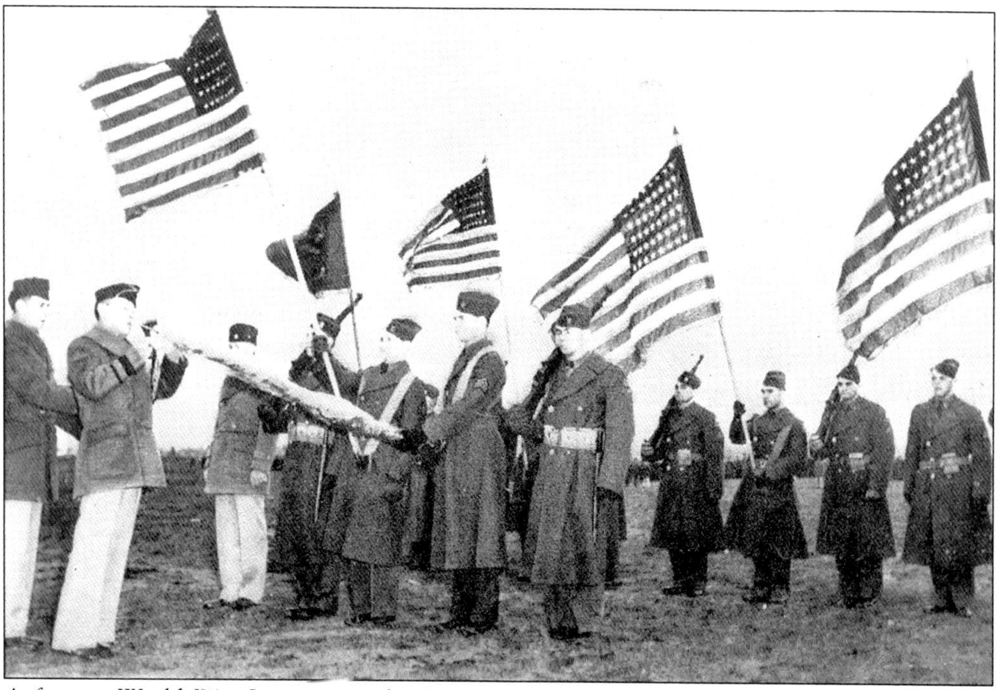

A famous World War I regiment, the 51st Armored Infantry, was reorganized on April 15, 1941, and assigned to Pine Camp. A presentation of colors ceremony welcomes the unit to the post.

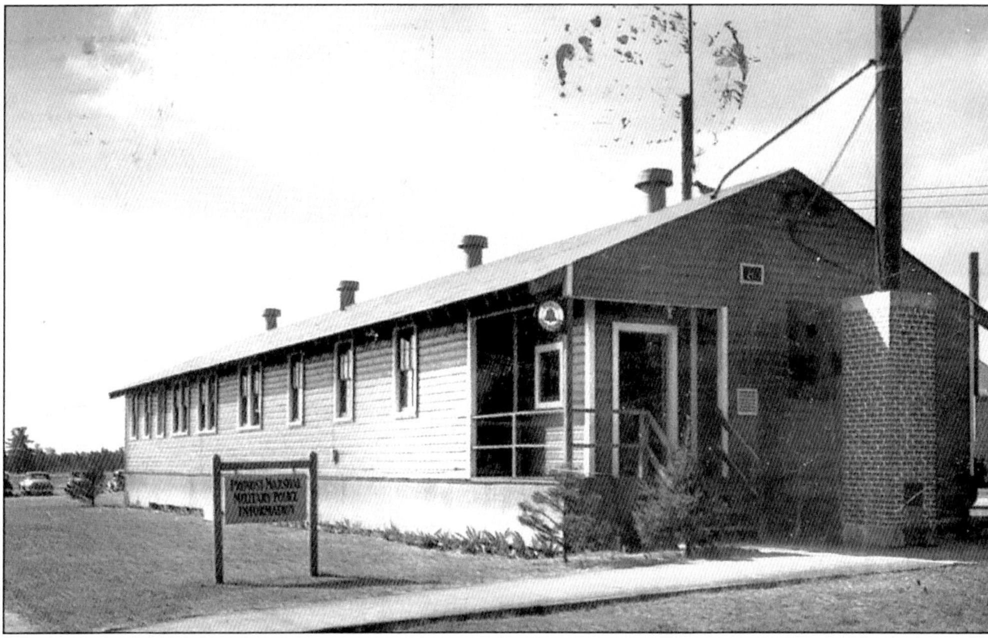

The office of the provost marshal, the chief of police for the camp, handled the tremendous task of security on the 167-square-mile military reservation. Also, military policemen were responsible for the orderly conduct of soldiers when on pass in local communities.

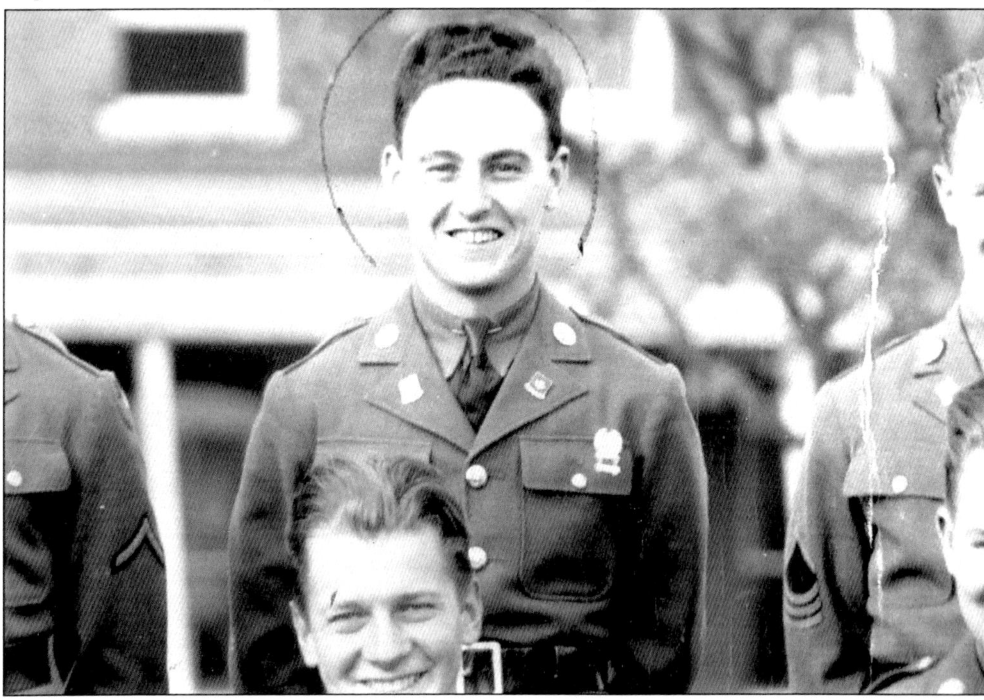

In 1936, Arthur Johns was a member of Battery D, 25th Field Artillery, stationed at Madison Barracks. In 1951, as a civilian at Camp Drum, he became provost marshal and chief of security police. He was the only civilian to hold that position in the 1st Army Command. He retired in 1970.

Three

FORT DRUM

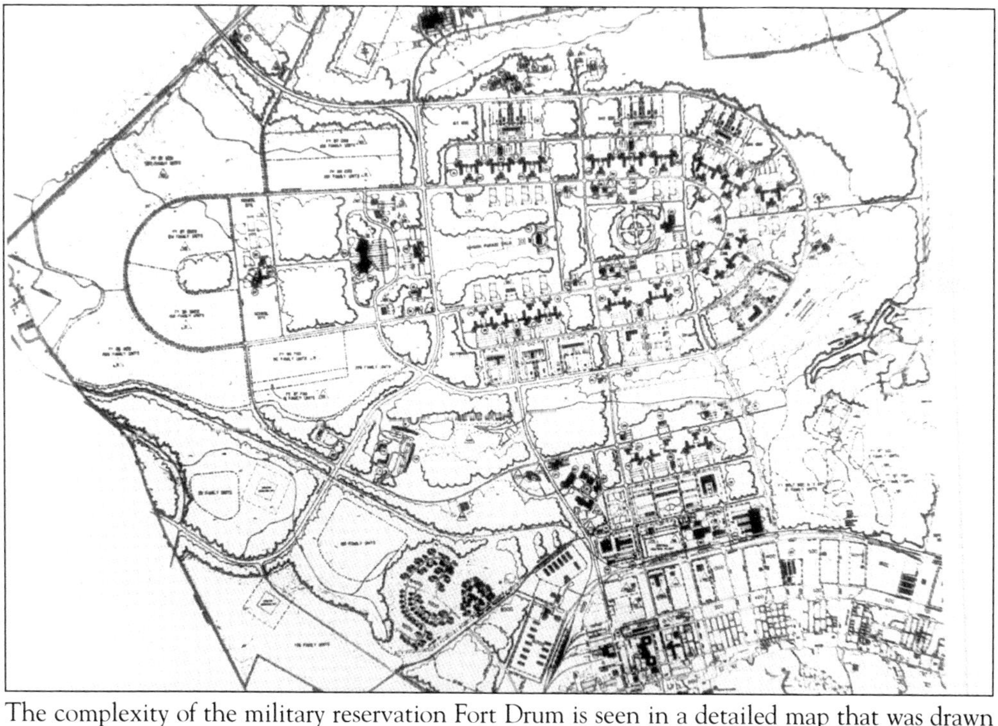

The complexity of the military reservation Fort Drum is seen in a detailed map that was drawn after the $1.3 billion expansion project between 1986 and 1992. A total of 130 new buildings and 35 miles of roads were constructed to create a facility capable of housing a light infantry division. In the foreground are buildings of the old post. The New York Army National Guard maintains the bulk of its deployable vehicles and equipment in this area. Units regularly train at the fort for weekend inactive duty training and annual training. On the left, family housing units are separated from military activities by a buffer and recreation zone. (Courtesy FDMHC.)

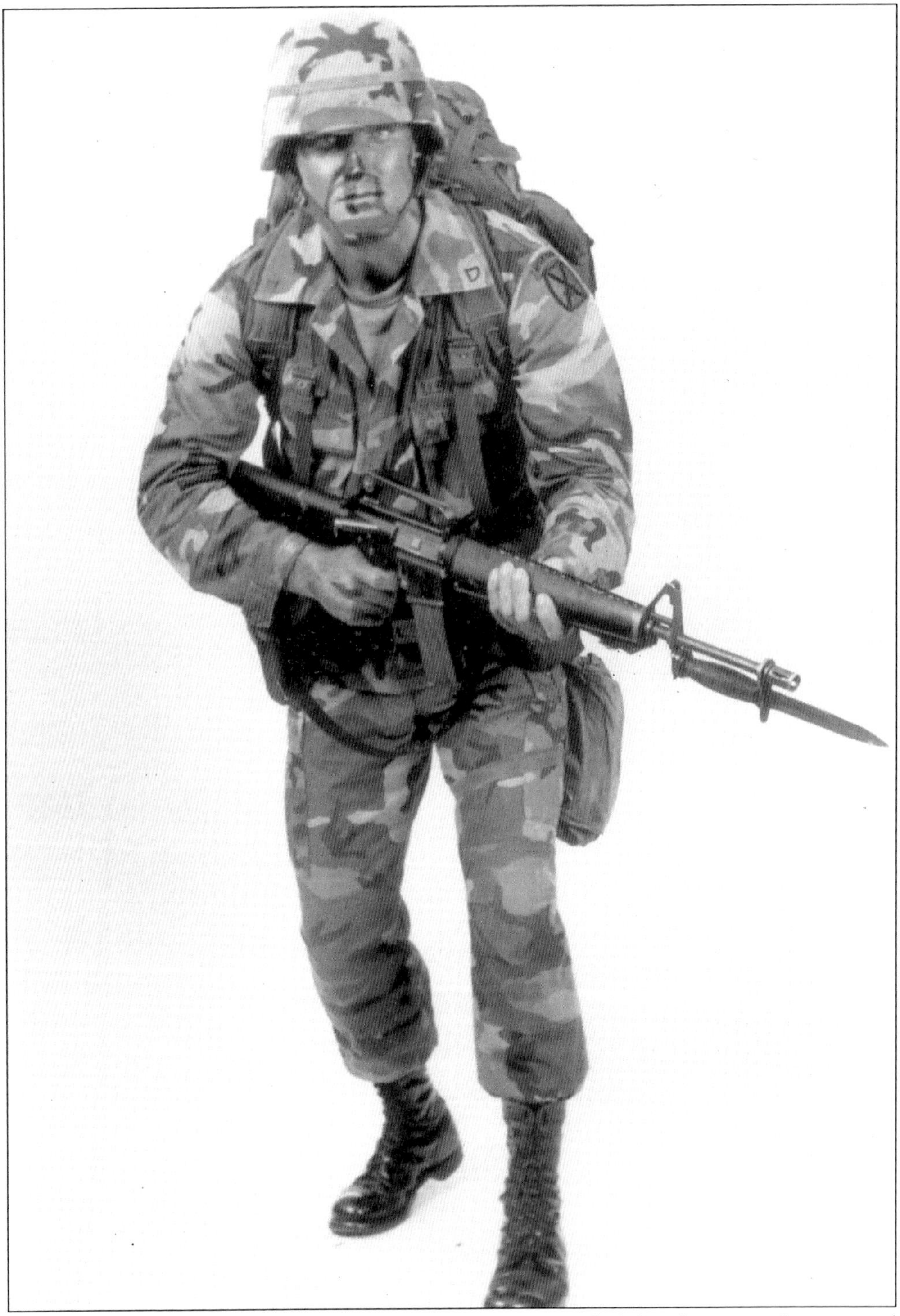

A camouflaged 10th Mountain Division soldier epitomizes today's "working army," committed to providing the United States with the best-trained light infantry division in the world. (Courtesy FDMHC.)

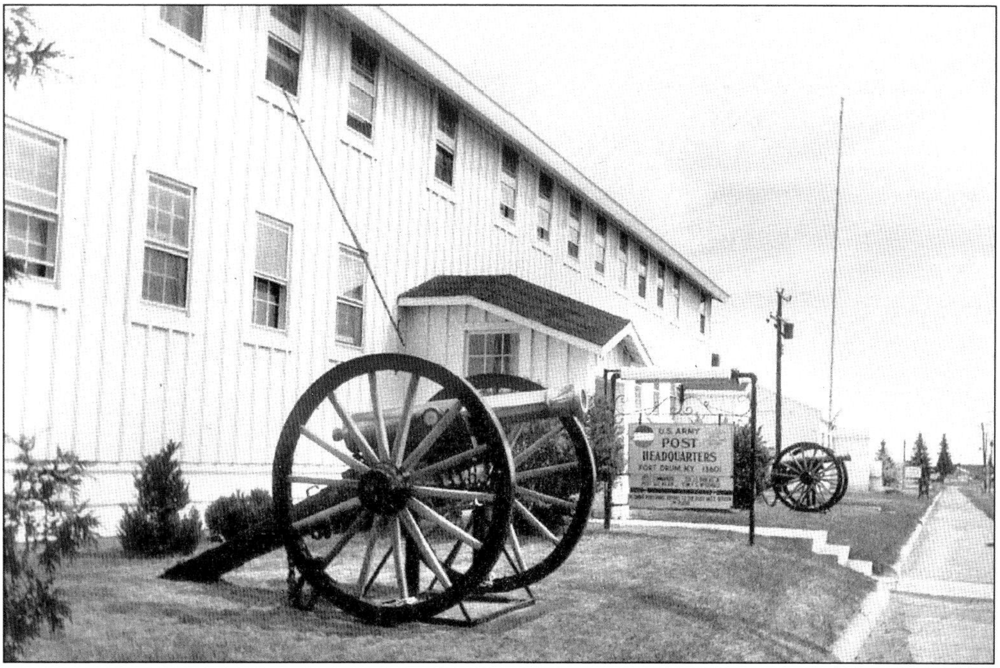

Two six-pound smooth-bore cannons, placed in front of the 1941 post headquarters, were manufactured in 1845 and 1851 by the N.P. Ames foundry of Springfield and Chicopee, Massachusetts. These cannons were presented *c.* 1940 to Fort Drum by Madison Barracks. (Courtesy FDMHC.)

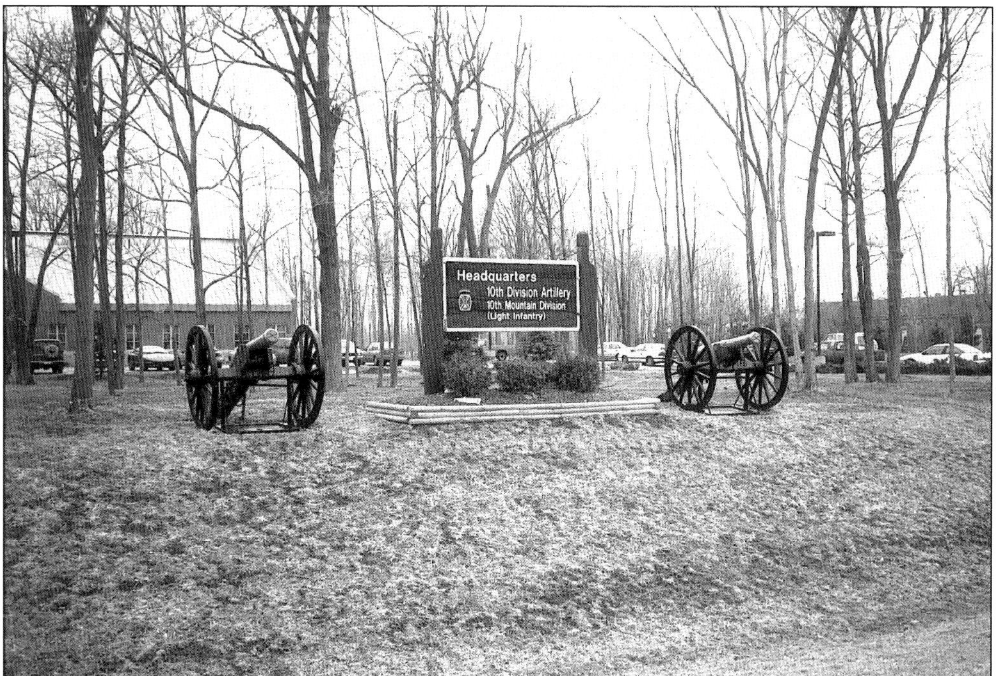

The cannons from post headquarters at Madison Barracks were relocated in front of the 10th Mountain Division Artillery headquarters on South Riva Ridge Loop at Fort Drum.

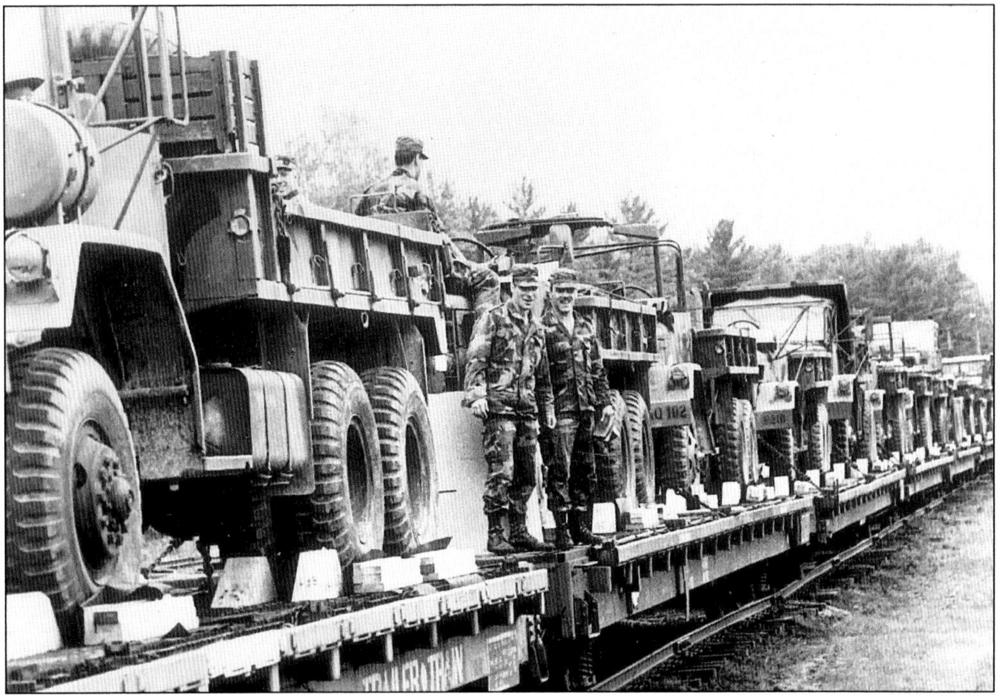

Vehicles and cargo carriers wait to be unloaded at Fort Drum. Equipment of the 194th Armored Brigade came from Fort Knox, Kentucky, for readiness command exercise Empire Glacier in 1985. (Courtesy FDMHC.)

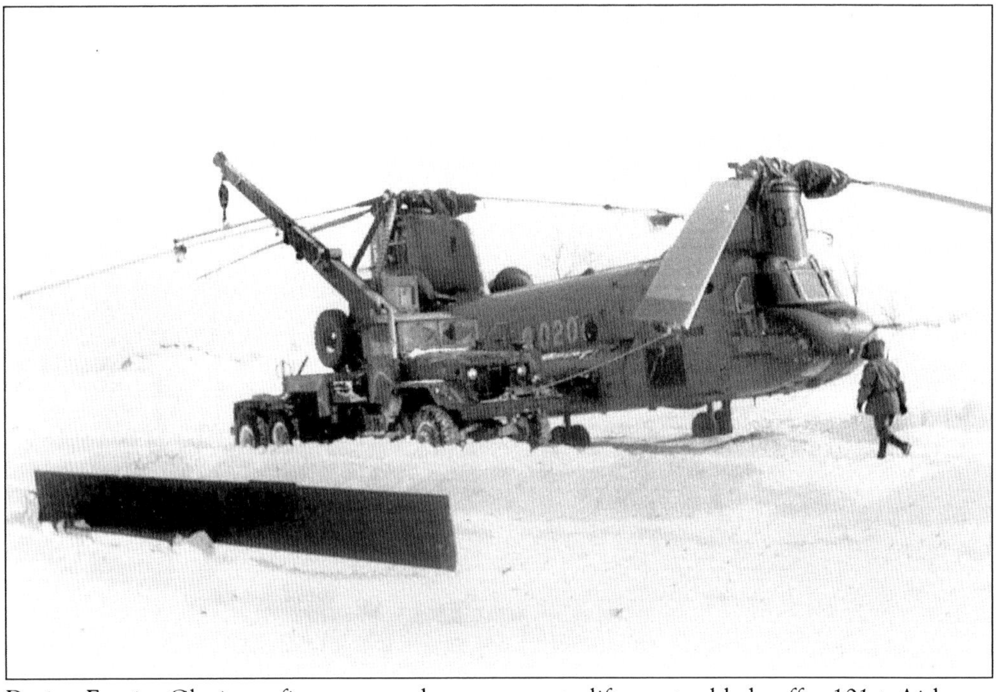

During Empire Glacier, a five-ton wrecker prepares to lift a rotor blade off a 101st Airborne Division Chinook helicopter. (Courtesy FDMHC.)

Marines receive their first skiing lessons. They are members of Battalion Landing Team, 1st Battalion 6th Marine Regiment, 2nd Marine Division, from Camp LeJeune, North Carolina. (Courtesy FDMHC.)

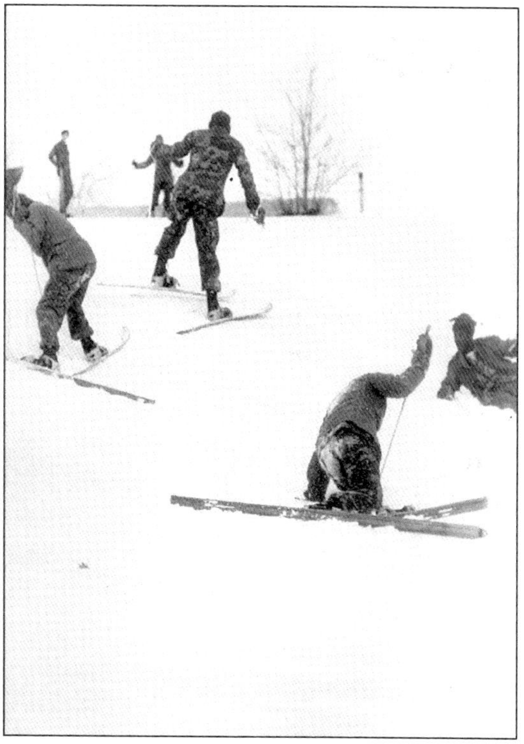

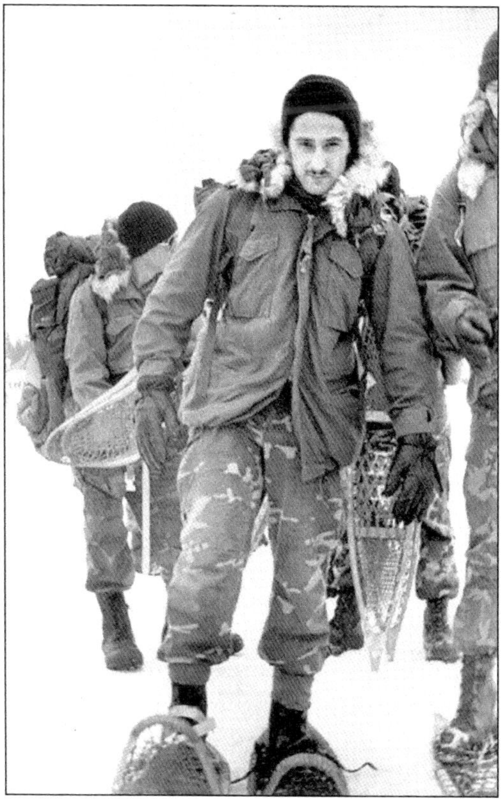

Another means of mobility during the Empire Glacier exercise is the use of snowshoes. (Courtesy FDMHC.)

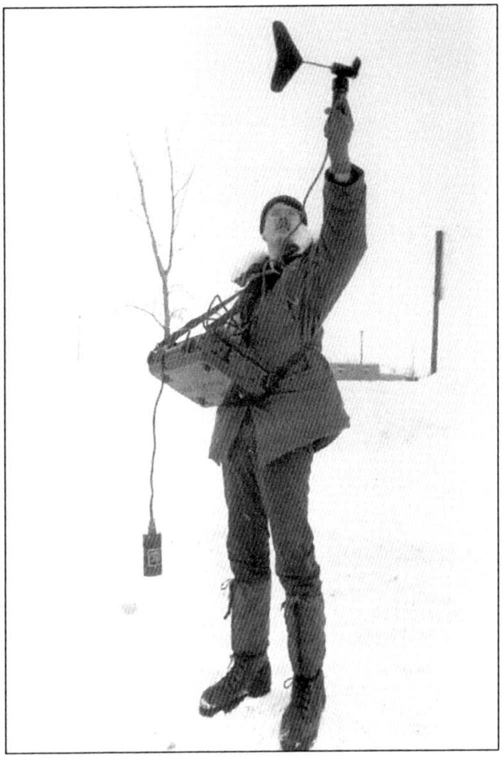

During Empire Glacier, Senior Airman Kim Runk, assigned to Detachment 3, 3rd Weather Squadron, Myrtle Beach, South Carolina, holds a TMQ 22 (tactical observation unit) to check wind speed and direction. (Courtesy FDMHC.)

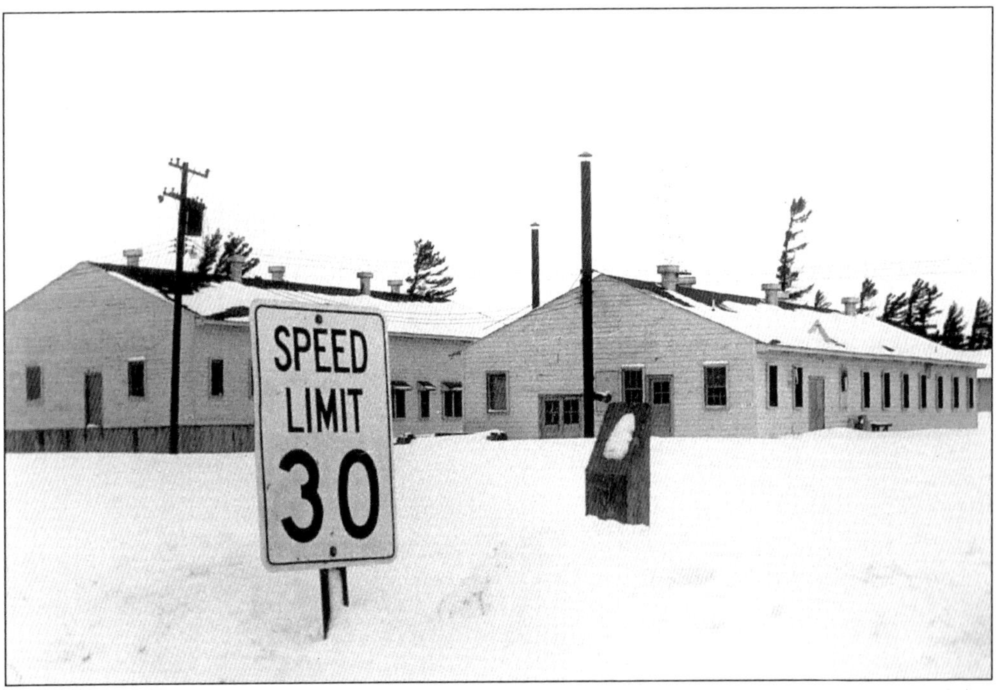

Winter conditions at Fort Drum cancel the need for a speed limit sign. (Courtesy FDMHC.)

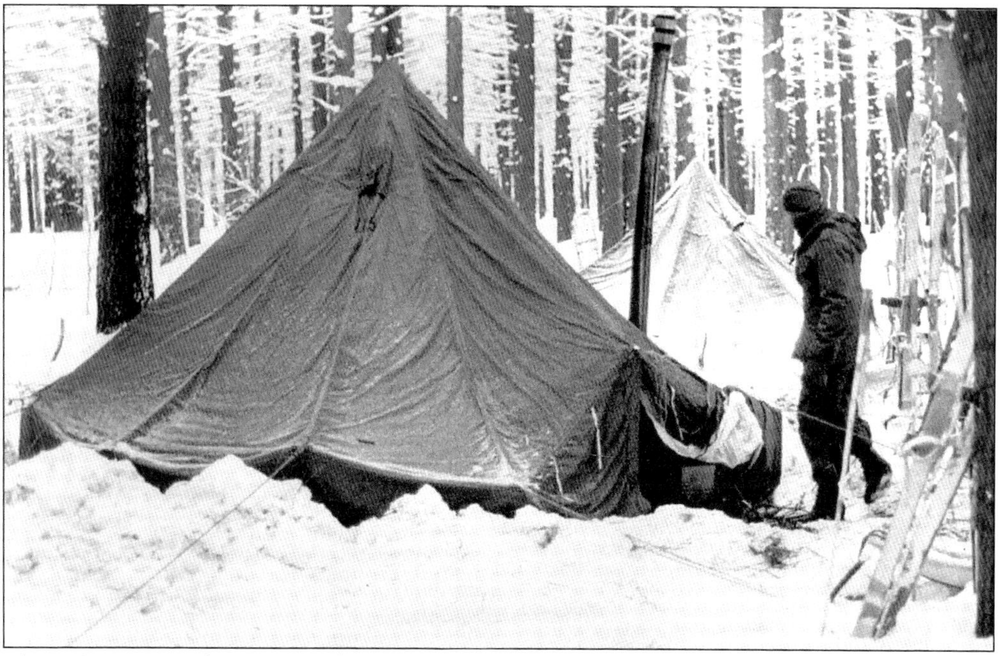

The 1978 quarters for Empire Glacier are Sibley tents. Marine Pvt. Charles Mitchell returns to his temporary home in the snow. (Courtesy FDMHC.)

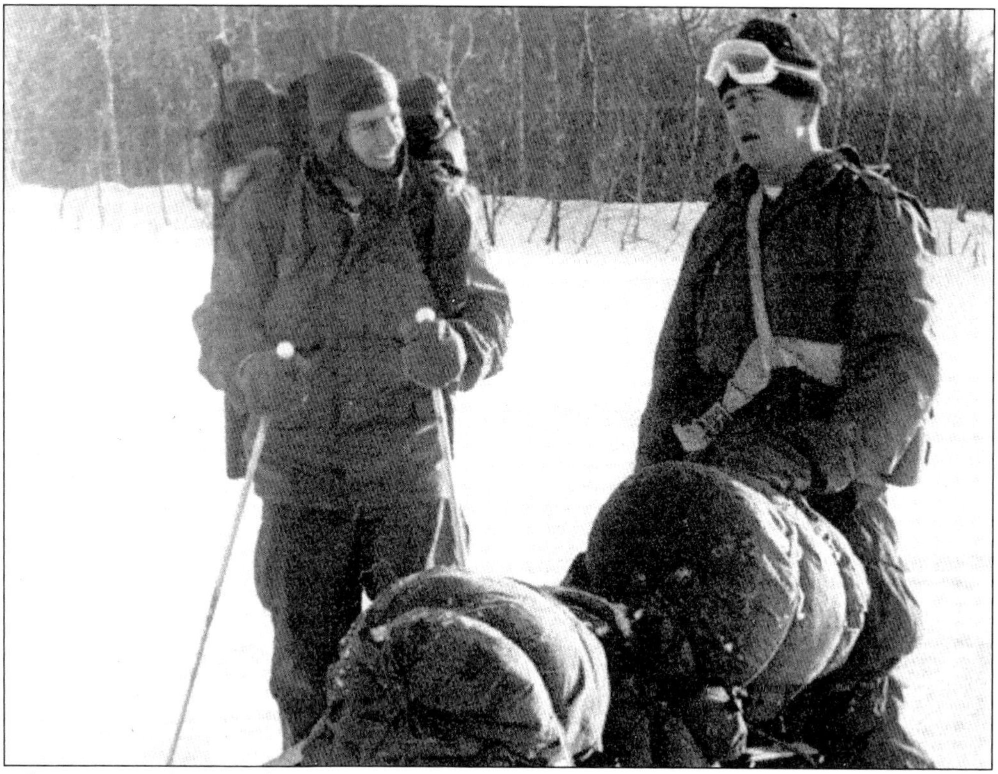

Taking part in Empire Glacier, Marines of the battalion landing team transport their gear on snow sleds. (Courtesy FDMHC.)

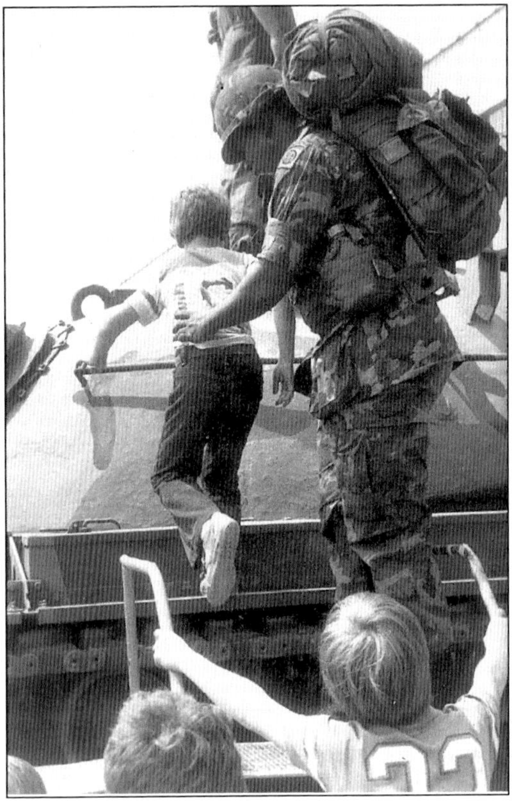

At a Fort Drum open house, children from neighboring communities clamber aboard one of the tanks on display. (Courtesy FDMHC.)

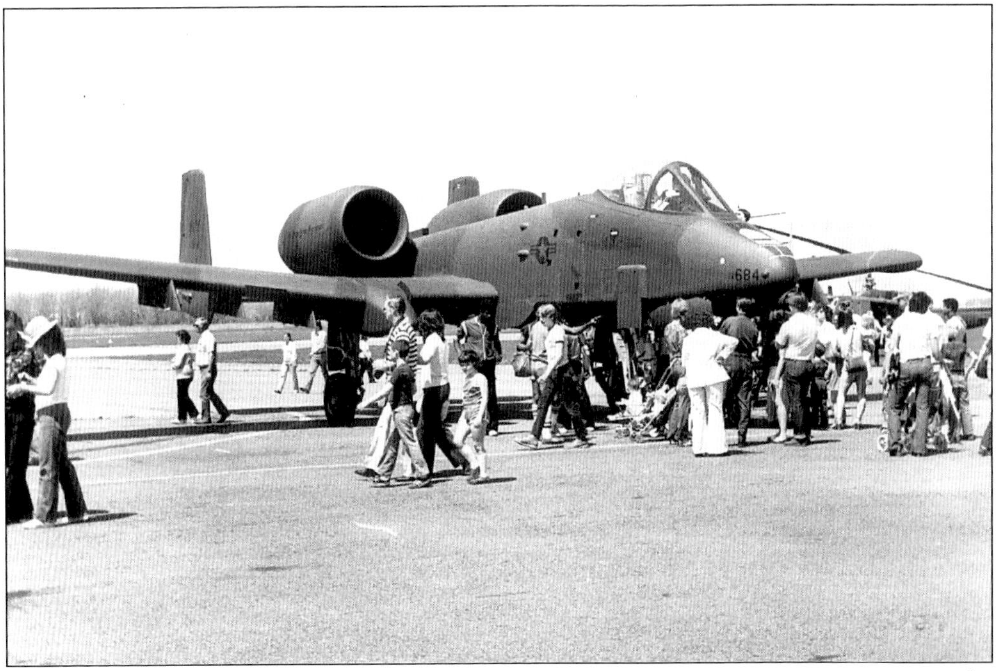

On Armed Forces Day each year, north country residents flock to the reservation to view the activities and exhibits. (Courtesy Watertown Daily Times.)

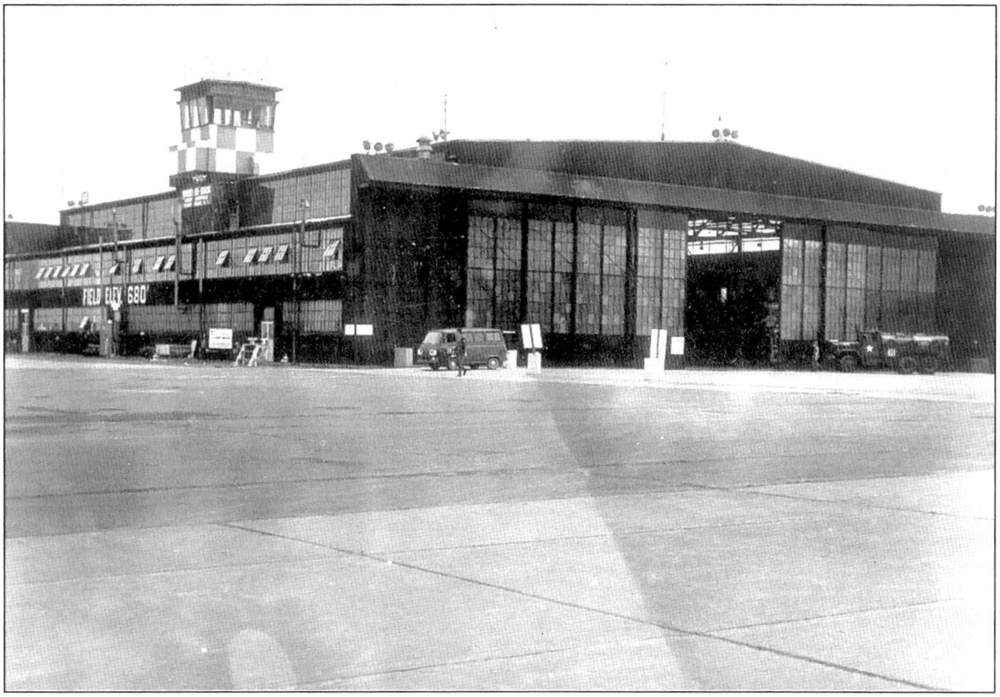

Wheeler-Sack Army Airfield hangar, completed on October 25, 1941, was first used by the 91st Observation Squadron. It remains the key transportation center located east of the World War II cantonment and northeast of the village Great Bend. (Courtesy FDMHC.)

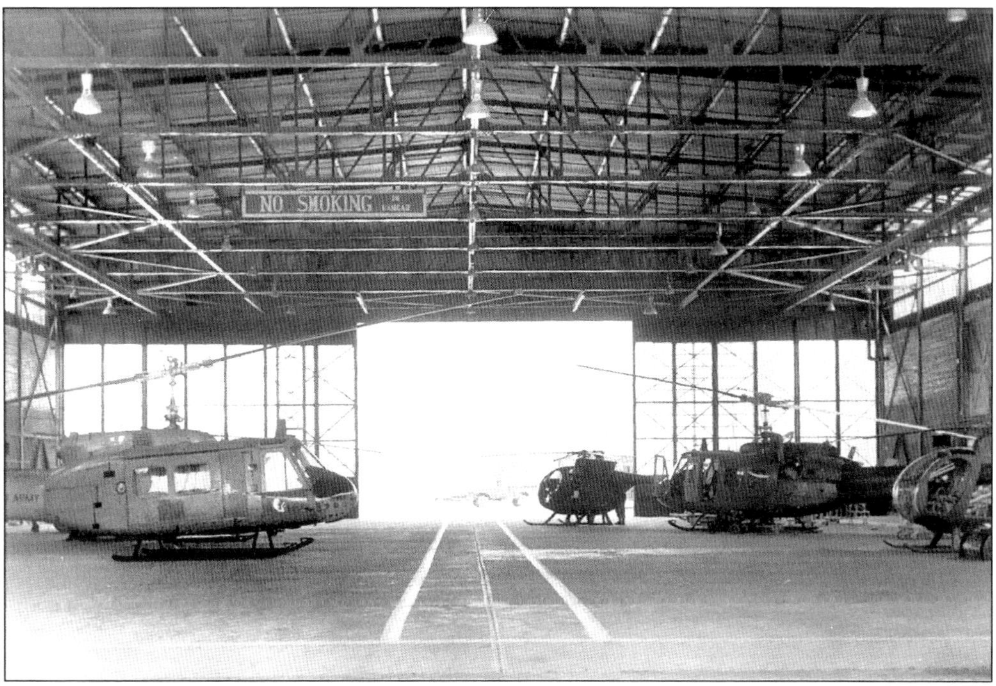

UH-IM Huey helicopters are parked in the original hangar at Wheeler-Sack Army Airfield. (Courtesy FDMHC.)

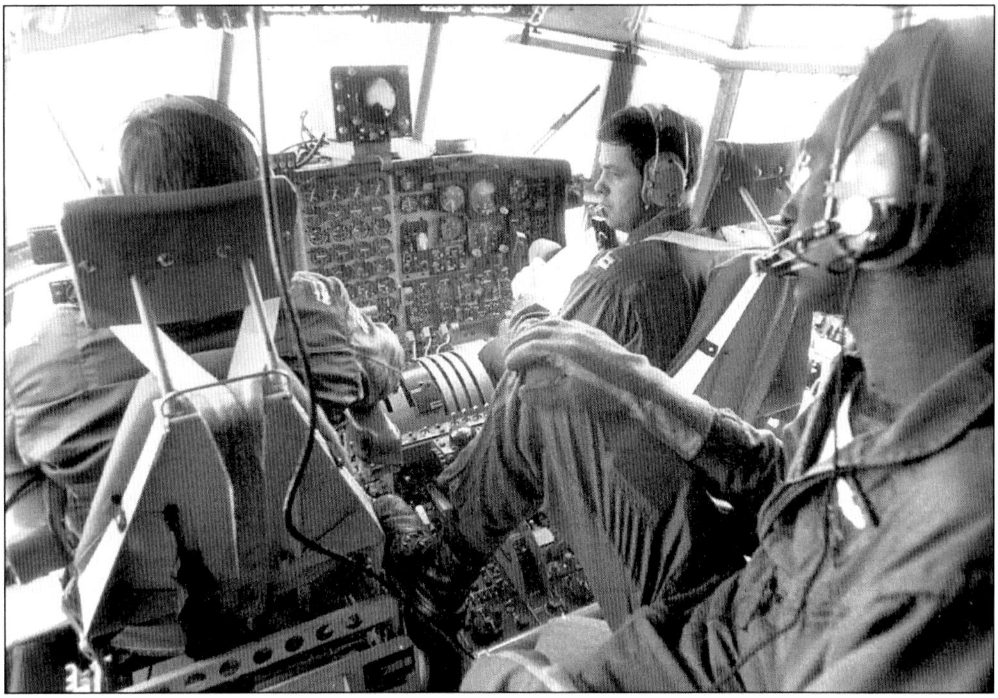

In the cockpit of a C-130, pilot and crew wait for takeoff clearance during one of the many 10th Mountain Division deployments. (Courtesy FDMHC.)

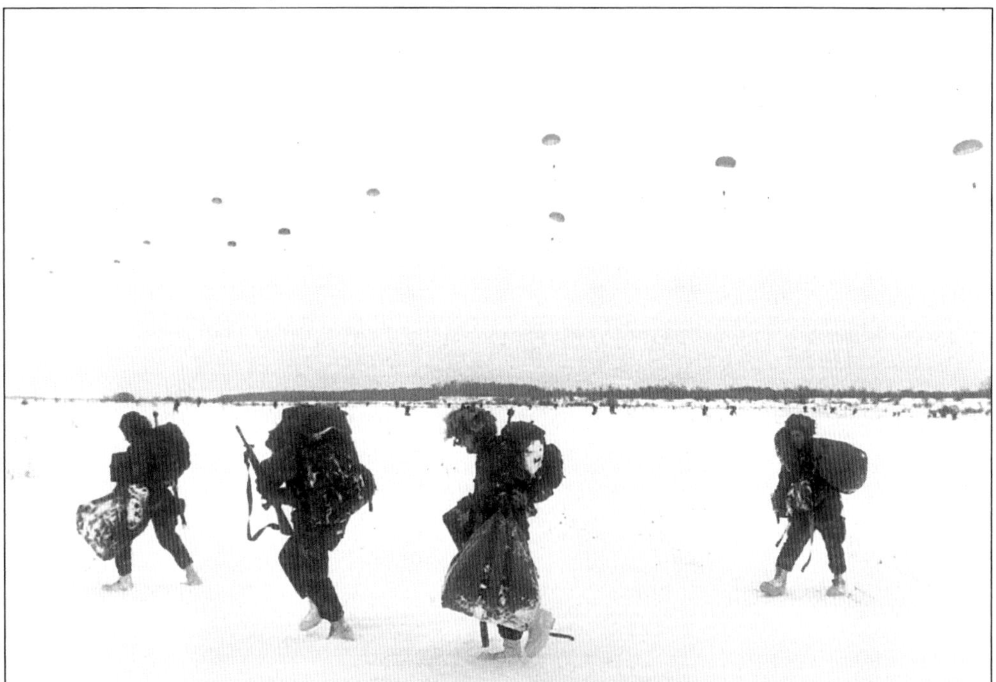

In February 1984, troops of the 82nd Airborne Division from Fort Bragg, North Carolina, drop from a C-130 aircraft onto a range near the village of Antwerp. (Courtesy Watertown Daily Times.)

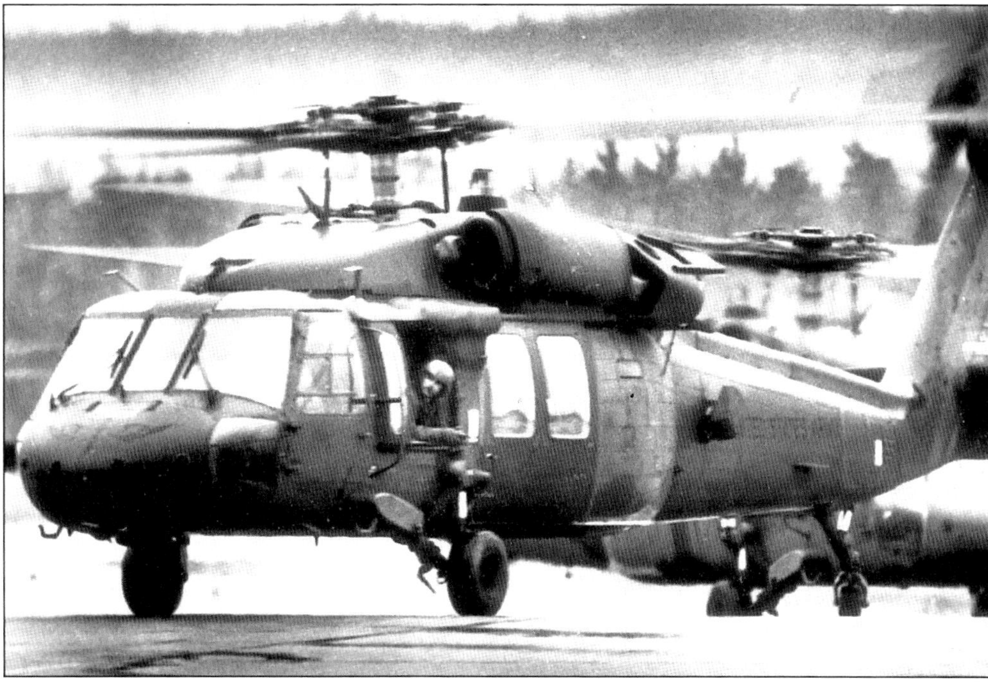

In April 1983, one of the 15 UH-60 Black Hawk helicopters arrives from Fort Ord, California. Traveling at speeds of up to 200 miles per hour and capable of carrying 8,000 pounds of load, they are stationed at Wheeler-Sack Army Airfield as part of the 10th Aviation Brigade. (Courtesy Watertown Daily Times.)

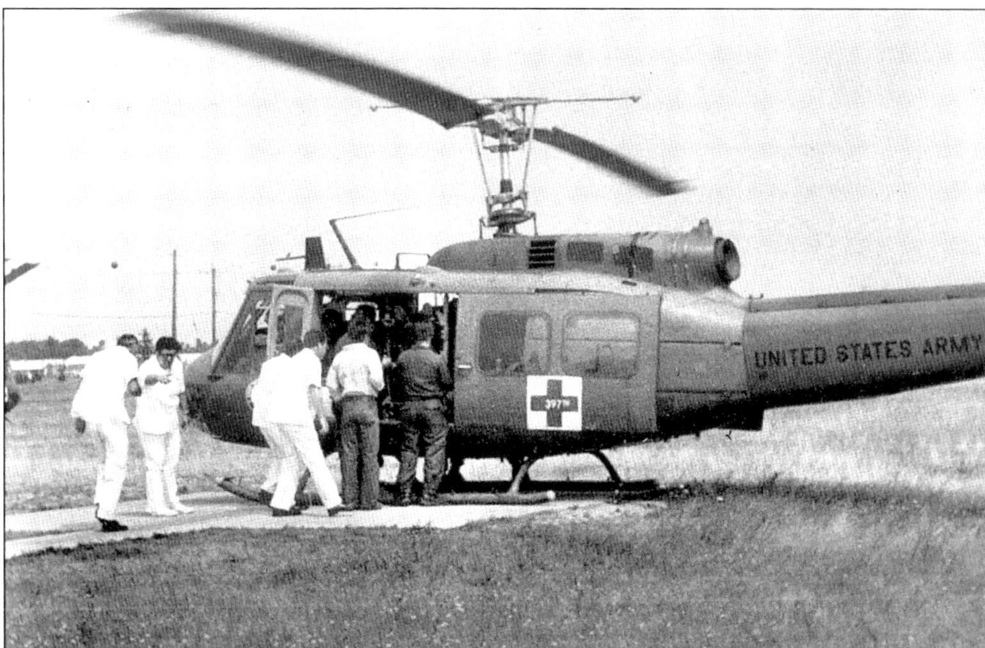

UH-IM Huey helicopters transport patients to Samaritan Medical Center in Watertown. (Courtesy FDMHC.)

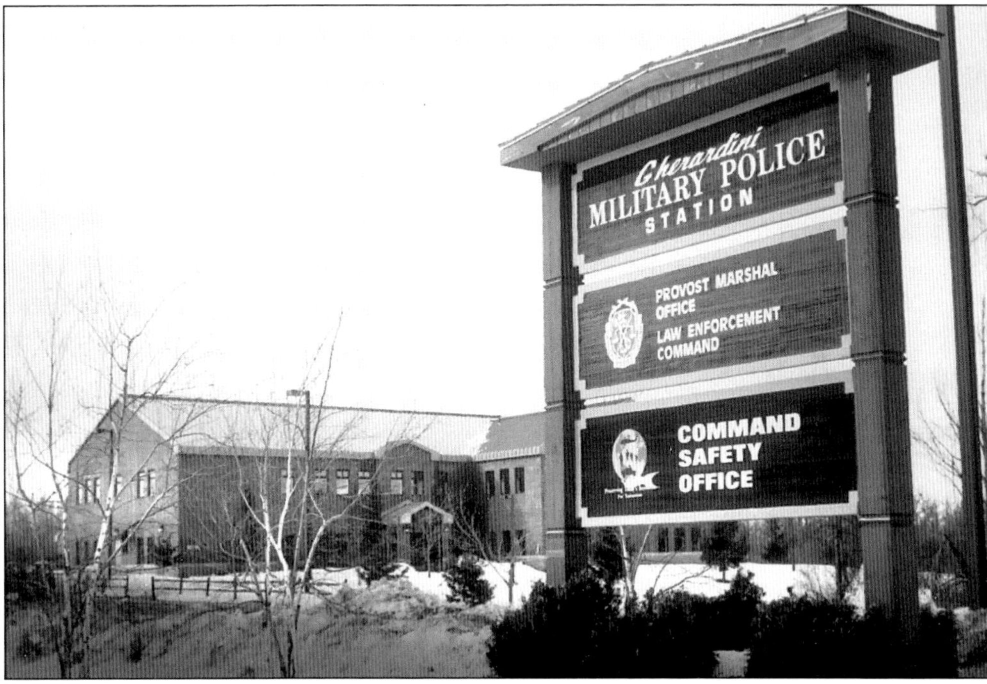

Headquarters for personnel responsible for civilian and military security are concentrated in this building on Mount Belvedere Boulevard.

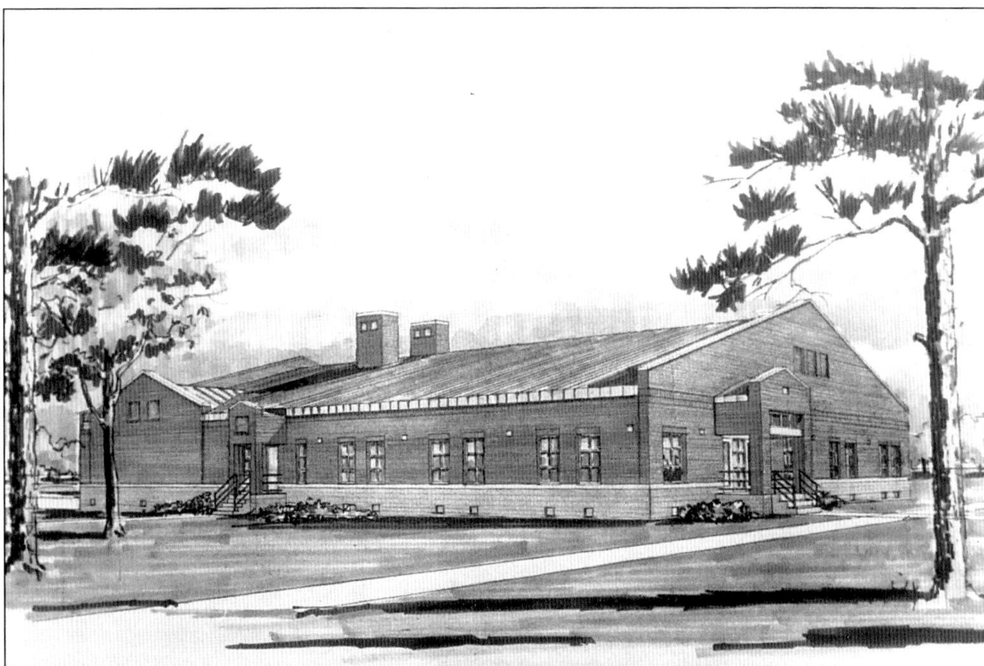

One of the many buildings constructed in the $1.3 billion expansion between 1987 and 1991 is the First Infantry Brigade dining hall. This 18,000-square-foot facility serves 651 to 1,000 personnel. (Courtesy Watertown Daily Times.)

The Family Readiness Center, located at the intersection of Po Valley Road and First Street, serves as a hub for family support during deployments. A communication center with six e-mail stations and two video-teleconference centers provides the family and deployed soldier instant contact.

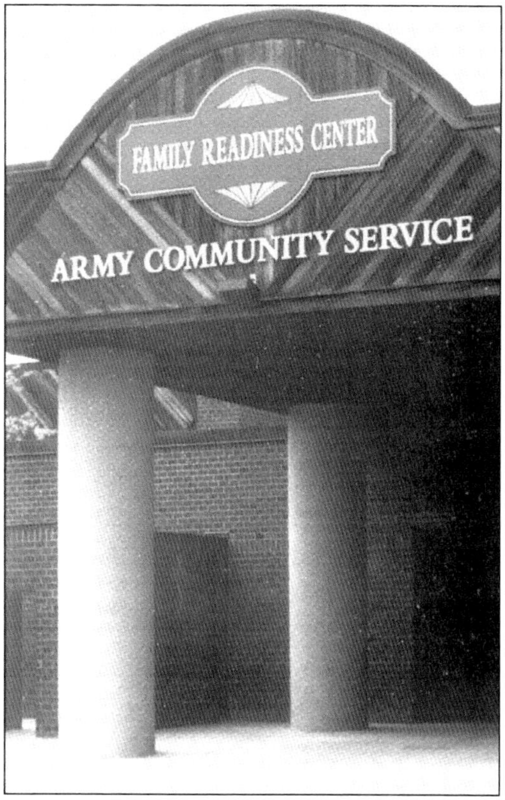

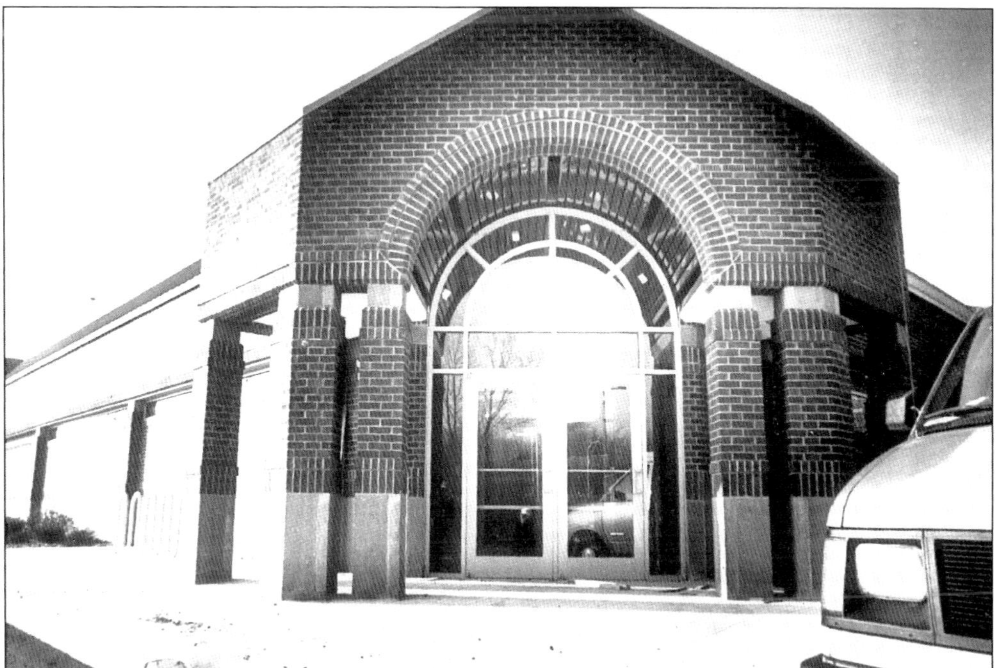

Located near Gate No. 1, at the intersection of North Memorial Drive and Chapel Drive, is a branch exchange convenience store with gas station. (Courtesy Watertown Daily Times.)

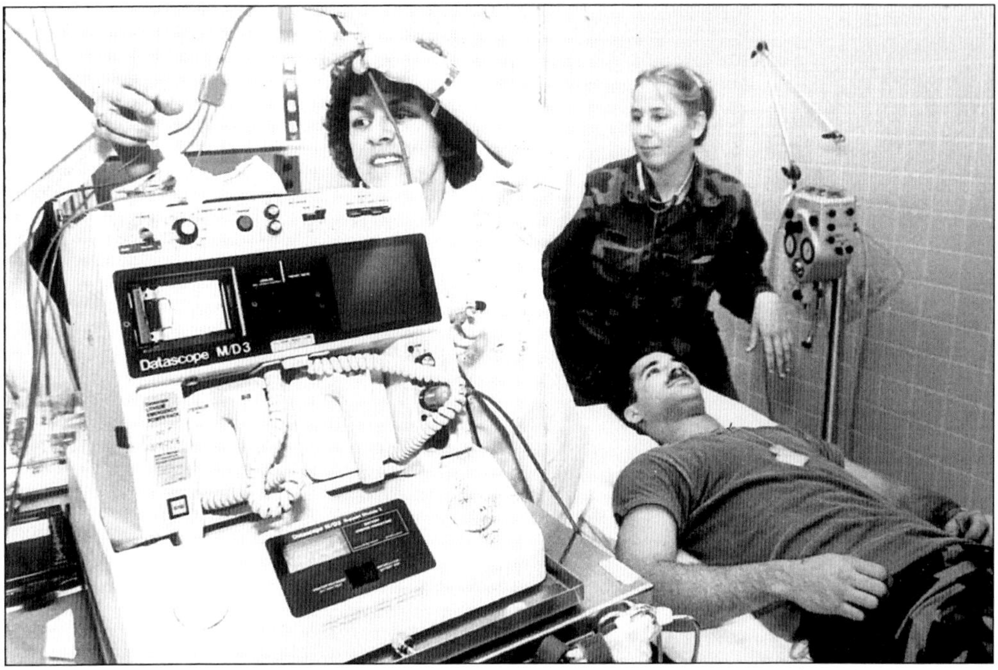

On December 13, 1984, emergency room supervisor Sharon Carlisle and medic EMT Pfc. Samantha Evers prepare to take an electrocardiogram. (Courtesy Watertown Daily Times.)

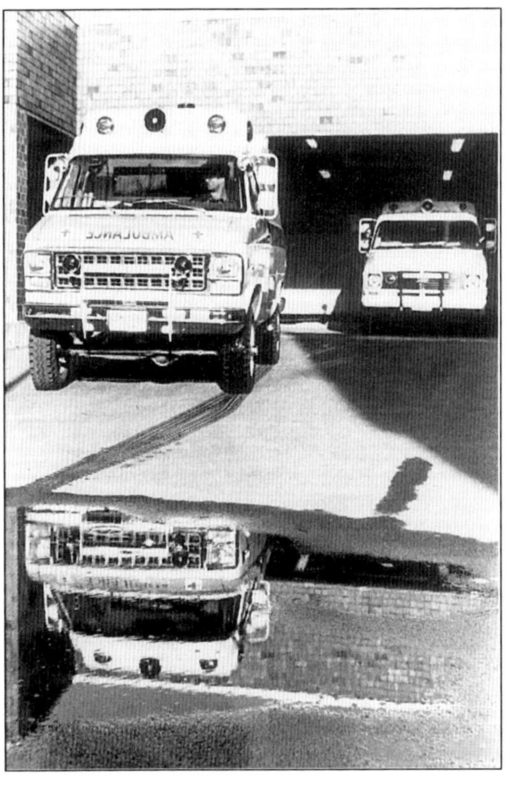

Wilcox Hospital clinic staff members provide care for army personnel and families. An ambulance returns to the clinic garage. (Courtesy Watertown Daily Times.)

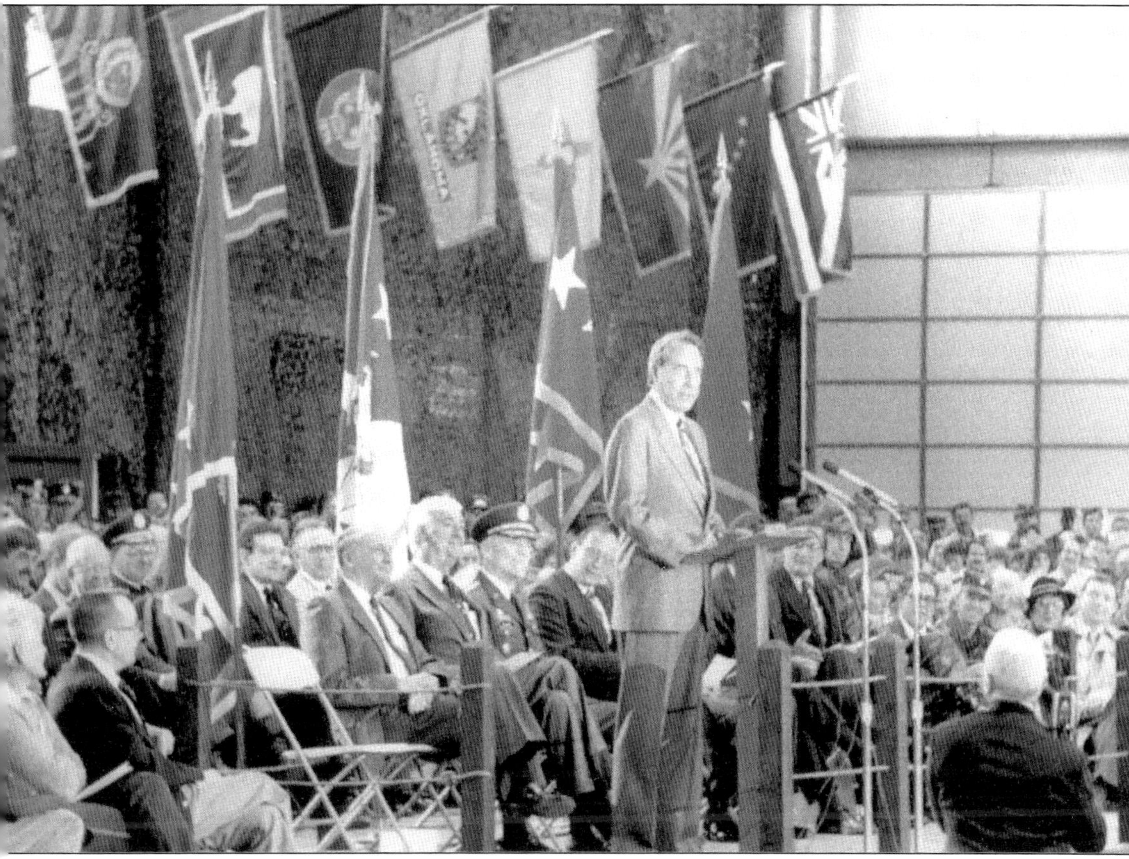

On February 13, 1985, at the activation ceremony, more than 1,500 people gathered to witness the 10th Mountain Division Light Infantry receive its newly made flag. The flag was made by the Institute of Heraldry, Cameron Station, Virginia. Sen. Bob Dole, a World War II veteran of the 10th Mountain Division, addresses 100 veterans of the division, along with a host of elected, invited, and uniformed dignitaries. Ceremonies were held in a hangar at Wheeler-Sack Army Airfield. Camouflaged netting covering the ceiling and walls was strung with a variety of flags. At 10:15 a.m., after four cannons fired a salute, Gen. Robert W. Sennewald, commander of the U.S. Forces Command, passed the colors to Gen. William Carpenter, division commander. Ceremonies concluded with "Ruffles and Flourishes," played by the 18th Army Band, Fort Devens, Massachusetts. A 19-gun salute was fired from a 105-millimeter howitzer manned by a salute battery from Headquarters Company Troop Command, Aberdeen Proving Ground, Maryland. (Courtesy FDMHC.)

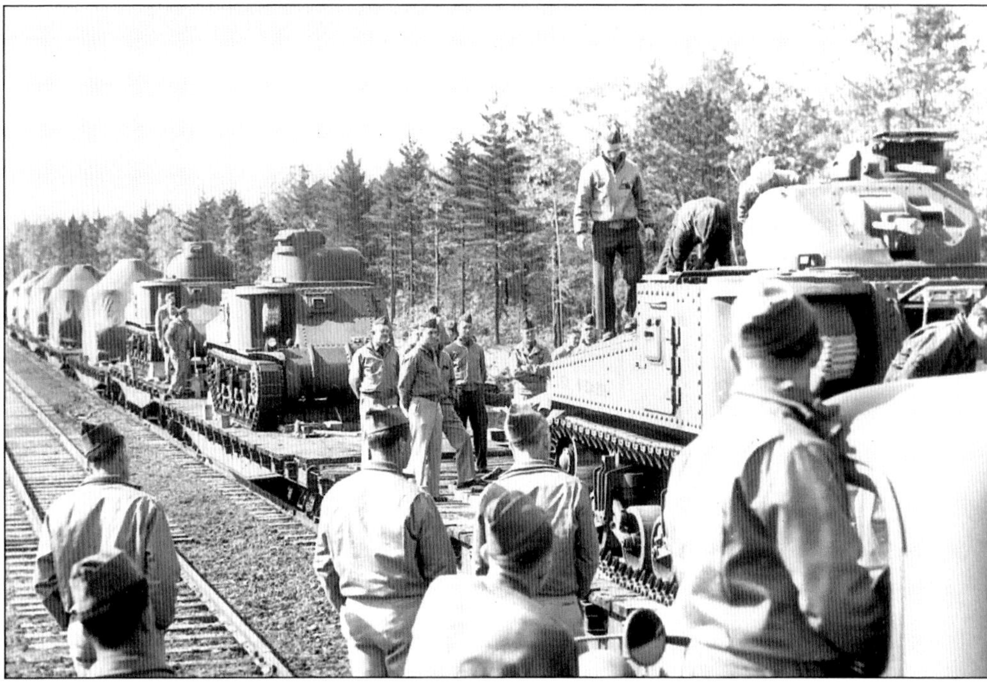

On June 13, 1945, equipment of the 76th Engineers Battalion is loaded on rail cars. The equipment, valued at $96.4 million, is headed for North Dakota National Guard, 142nd Engineers Battalion. (Courtesy Watertown Daily Times.)

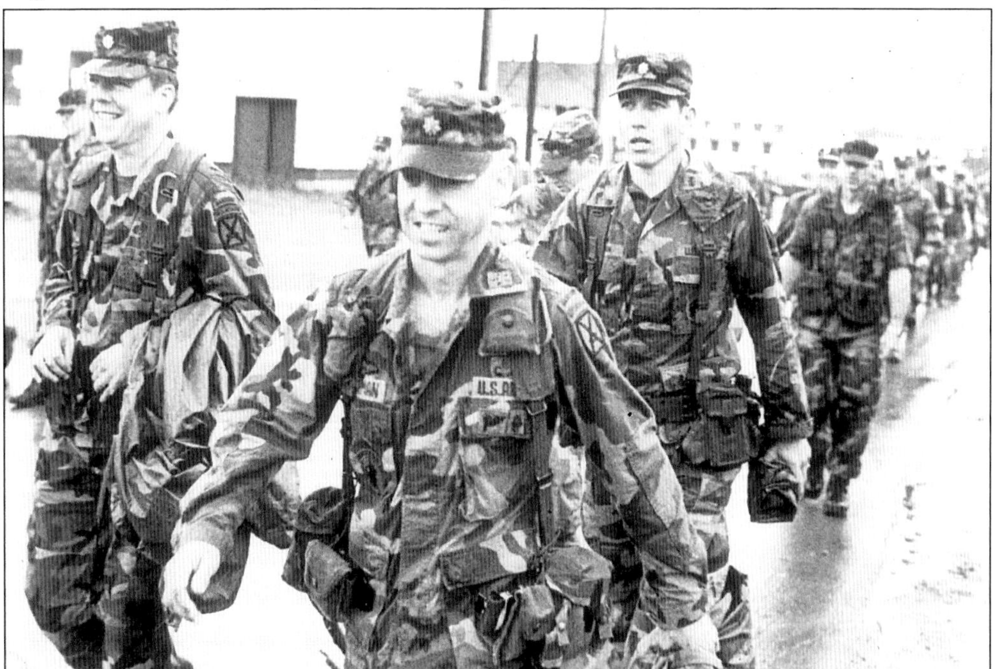

On June 14, 1985, 10th Mountain Division Headquarters enlisted men and officers Lt. Col. Al White, Maj. Bruce Newman, and Maj. Clay Vaughn join in a 25-mile march around the reservation. (Courtesy Watertown Daily Times.)

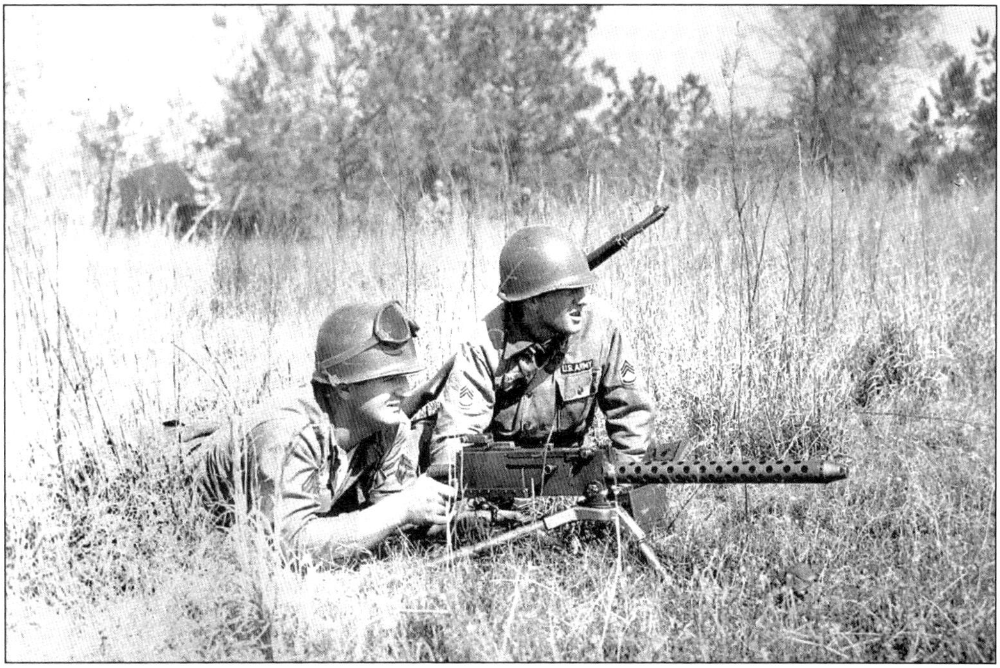

In June 1988, soldiers prepare to fire an M-60 machine gun during summer training exercises. (Courtesy FDMHC.)

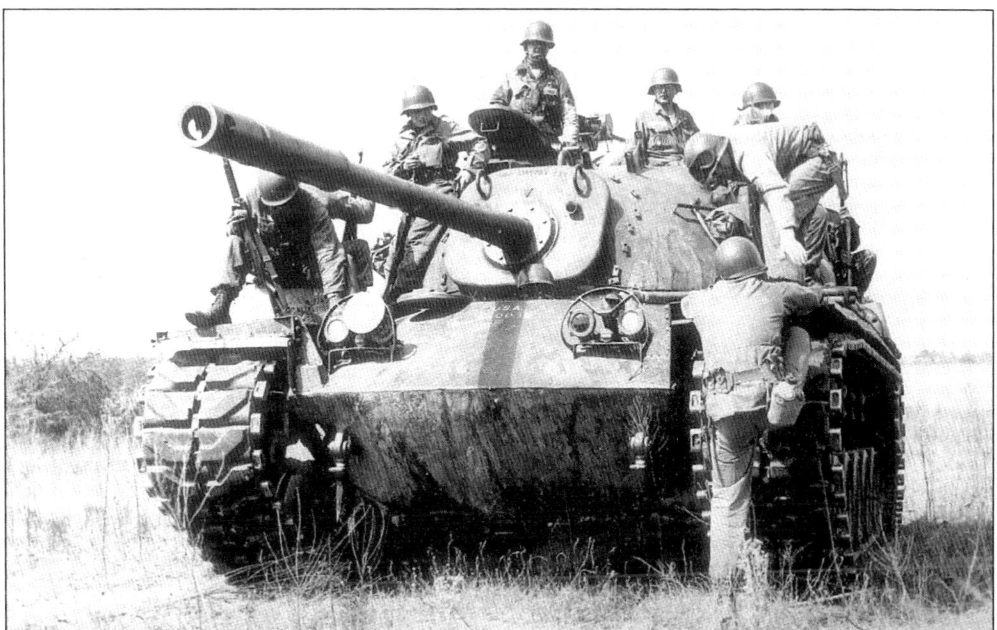

Out in the field, an M-48 Patton tank with a crew of four becomes a photographer's target. (Courtesy FDMHC.)

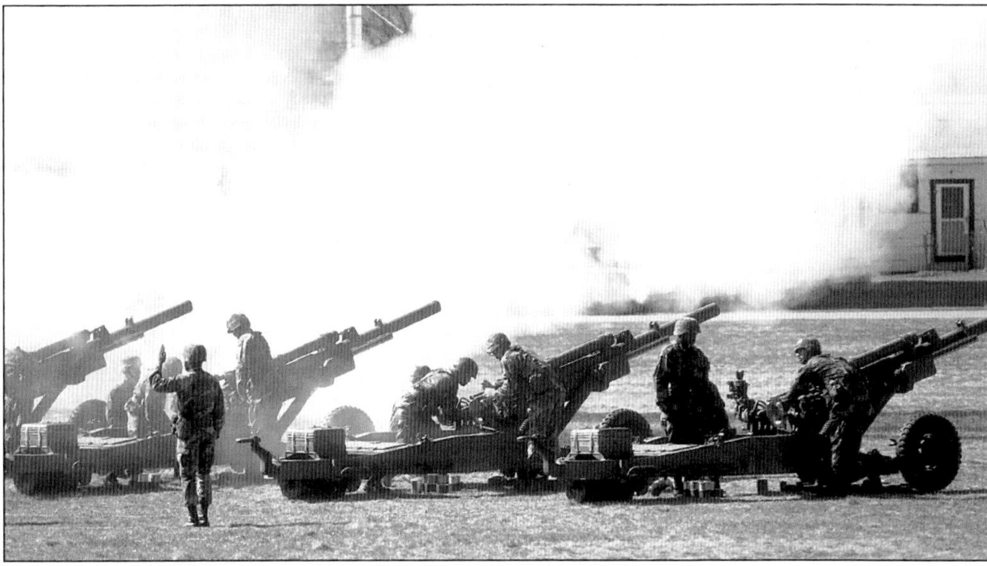

On April 23, 1988, members of the 7th Field Artillery Regiment of the 10th Mountain Division from Fort Drum traveled to Madison Barracks in Sackets Harbor for a ceremony to activate the regiment. The 7th Field Artillery Regiment was stationed at Madison Barracks from 1922 to 1934. The ceremony, held on the parade grounds at Madison Barracks, was attended by William Clark, assistant secretary of the army. Clark's father, Gen. Mark Clark, was born at Madison Barracks and incorporated the 10th Mountain Division into the 5th Army during the liberation of Italy in World War II.

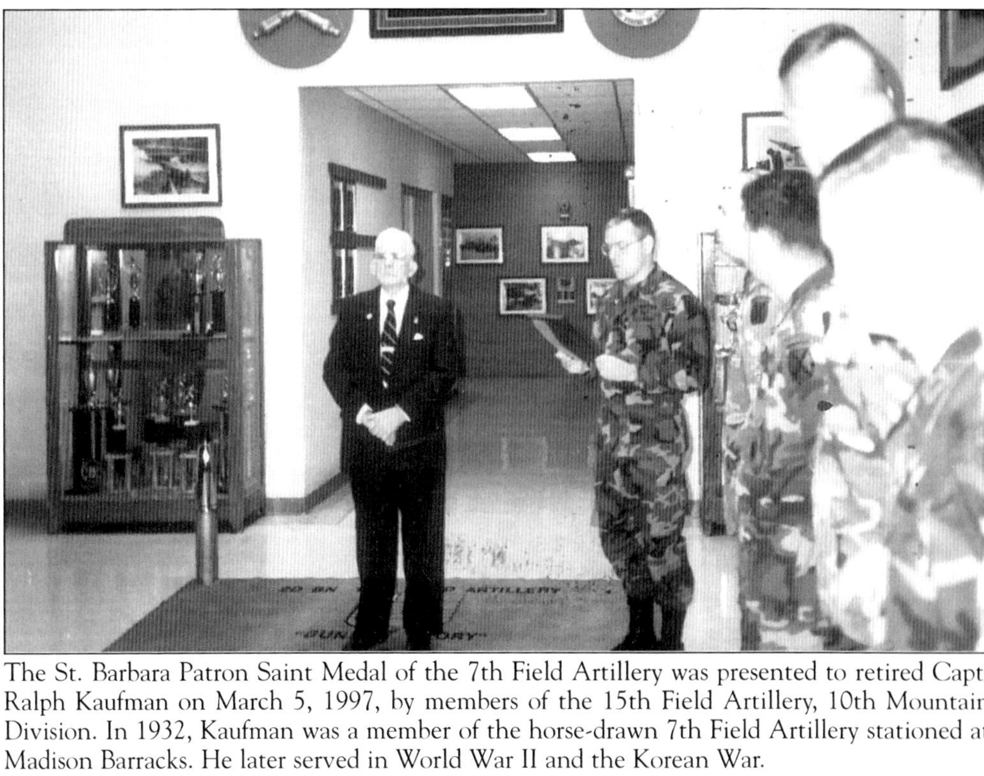

The St. Barbara Patron Saint Medal of the 7th Field Artillery was presented to retired Capt. Ralph Kaufman on March 5, 1997, by members of the 15th Field Artillery, 10th Mountain Division. In 1932, Kaufman was a member of the horse-drawn 7th Field Artillery stationed at Madison Barracks. He later served in World War II and the Korean War.

A CH-54, or Flying Crane, of the 1028th Transportation Company, Pennsylvania National Guard, is engaged in clearing land for an upcoming expansion project. (Courtesy Watertown Daily Times.)

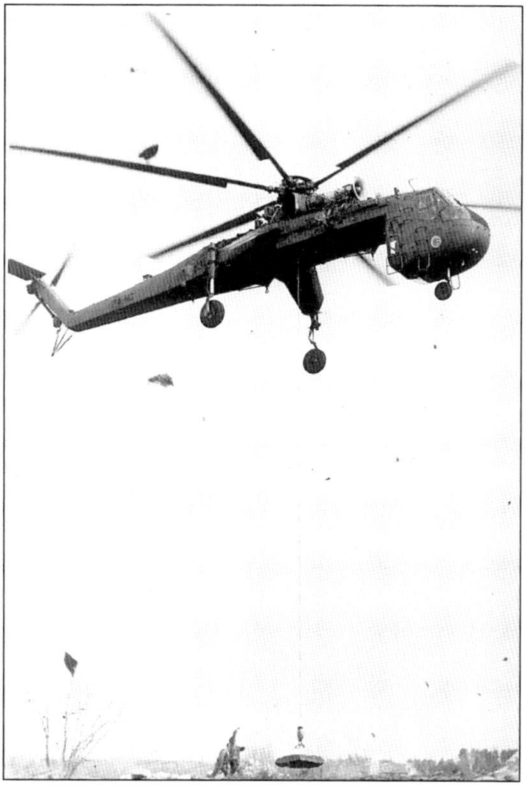

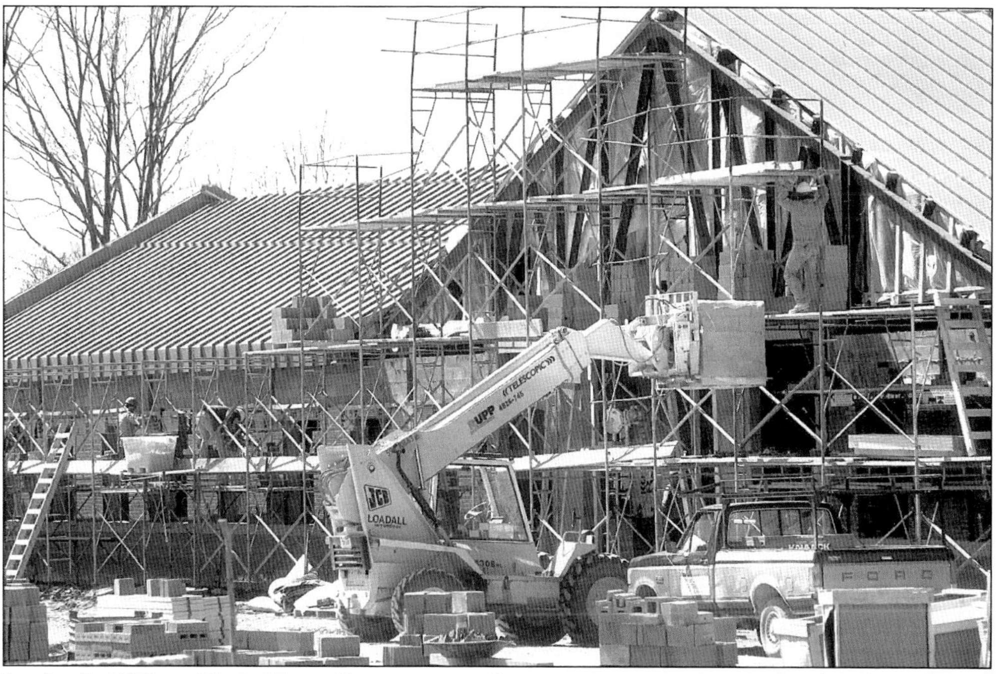

In April 1988, a Black River Construction Company crew works on the first brigade and battalion headquarters being constructed under a \$5.17 million contract. The buildings were designed to represent those of Madison Barracks. (Courtesy Watertown Daily Times.)

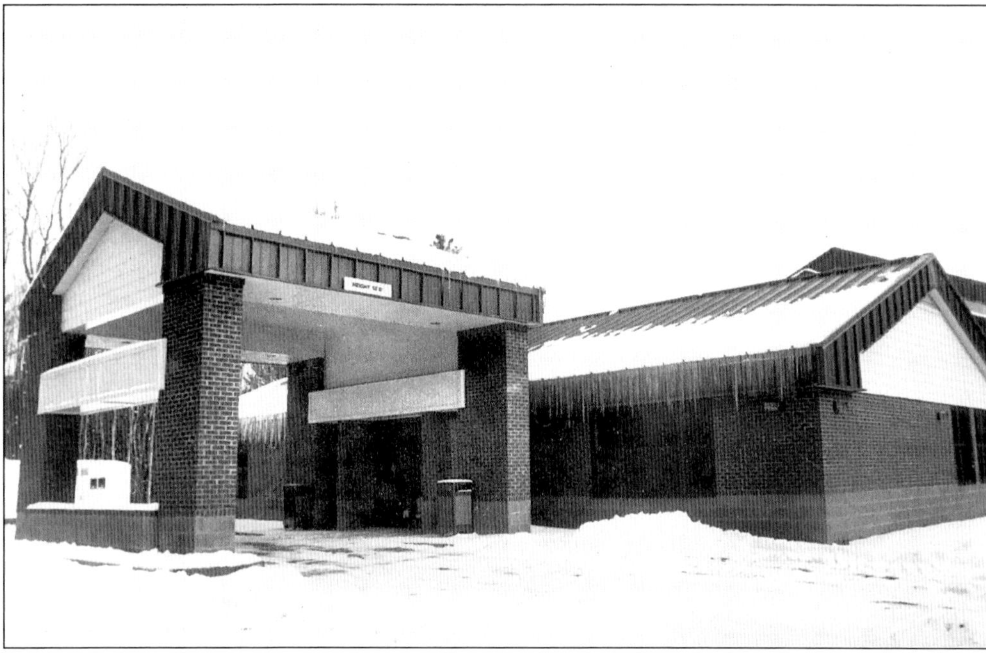

On February 15, 1989, the Inn at Fort Drum, a motellike transient lodging facility located off Po Valley Road, was ready for guests. (Courtesy FDMHC.)

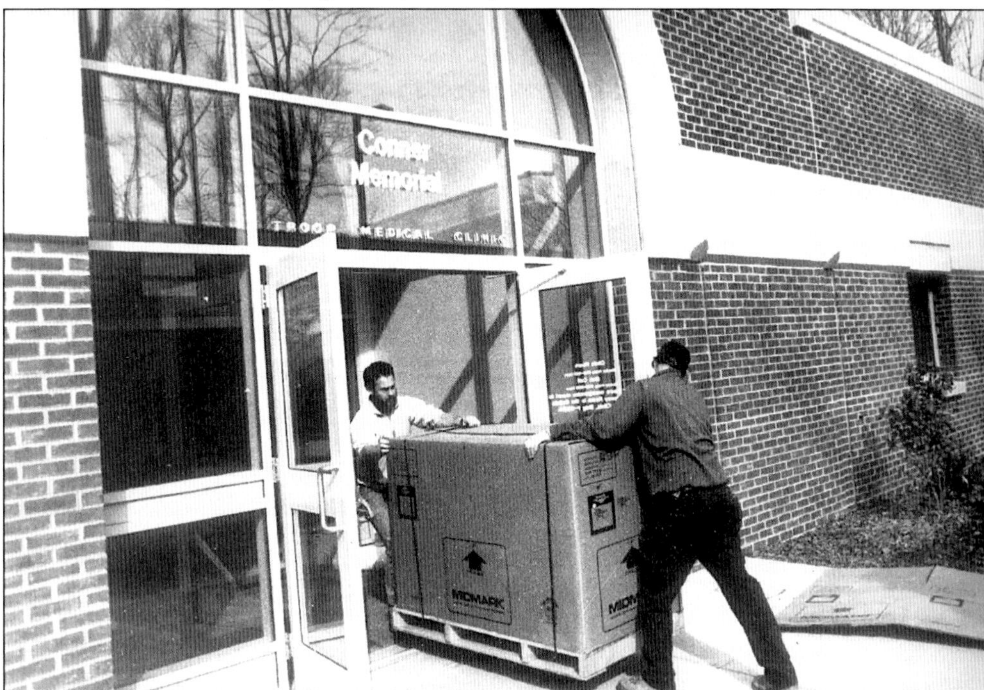

Gordon W. Myers, on the left , and Al Britt, of Livingston Moving and Storage, wheel boxes into the new Conner Troop Medical Clinic. This primary medical care clinic for active duty soldiers is located on the corner of Second Street and North Country Lane. (Courtesy Watertown Daily Times.)

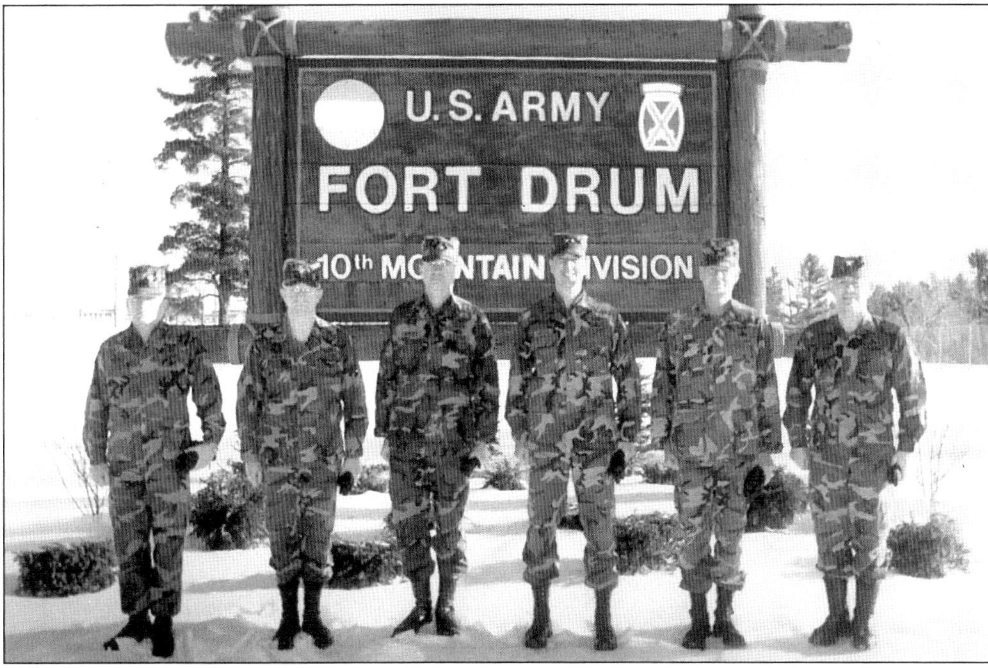

On a winter day c. 1989, officers of the 10th Mountain Division stand proudly by the division sign located at Gate No. 1 at the entrance to the World War II cantonment. They are, from left to right, Sgt. Maj. Southern "Buddy" Hewitt, Col. James Moore, Brig. Gen. John D. Howard, Maj. Gen. Peter J. Boylan, Col. Michael T. Plummer, and Col. Frederick Van Horrn. (Courtesy FDMHC.)

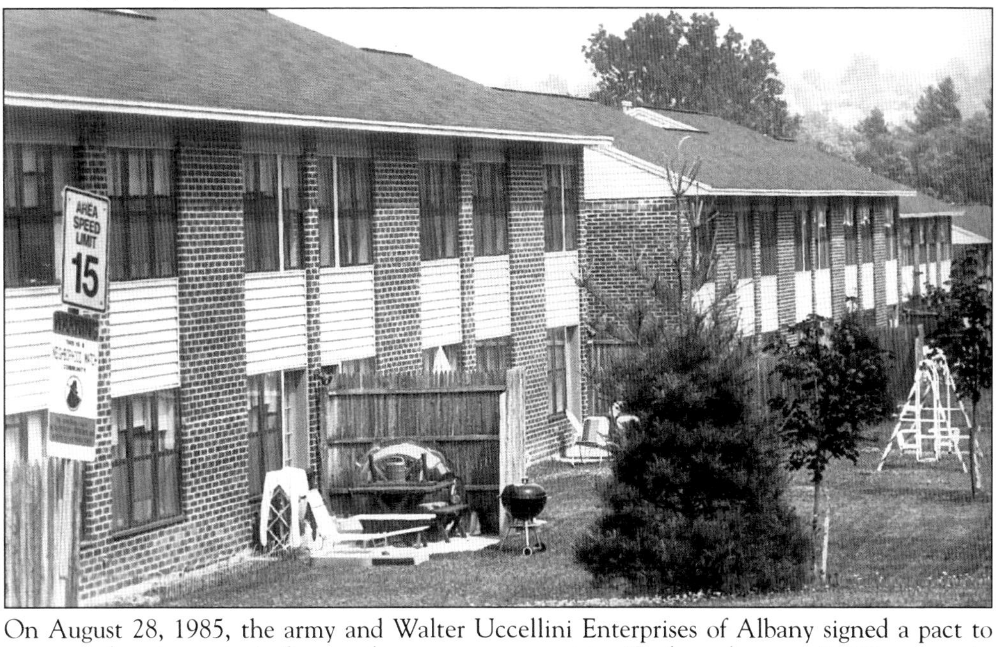

On August 28, 1985, the army and Walter Uccellini Enterprises of Albany signed a pact to construct housing units in five north country communities. To date, there are 2,000 quarters in 13 communities. Seen here is a typical row of living accommodations. (Courtesy Watertown Daily Times.)

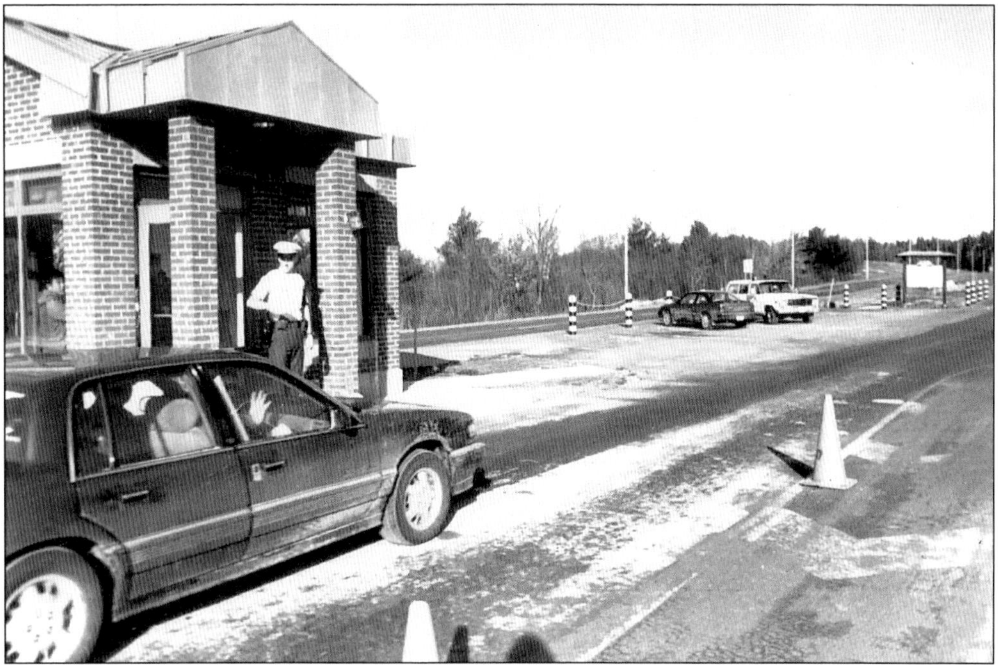

Gate No. 1 on Entry Road 1, North Memorial Drive, is manned by military police. All vehicles are required to stop for identification. Only those with passes are allowed access to the reservation. (Courtesy Watertown Daily Times.)

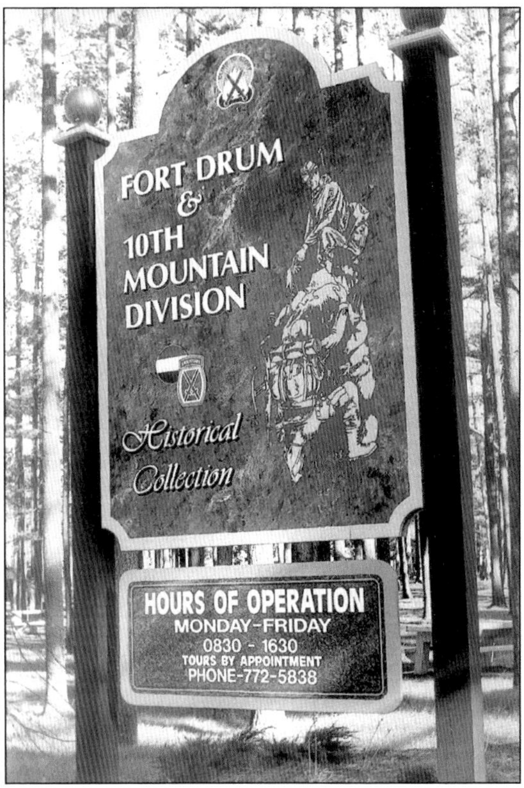

Located on Nash Boulevard, the Fort Drum and 10th Mountain Division Historical Collection Museum is the repository of historical memorabilia from 1907 to the present. Director James Neville provides research material, conducts tours, and preserves the artifacts. (Courtesy FDMHC.)

In the summer of 1990, 10th Mountain Division troops await deployment to Bosnia. The division served as controlling headquarters for the region of Bosnia known as Multidivisional Division-North. This deployment was the division's fourth since its reactivation in 1985. (Courtesy Watertown Daily Times.)

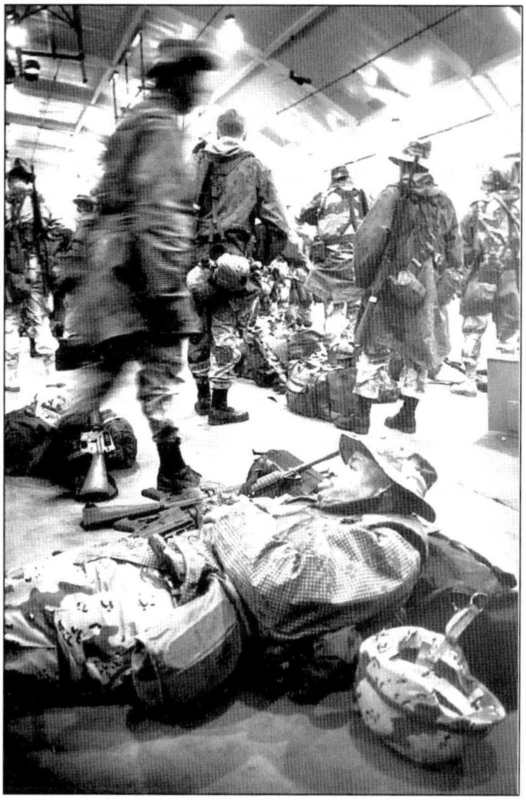

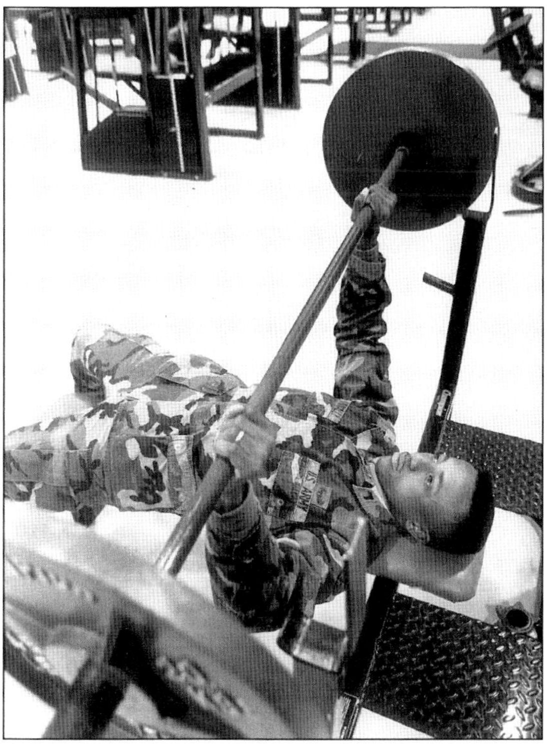

Opening ceremonies were held on December 14, 1990, at the Soldiers Sport Complex. Noncommissioned Officer of the Year Cpl. Eric L. Nunnally tries out some equipment in the Nautilus and weight training center. (Courtesy Watertown Daily Times.)

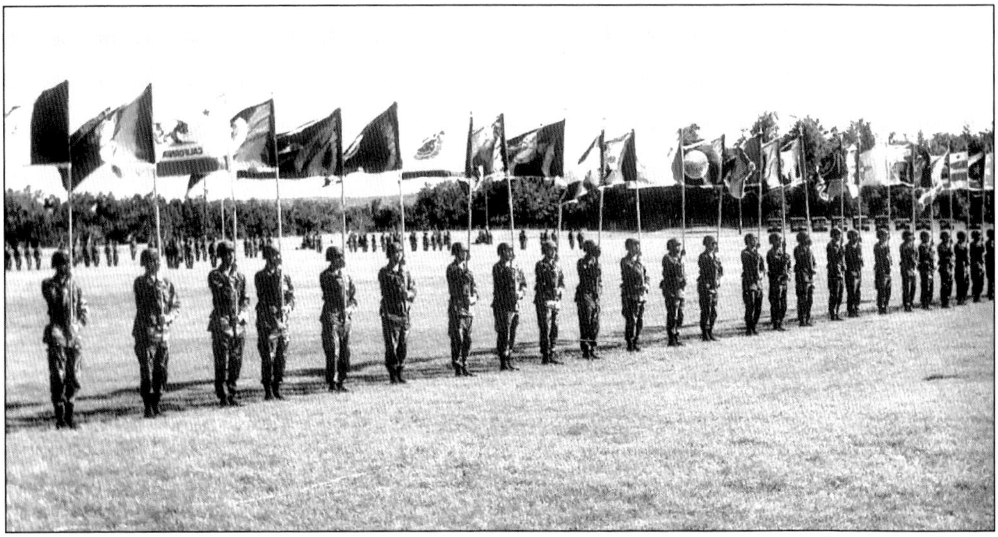

From June 29 to July 4, 1991, the first 10th Mountain Division Mountain Fest was held at Division Hill. On July 4, the division of approximately 8,000 soldiers stood in formation on the parade field. (Courtesy FDMHC.)

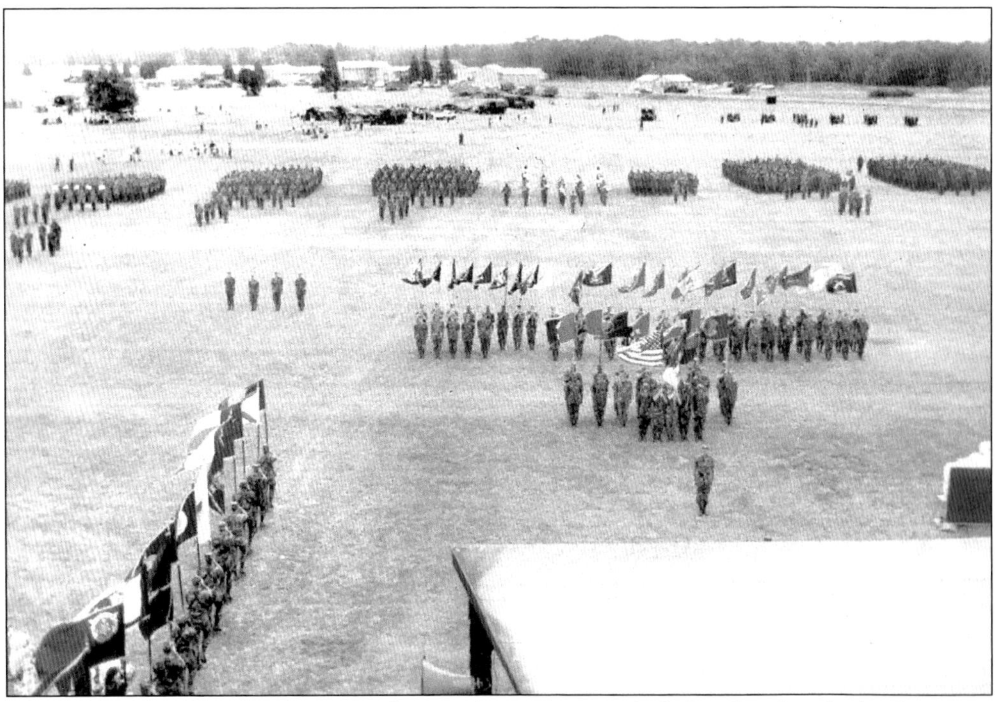

On July 4, 1991, a 50-gun cannon salute to the nation concluded with a flag display honoring each state. (Courtesy FDMHC.)

A 16-foot-tall bronze statue to honor the 10th Mountain Division was dedicated on October 5, 1991. The sculpture sits at Mount Belvedere and Memorial Drives at Fort Drum. In 1987, Susan Grant Raymond of Boulder, Colorado, was selected to design and sculpt the statue. Money for the work was raised by veterans of the 10th Mountain Division. It depicts a 10th Mountain Division soldier of World War II reaching down and hauling on a rope to help an infantryman of today. (Courtesy FDMHC.)

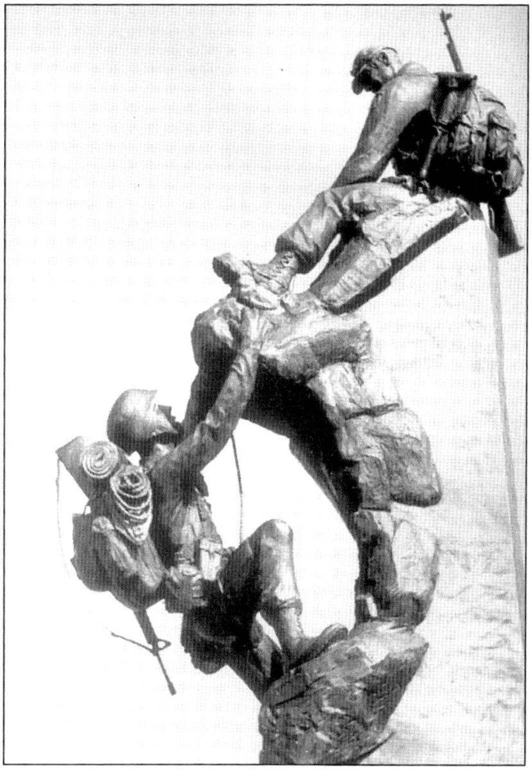

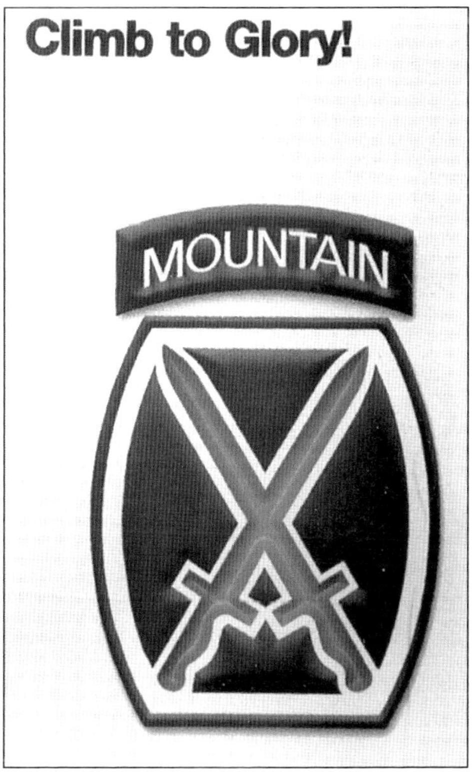

The shoulder patch of the 10th Mountain Division is a blue powder keg bordered in white. Superimposed on it are two red bayonets crossed to from the Roman numeral X, the numerical designation of the division.

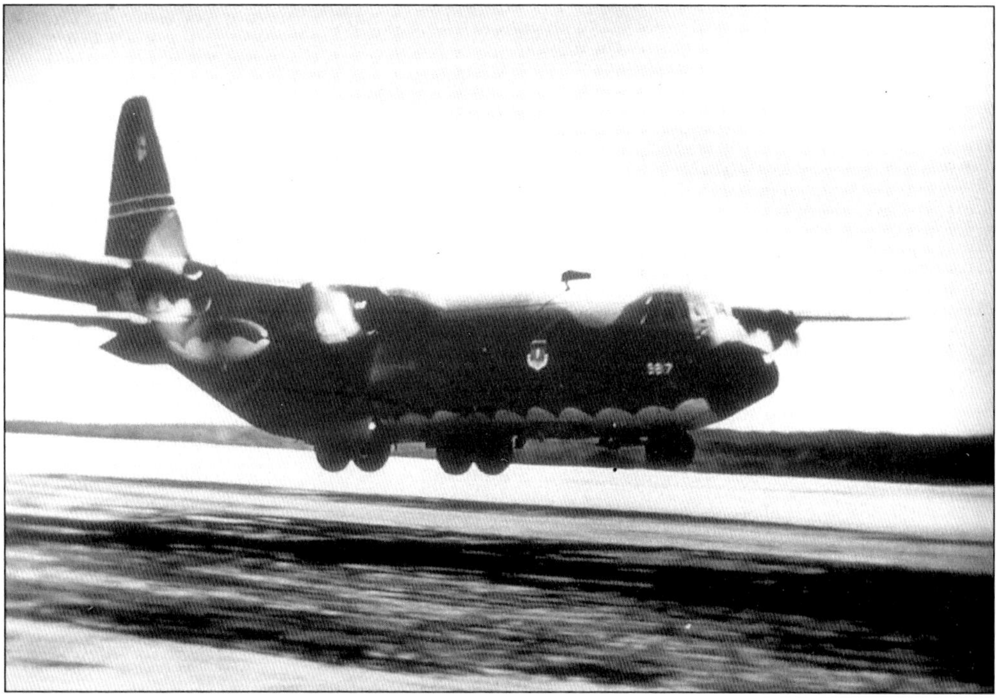

The 16,000-foot runway at Wheeler-Sack Army Airfield accommodates the C-130 transport planes used to deploy troops and equipment. (Courtesy FDMHC.)

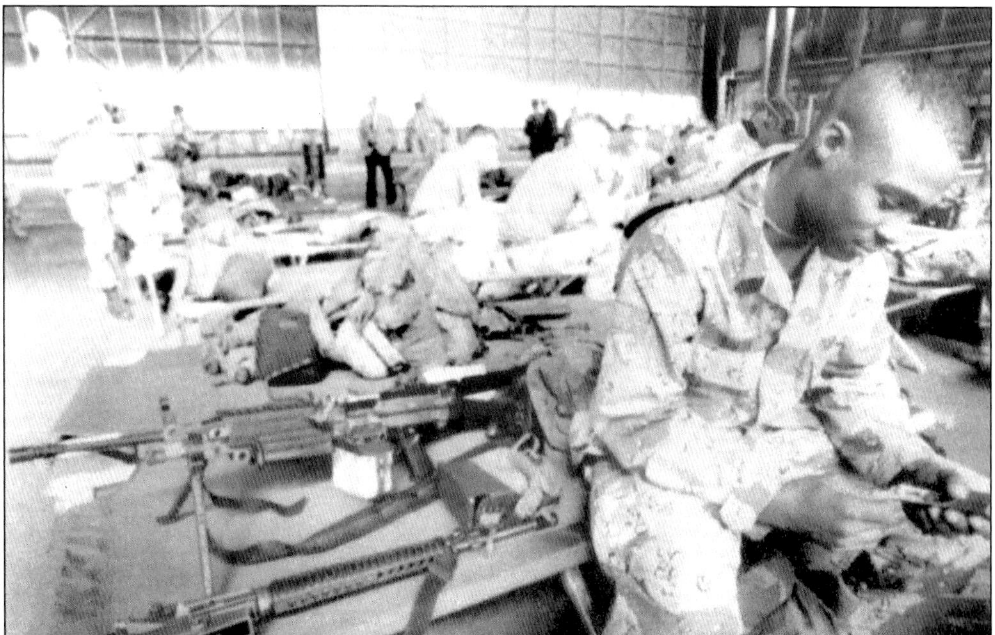

On October 11, 1993, Pfc. James Simon, 10th Mountain Division, waits at Griffiss Air Force Base in the town of Rome to board a transport plane to Somalia. Before expansion of runways at Wheeler-Sack, troops were transported by bus to Griffiss Air Force Base. (Courtesy FDMHC.)

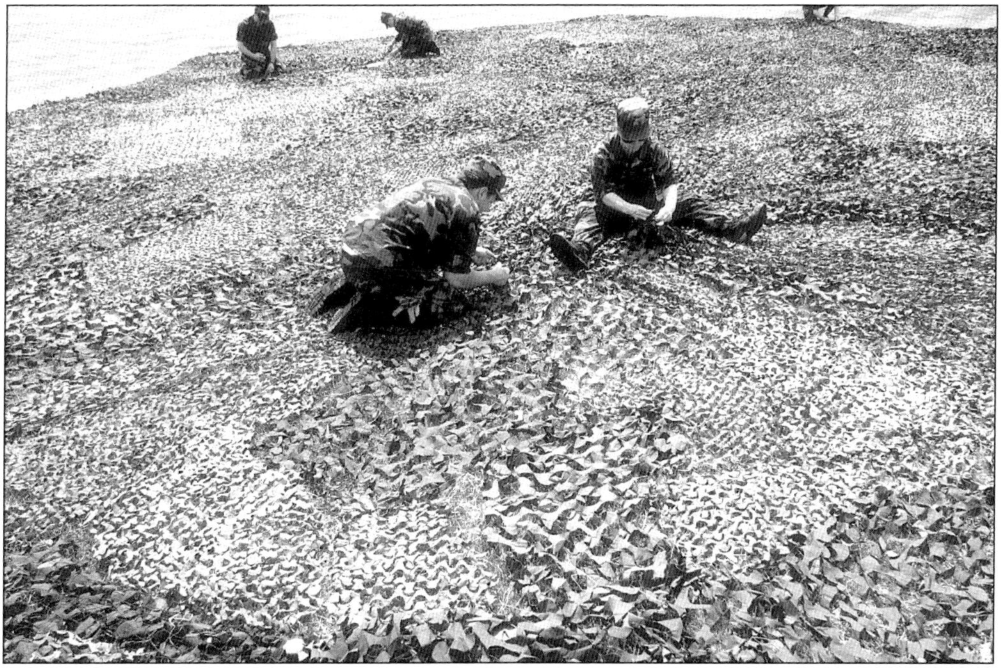

On June 5, 1995, troops from the New York State Air National Guard and fighter plane units from the Midwest join in operation Global Yankee '95. National Guard members piece together camouflage nets used to cover vehicles and equipment. (Courtesy Watertown Daily Times.)

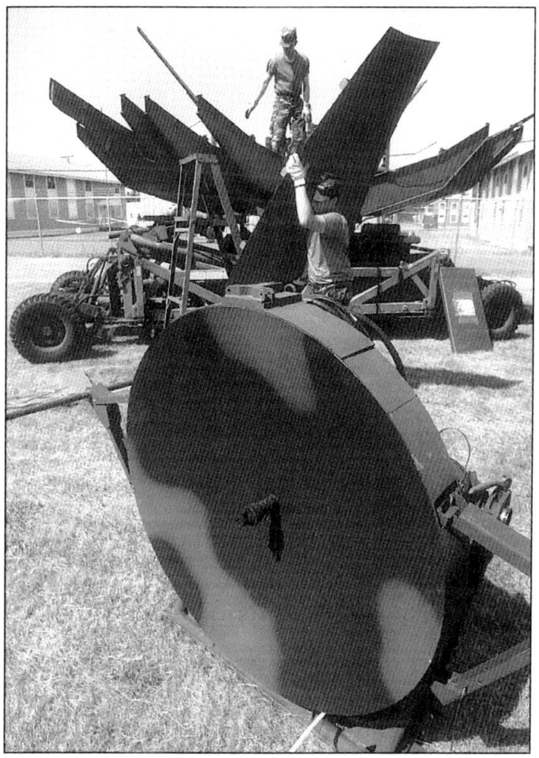

Members of the 264th Combat Command Squadron, based in Chicago, Illinois, assemble a satellite dish to be used during Global Yankee '95 training exercises. (Courtesy Watertown Daily Times.)

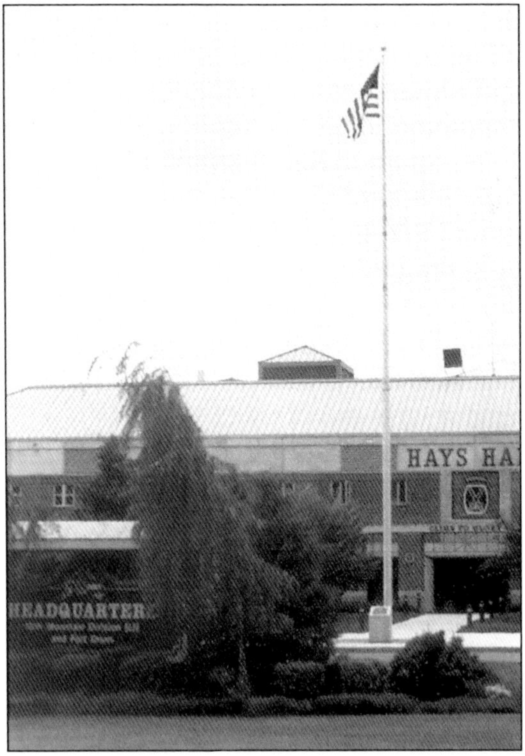

On September 19, 1998, post and division headquarters building F-10,000, was renamed Hays Hall and officially dedicated in honor of Lt. Gen. George P. Hays, commander of the 10th Mountain Division during World War II. (Courtesy FDMHC.)

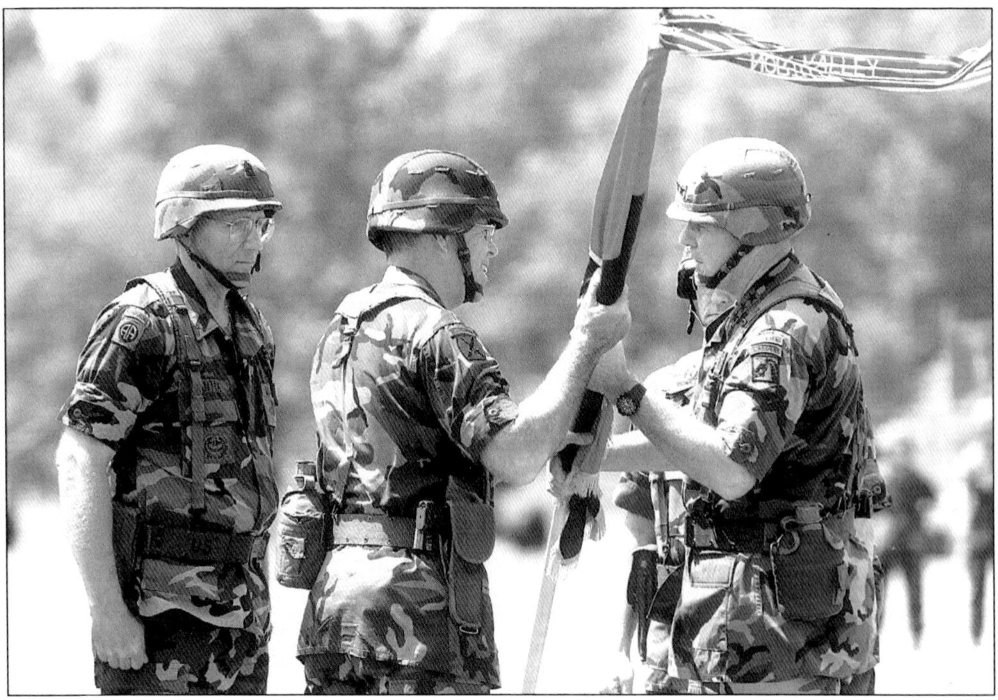

A change of command at Fort Drum shows Maj. Gen. Lawson W. Magruder III receiving the 10th Mountain Division colors from Lt. Gen. John M. Keane, commanding general of the 18th Airborne Corps. (Courtesy Watertown Daily Times.)

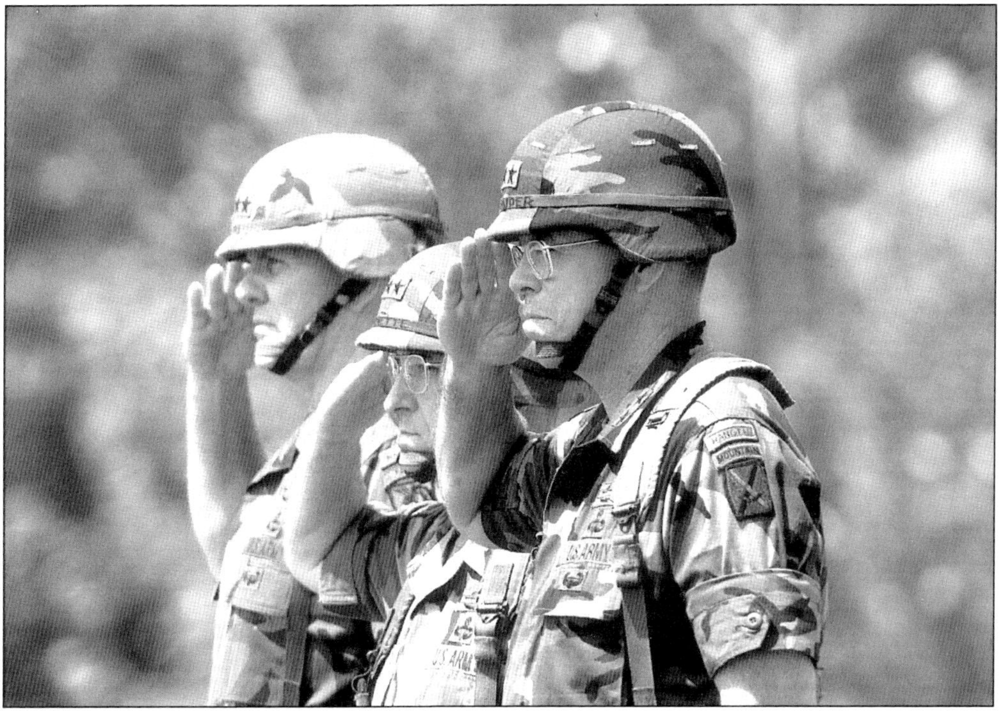

A salute to the flag during the playing of the national anthem is honored by Lt. Gen. John M. Keane, Maj. Gen. Thomas N. Burnette Jr., and Maj. Gen. Lawson W. Magruder III. (Courtesy Watertown Daily Times.)

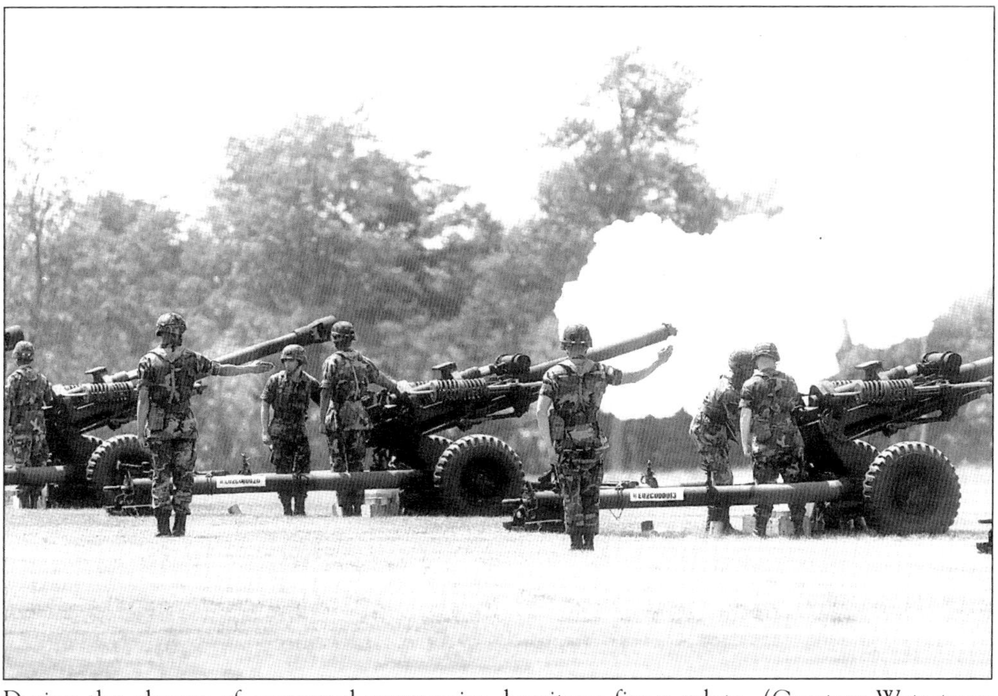

During the change of command ceremonies, howitzers fire a salute. (Courtesy Watertown Daily Times.)

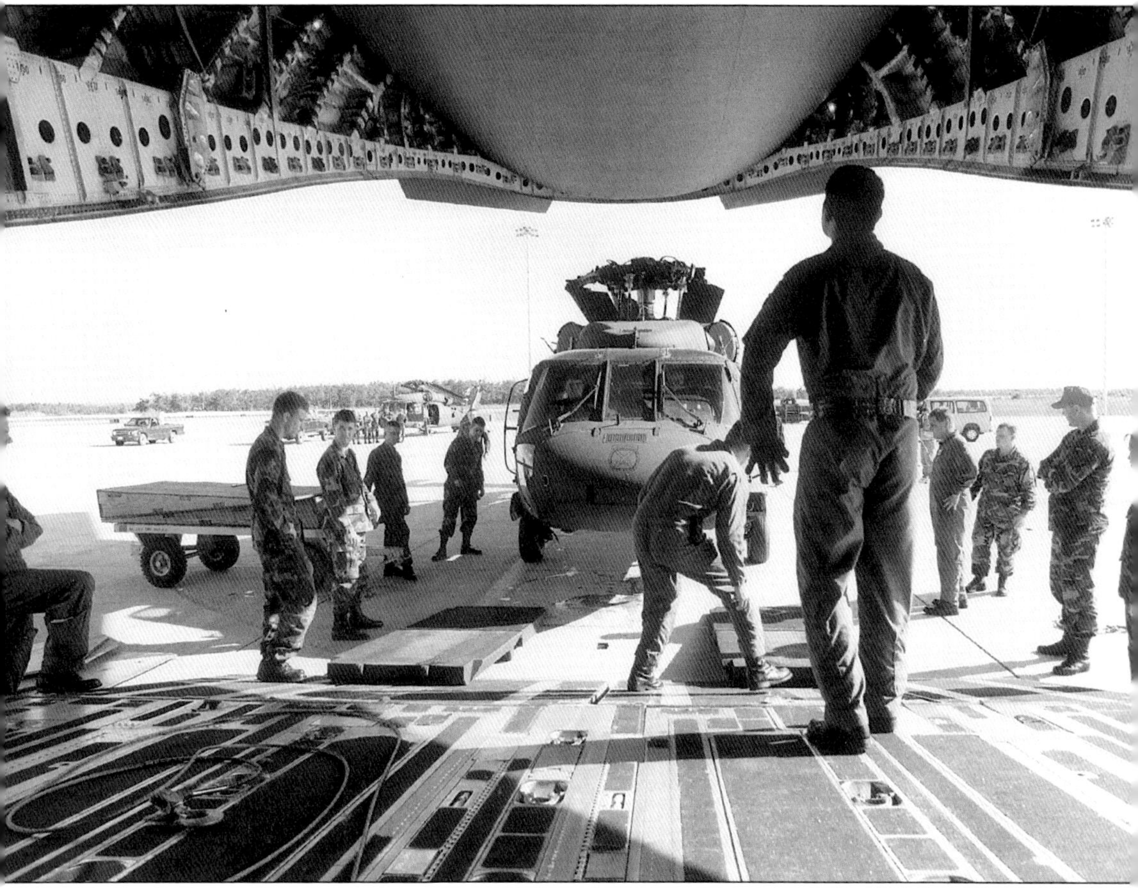

On May 28, 1999, at Fort Drum, crews from the 10th Aviation Brigade, 2nd Battalion, 10th Aviation Regiment, load UH-60 Blackhawk command and control helicopters onto a C-17 transport aircraft for deployment to Albania. (Courtesy Watertown Daily Times.)

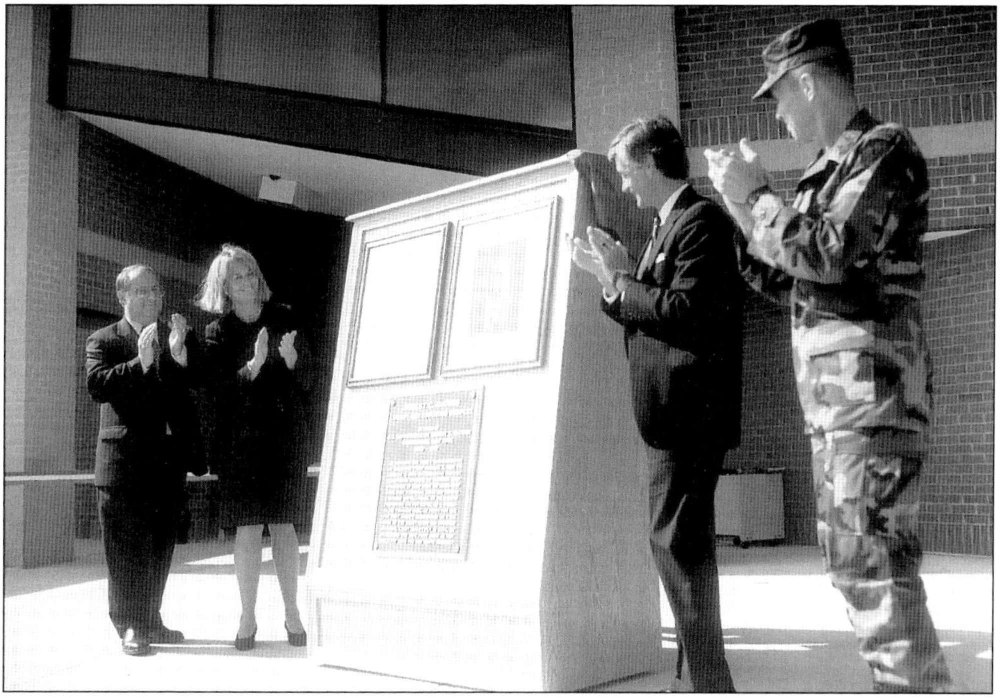

On September 1, 2000, the McEwen Library and Education Complex is dedicated in memory of Robert C. McEwen of Ogdensburg, a member of Congress from 1965 to 1981. Present at the ceremony, from left to right, are Cary Brick, Mary Fitzpatrick (McEwen's daughter), Rep. John M. McHugh, and Maj. Gen. James L. Campbell (Fort Drum commander). (Courtesy Watertown Daily Times.)

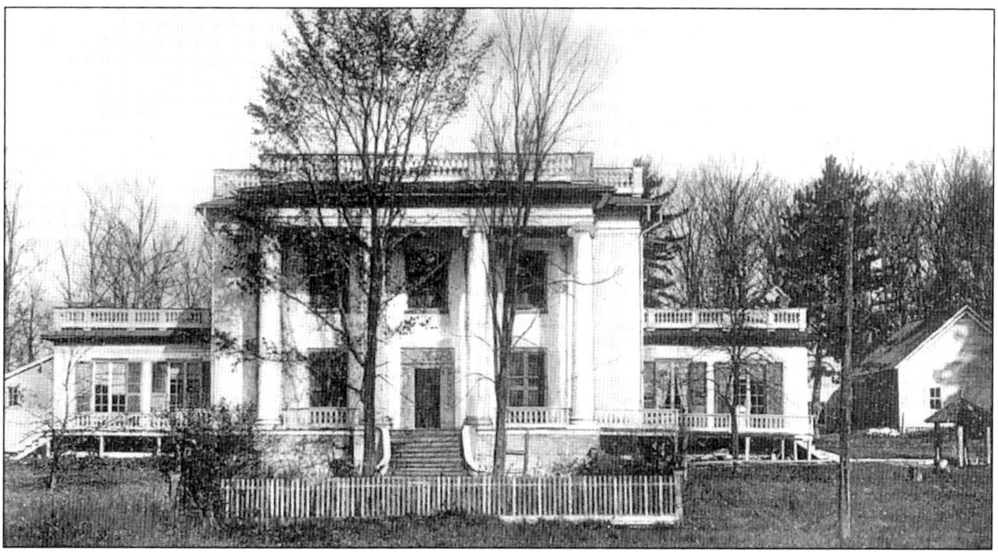

For over 60 years, the LeRay de Chaumont Mansion has housed visiting dignitaries. The original mansion, built for James LeRay de Chaumont in 1808, burned and was replaced in 1827 by the present structure. Located near the village of Leraysville, it was privately owned. In 1943, the federal government purchased the structure for $150,000 from the owners, Col. and Mrs. Harold Remington.

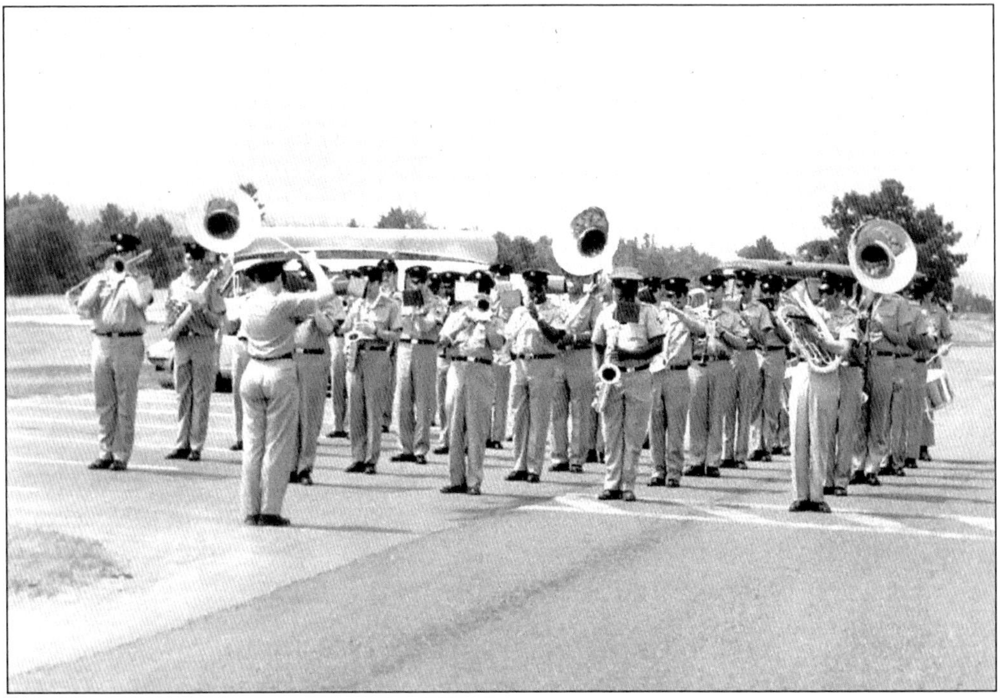

A reserve component band practices at Fort Drum. Communities throughout northern New York enjoy performances by these musicians. (Courtesy FDMHC.)

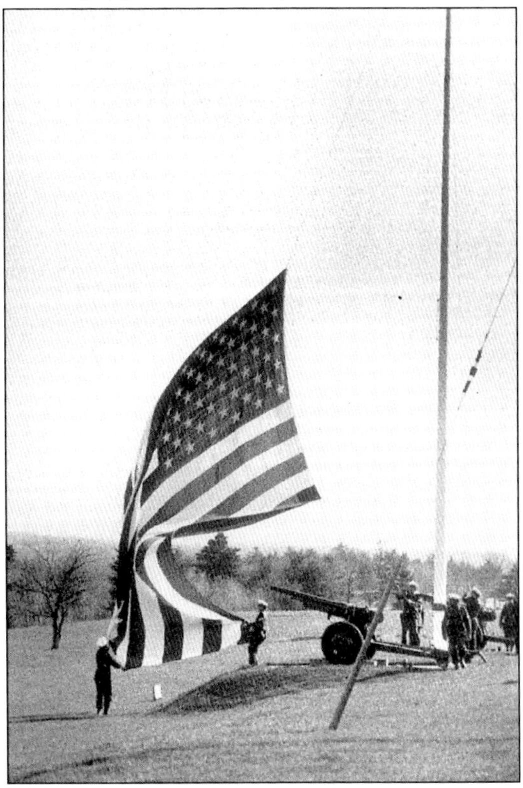

A detail of military police conducts the retreat ceremony with the lowering of the garrison flag at the flagpole on Nash Boulevard. (Courtesy FDMHC.)